W9-DIR-688

TAKEN BY STORM

AMERICAN POLITICS AND POLITICAL ECONOMY SERIES
EDITED BY BENJAMIN I. PAGE

TAKEN BY STORM

The Media, Public Opinion, and U.S. Foreign Policy in the Gulf War

Edited by
**W. Lance Bennett
and
David L. Paletz**

THE UNIVERSITY OF CHICAGO PRESS
CHICAGO AND LONDON

The University of Chicago Press, Chicago 60637
The University of Chicago Press, Ltd., London
© 1994 by The University of Chicago
All rights reserved. Published 1994
Printed in the United States of America

03 02 01 00 99 98 97 96 95 94   1 2 3 4 5

ISBN: 0-226-04258-8   (cloth)
        0-226-04259-6   (paper)

Library of Congress Cataloging-in-Publication Data

Taken by storm : the media, public opinion, and U.S. foreign policy in
  the Gulf War / edited by W. Lance Bennett and David L. Paletz.
      p.   cm. — (American politics and political economy series)
  Includes bibliographical references and index.
    1. Persian Gulf War, 1991—Press coverage—United States.
  2. Press—United States—History—20th century.   3. Persian Gulf
  War, 1991—Foreign public opinion, American.   4. Public opinion—
  United States.   I. Bennett, W. Lance.   II. Paletz, David L., 1934–   .
  III. Series: American politics and political economy.
  DS79.739.T35   1994
  956.7044'28—dc20   93-45527

To my parents, Walter and Anna Bennett, with love and appreciation.
WLB

For my mother, Hetty Rochlin, who has experienced too many wars, but through her courage, individuality, and independence prevailed over them all.
DLP

contents

CONCLUSION

preface

In late 1990, the Social Science Research Council brought together two dozen of the leading scholars in political communication, U.S. government and politics, the news media, and public opinion. Their mission: to propose and undertake fresh, original research on the relations between the news media, the public, and U.S. foreign policy. At the time of our first meeting, there were some 400,000 U.S. troops deployed as part of an international coalition seeking to pressure Saddam Hussein to withdraw his occupying army from Kuwait. In the name of Iraq, Saddam Hussein had invaded Kuwait in August of that year and driven the ruling royal family into exile, upsetting the fragile balance of power and oil wealth in the strategically important Persian Gulf region. As our group began its discussions, we quickly decided that, whether or not it eventuated in war, the looming crisis in the Gulf offered a unique opportunity to study the complex relationships of news, foreign policy, and public opinion in action.

This book is the result of that decision. The authors assembled here draw upon broad knowledge of political communications, public opinion, and foreign policy. The goal throughout the development of our case study was to expand the normal academic boundaries to comprehend the complex ways in which foreign policy options are managed by various political players as they undergo the often sensitive process of public scrutiny. Beyond producing a thorough case study of the Gulf War, our purpose was to demonstrate the broad applications of knowledge gained from research in our different fields.

Case studies provide the advantages of interesting and often dramatic applications for academic knowledge. Their sometimes idiosyncratic features also present intellectual challenges to rethink and modify the conventional wisdom (what we know or think we know). We have avoided turning the Gulf War into a model for other foreign policy situations. To the contrary, many of our discussions in the group were aimed at trying to understand where this situation, as it was reported by the mass media, fit within a broad range of policy episodes from Vietnam to the invasion of Panama, and from Tiananmen Square to world-trade policy. The many distinctive elements of the Gulf Crisis stood as challenges to see what could be explained on the basis of existing research and theories, and what had to be thought about anew.

Thus this book is divided into five parts. It begins with three contrasting perspectives from, respectively, the distinguished journalist, lately turned academic administrator, Marvin Kalb; Lieutenant General Thomas Kelly, the chief operations officer for the U.S. effort in the Gulf and the top Pentagon briefing-officer during the war; and Professor Bernard Cohen, the dean of foreign policy and media studies. These "provocations" are followed by Lance Bennett's discussion in Chapter 1 of the often contradictory arguments and assertions about the relationships between the media, foreign policy, and public opinion that he connects to and integrates with the book's research and findings.

The three chapters in Part II analyze the news as political information during three prewar periods. In Chapter 2, Gladys Engel Lang and Kurt Lang chronicle (the inadequacies of) media coverage of Saddam Hussein from 1979 to 1990. William Dorman and Steven Livingston dissect in Chapter 3 news coverage during the establishing phase of the Persian Gulf policy debate. And in Chapter 4, Robert Entman and Benjamin Page identify the limits of media independence during the crucial period following the administration decision to double U.S. troop strength in the Gulf.

Part III deals with the politics, journalistic conventions, and cultural foundations of news construction. Timothy Cook shows in Chapter 5 how the content of news stories after the Iraq invasion of Kuwait was determined by reporters' reliance on Washington newsbeats. Jarol Manheim reveals in Chapter 6 the ways in which Kuwait's image was successfully managed during the Gulf conflict. And in Chapter 7, Daniel Hallin and Todd Gitlin analyze media war coverage as popular culture and television drama.

Part IV explores the impact of these coverage patterns on public opinion. The effects of news coverage of the Gulf Crisis on the public are the subject of Chapter 8, by Shanto Iyengar and Adam Simon. In Chapter 9, John Zaller uses opinion data from the Gulf Crisis and other foreign policy episodes to explain elite leadership of mass opinion. And in Chapter 10 Richard Brody discusses the relationship between the media and public support for the president in two phases of the Persian Gulf confrontation.

Part V focuses on the impact of news and opinion on policy-makers. In Chapter 11, Patrick O'Heffernan looks at the role of the media in foreign policy decisions from the perspectives and experiences of government officials. John Zaller considers in Chapter 12 the political calculations of the president and the Democratic opposition in Congress during the unfolding crisis. The final chapter contains David Paletz's overview and reactions to the ideas, arguments, and analyses of his colleagues in the rest of the book.

By bringing together in one volume perspectives from political communication, public opinion, policy analysis, and journalism, we hope to display the benefits of interdisciplinary research and to stimulate it in the future. Only by initiating a dialogue across academic fields and among academics, journalists, and government officials can we begin untangling the many different and often opposing claims that have been made about the involvement and effects of the media in the foreign policy process.

acknowledgments

One of the many pleasures provided for us by this book was the opportunity to engage in a dialogue with, and benefit from the knowledge and expertise of, our fellow scholars. We were joined by journalists and practitioners in communications and public relations in a series of three conferences held in New York, Seattle, and Washington, D.C. Although some of these individuals did not contribute chapters to this volume, their insights were most helpful in stimulating discussion and challenging our ideas and approaches. We would like to thank Don Bates of the Institute for Public Relations Research and Education, Patricia Ellis of the American University, Doug Frantz of the *Los Angeles Times*, Lynne Gutstadt of CNN, John Kirton of the University of Toronto, James Larson of the University of Singapore, Robert Manoff of the Center for War, Peace, and Media Studies at New York University, Albert Pearce of the National War College, Leon Sigal of the *New York Times*, and Barry Sussman of Barry Sussman Associates for joining our group sessions.

In addition, we thank Robert Huber and Stanley Heginbotham of the Social Science Research Council for their generous support which made our meetings possible. We hope that their vision of expanding the intellectual boundaries of both foreign policy studies and political communication research has been advanced by our work. The Social Science Research Council staff was nothing short of superb in facilitating the meetings and communication among our large group. In particular, Valli Rajah and Jill Finger handled our complex conference arrangements smoothly, making meetings both stimulating and productive.

All the chapters were written expressly for this volume. However, while the book was being prepared for publication, Shanto Iyengar and Adam Simon's essay, "News Coverage of the Gulf Crisis and Public Opinion," appeared in the journal *Communication Research* 20, no. 3 (June 1993): 365–83, © 1993 by Sage Publications, Inc.; we therefore acknowledge that the essay is reprinted here by permission of Sage Publications, Inc. The chapter by Dan Hallin and Todd Gitlin was published by prior agreement in a special issue of *Political Communication* that includes other articles by members of the SSRC working group; it appears here with permission of Taylor and Francis, Inc.

Members of Paletz's fall 1992 seminar devoted to the media and the Gulf War, enjoyed (relished) the opportunity to critique (eviscerate) early versions of most of the chapters herein. Scott Altes, Jon Aronie, George Brickhouse, Will Cox, Karin Goetz, Courtney Hentz, Peter Lemieux, Karen Lloyd, Kristina McGowan, Melinda Mische, Rachel Pearce, Michael Scholl, Moorari Shah, Leah Shahum, and Dade Van Der Werf enthusiastically undertook their task with a tough-minded disdain for reputation and renown.

Paletz appreciates the many contributions of his friend, journalist Terry Pristin; Beryl Slome, for advice and counsel; the inexhaustible Lillian Fennell; the oft incomparable Judith Olney, who was in on the inception; and the timely support of the Duke University Research Council.

Special recognition and warm appreciation are due to Ann Buscherfeld, who helped coordinate all of our conferences and took primary responsibility for our session at the University of Washington. Above all, Ann attended to the myriad details required to produce a single volume from the collection of computer disks submitted by the authors. We are indebted to her.

Professors John Mueller and Russell Neuman evaluated the book proposal and Professors David Swanson and Holli Semetko reviewed all the individual chapters in perceptive detail for the University of Chicago Press; the book has benefited immeasurably from their comments and suggestions.

At the Press, senior editor John Tryneski recognized our proposal's appeal and acquired the manuscript before other publishers reacted. John is a pleasure to work with and is, in his delightful way, a continual source of support.

Lance Bennett is indebted to Bettina Lüscher for her friendship, intellectual support, and patient discussions about journalism.

Gabriel Michael Paletz from Prague and Ravenna, and Susannah Batyah Felicity Paletz from Middletown and Hove, provide, by e-mail, letters, and telephone, the news, views, and, above all, the love that sustain and enrich life.

WLB
Seattle, Washington

DLP
Durham, North Carolina

part one

Introduction to the Media and Foreign Policy

Provocations

A View from the Press

MARVIN KALB

When America goes to war, so too does the press, wrapped in the flag no less proudly than the troops themselves. Thus, it seems it has always been, even if the journalists have been saddled with censorship in one form or another from the Civil War to the Gulf War.

Up until the discovery of the telegraph in 1843, the military could safely accommodate journalists, even on the battlefield, because press dispatches were so slow getting into print that there was little chance of providing comfort to the enemy or embarrassment to the generals—or the politicians in Washington. However, once the telegraph in the mid-nineteenth century and television in the late-twentieth century accelerated the process of reporting, the generals could no longer be indifferent to the power of the press to influence public opinion. In different ways, they have attempted, in modern parlance, to control the spin on their tactics and strategy.

Theodore Roosevelt invited prominent journalists, such as Richard Harding Davis, to observe his heroics during the assault on San Juan Hill. Their cables at the turn of the century advanced his presidential career. Walter Lippmann, as a young man, worked for the Committee on Public Information, the first U.S. propaganda and censorship agency, during World War I. Edward R. Murrow directed the United States Information Agency during the Kennedy administration. John Chancellor succumbed to Lyndon Johnson's entreaties during the Vietnam War and, for a time, ran the Voice of America. A string of journalists, from Hodding Carter to Bernard Kalb, served with distinction as State Department spokesmen. General Colin Powell, then chairman of the Joint Chiefs of Staff, got on television and urged journalists to "trust me" during the Gulf War. They did, almost all of them, and they were then subjected to the most sophisticated massage in the history of Pentagon salesmanship. The upshot was an upsurge of unchecked patriotism that fired U.S. troops towards a limited victory in a blessedly short war (limited, in the sense that the Iraqis were driven out of Kuwait but Saddam Hussein was not driven out of power) but also robbed U.S. reporters of their most important function during the spilling of blood in pursuit of national objectives: the ability to think critically, act in a detached manner, ask questions, remain unemotional, and resist—always resist—the strong temptation during war to cheer for the American side and denounce the enemy. From whom, if not from the press, are the American people to get the information on which to base an intelligent decision on the worthiness of a particular war, or the soundness of their government's strategies and policies, or the actual conditions on and above the fields of combat?

Unfortunately, during the Gulf War, the American people were shortchanged, in part because the press engaged in that most dangerous of professional practices, namely, patriotic journalism.

Ever since the Vietnam War, U.S. military journals have been stuffed with antimedia cant designed to prove that the press—not the Pentagon, not the U.S. government, not the nature of revolutionary struggle, not, as Dean Rusk once put it, "the tenacity" of the North Vietnamese—lost the war. Nonsense—foolish, self-deluding, destructive nonsense. And, ever since the Vietnam War (and Watergate), the press has been determined to prove not only that it did not lose the war but that it is also composed of "the right stuff," the stuff of red-white-and-blue-blooded, pork-rinds-eating, beer-drinking, flag-waving Americanism, hardly the sort of press that would undermine a war effort by raising embarrassing questions about an administration's earlier dealings with Saddam Hussein or about its involvement in the Iran/Contra affair. No one wanted another Watergate.

Ever since Ronald Reagan rode to office in 1981 and George Bush rode to war in 1991, the press has, with rare exceptions, tamely embraced the role of populist booster, perhaps to increase its ratings and circulation, perhaps to play it safe in an environment of uncertain economic and competitive pressures. At no time was this saccharin journalism more on display, from early morning until late at night, than during the Gulf War—so much so that even Sam Donaldson, one of TV's most aggressive reporters, expressed "surprise" and "dismay" about "the jingoist tone of some of my colleagues."

Anchors and reporters struck up a we-vs.-they form of dialogue, which had the effect of suffocating press skepticism. We, the American and allied side; they, the Iraqi side. We, "virtuous" and "united" against aggression, Saddam Hussein, portrayed as the Middle East equivalent of Adolf Hitler. As Ed Siegel of the *Boston Globe* put it, "television has been giving us . . . black-and-white stories of the forces of good vs. the forces of darkness."

Experts paraded their military expertise across the TV screens, almost all of them former generals or admirals who seemed to roll up their sleeves and gleefully play war games on the tube. "We'll clean their clocks," pronounced Admiral William Crowe, former chairman of the JCS, with hardly a bow in the direction of objective analysis. The air was filled with an unquestioning acceptance of the Pentagon line—official footage of pinpoint target bombing ("right down their chute"), which, months after the war, proved to be much less than "pinpoint" in its accuracy.

CNN's Peter Arnett, one of the few Western journalists operating out of Baghdad during the war, was savagely attacked by conservative politicians in Washington for doing no more than reporting what the Iraqi government said and did—all the while functioning under severe restrictions. Still, Senate minority whip Alan Simpson referred to Arnett as a "sympathizer" (Simpson was later to apologize) and critics called CNN the "Saddam Network News."

ABC and NBC, more than CBS, showed "video postcards" from the war front—smiling soldiers sending love and kisses to moms, dads, and girlfriends, also holiday greetings. These "postcards" usually preceded commercials, so that there was an impression of a blissful blending of homespun patriotism and profit. "I'm worried," said Tom Shales of the *Washington Post*, "the networks are whooping up war fever."

Magazines and tabloids were equally jingoistic. A *New York Post* front-page headline read: UP YOURS. *Newsweek*'s read: BAGHDAD'S BULLY. The *New York Times*, of all newspapers, ran a special supplement months later, which featured the following salutation over a photo of two African-American soldiers embracing, with one holding an American flag: "New York Celebrates, Operation Welcome Home, Monday, June 9, 1991."

Was it then any wonder that the overwhelming majority of the American people supported the Gulf War? Any wonder that President Bush closed down U.S. military operations with a popularity rating of 89 percent, which conveyed the totally inaccurate impression that he was unbeatable in 1992? Any wonder that there was so little sensible and informed public discussion of the pros and cons of the war, or of the buildup and follow-up to the war? Any wonder then that Iraqgate came as such a surprise to the American people, not to mention the American press?

In the age of television, which does so much to fashion our political and cultural discourse, passions and patriotism can be easily aroused, critical faculties can be easily suppressed. Question: If Hitler had had television in the early 1930s, would the German people have rushed to his support with even more enthusiasm, or would they have been repelled by his fascist, racist message, and blocked his ascent to total power? In the 1990s, with wars now being waged in "real time," with public opinion so effectively fashioned by handlers and manipulators, with the line between perception and reality so naturally blurred, the responsibility of the press to monitor the affairs of state has never been greater.

And yet, during this particular war, technology globalized the news process, obliterating time and distance and setting new and not always higher standards of performance. CNN wired the world. Network anchors got teary-eyed as they shook hands on television with generals who were about to leave on missions. Local reporters who had never been abroad flew into Saudi Arabia, where they had little or no knowledge of the history, culture, language, or politics of the country, to cover a strange conflict, which they rarely if ever saw or heard, except on television, and they were expected to satisfy not only the professional norms of war coverage but the specific needs of their communities. In this journalistic revolution, news organizations were routed by the Pentagon through a clever use of pools and restrictive practices. The press objected strenuously on occasion, but the public, by a huge majority, applauded the Pentagon and showed no sympathy for the press. Too bad, because now there is no record, no witness, to most of what happened in the war. No understanding of why the war, which seemed to end so decisively, continues in different ways. Norman Schwarzkopf's briefings were TV highlights that featured his toughly worded brilliance pitted against the press's awkward and occasionally stupid questions. There was little perspective—and there was excessive emotionalism—in the reporting. Jonathan Alter of *Newsweek* wrote that "real reporters keep their feelings from getting in the way." But they did not.

Patriotic journalism was—and is—dangerous, because it denies to the public the information and detached perspective people need to make sound decisions. Saddam Hussein was—and is—evil enough: Hitler-style comparisons not only exaggerate and twist the truth, they do an injustice to history. They are more propaganda than news. And what is the difference? Walter Lippmann, many years after his days as government flack, wrote: "We must remember that in time of war what is said on the enemy's side of the front is always propaganda and what is said on our side of the front is truth and righteousness."

And what happens next? What happens when another Gulf War erupts? Will the press regroup, and serve the people? Will the public interest be addressed? Or, will the Pentagon, feeling no pain or popular constraints and encouraged by its recent successes in controlling a not terribly popular press, again establish its pools, its censorship, its vision of reality—and sell it in prime time? If there was ever a time for the press to reconsider its function and purpose, it is now. The press does not have to be popular or patriotic, it has to be energetic, purposeful, detached, unemotional, cool, skeptical, determined.

A View from the Military

LIEUTENANT GENERAL
THOMAS W. KELLY (RET.)

Our most important "possession" as Americans is freedom. Because we have never lacked it, we don't think about it much but, friend, it's vital and if we ever lost it, we'd notice! There are a number of institutions in America that guard it. First, there is the bedrock of our magnificent Constitution; then our political process itself. Beyond these, there are two crucial institutions that are among the principal guarantors of freedom and democracy in America, the military and the press. For 217 years, the military has stood like a rock in its constant devotion to the nation, sometimes imperfect but always striving to do its duty. And then there is the press. Ours is the best and worst in the world, but always vital to the democratic process in our country. From the ponderous *New York Times* to the supermarket tabloids, it blares out, on a daily basis, the facts and fantasies of our time. The pundits punditize, the sensationalists sensationalize, the electronic media view with alarm, and all of the press devotes itself to a full measure of 20-20 hindsight.

As a soldier who served almost thirty-five years in the army as a combat officer, how do I view their success or lack thereof? Strange as it may seem, I view the U.S. press as the best in the world, by far. More important, our press has been successful. The American people are the best-informed of people anywhere, and the press has made an almost sacred contribution to American freedom since the very beginning.

Not that it doesn't have warts. It sure does (so does the military and all other institutions). I recently participated in a seminar at George Washington University on the subject of the media and foreign policy. It was full of press academics, working-press people—and me. The question was whether the press influenced policy-making (the Gulf War was the case study) and if so, how much. The answer was, yes it does—a lot. But then we got down to cases with me defending the government regarding the war and "them" attacking it because of a perceived secrecy/conspiracy idea which was deeply held.

I once attended a press gathering in New York where the leading paladins of the press gathered to honor themselves. During the proceedings, a very respected TV news anchor got up and said that a major casualty of the Gulf War was the truth. This thought was clearly reflected in the seminar at George Washington University. Baloney. The truth was quite healthy during the war, the government told its story, and the American people believed it. The war was quick, it was successful, and there were blessedly few casualties. If that scenario didn't satisfy the press, tough luck. Press members may have thought that they were badly treated but they weren't. There were accusations of secrecy. True, yet secrecy in military operations is valid and vital. There were accusations of "a conspiracy." That's a real biggie with the press. Uncover one and you are made as a professional journalist—but it just wasn't there. We, the military, did a good job and so, incidentally, did the press. My advice is to stop carping and report the facts. Stop the postmortems and look to the future. Don't look for a conspiracy behind every tree, there isn't one. But if one comes along, hammer it. You know, military people are Americans too. We work very hard to keep our country free and we often do it under some pretty trying circumstances. Try to understand and interpret what is going on. Don't try to make news, it doesn't work. And the press shouldn't expect the government to cater to its every whim; it won't and it shouldn't. The press, however, should keep the pressure on to insure that the bureaucracy keeps straight. The media do a pretty good job of that, always have. That's one of the main reasons we are still free.

A View from the Academy

BERNARD C. COHEN

The study of the media and foreign policy, a cottage industry thirty years ago, has become big business today. It was natural, therefore, that the Gulf War, a signal media event, would stimulate intensive inquiry, both among media practitioners and scholars. Never before had so many

Americans been given the opportunity, in the comfort of their homes, to witness a war from the vantage point of actual participants. Does the Gulf War signify a fundamentally new relationship between the media and the world of foreign policy, or does it strengthen the intellectual underpinnings of existing theory? Is it a seminal event, or simply a strikingly different one?

It is the purpose of this book to explore aspects of these questions in systematic ways. Rather than hazard my own answers here ex cathedra, I would like instead to reflect briefly on what I believe has changed in the structure of media-foreign policy relations over the past thirty years, and what its potential significance might be, for this country at least. Beyond that, where should we go from here, by way of research?

There has been much discussion, mostly in the media, of what has been called the CNN phenomenon: the so-called internationalization of television news. Although CNN seems to have played a distinct role in the Gulf War, I have serious doubts that it has "internationalized" television news. More to the point, it is not the arrival of CNN that has been the source of structural change; it is television itself that has finally become a major force in the media-foreign policy equation.

National network television is now over forty years old, but its capacity to "move and shake" independently is quite recent. Two things have come together to make it a force to be reckoned with: the technical capacity to cover the entire globe in "real time," as it were, and in ever-sharper clarity and color; and the liberation of the medium from the norms or conventions of traditional journalism. The latter is the more important, and deserves some elaboration.

The media in general have always been able to force an "external" set of priorities on foreign-policy makers; by the concerted application of the norms of "the news," what was of interest to the media often became, willy-nilly, of interest to officials. Television participated in this process, along with the press and other media, simply by following the same operating rules as the others. And during the Gulf War, in fact, effective government management of all the media actually forced television into behaving like the other media. In short, the real significance of TV was not revealed by the Gulf War; but it was rumbling underneath, as in fact it had begun to during the Vietnam War.

It has really been in the months since the Gulf War that television, freed from management by the Department of Defense, has also freed itself from the constraints of conventional news journalism, and has demonstrated its power to move governments. By focusing daily on the starving children in Somalia, a pictorial story tailor-made for television,

TV mobilized the conscience of the nation's public institutions, compelling the government into a policy of intervention for humanitarian reasons. But the causes of the starvation in Somalia did not make nearly as good television, and as a consequence there was no discussion of the costs and risks of possible cures. Once intervention was an accomplished fact, however, the starving children of Somalia disappeared almost immediately from the TV screen, leaving in their place crates of food, soldiers, armed convoys, and a host of unresolved military and political problems.

Similarly, by concentrating almost exclusively on the eminently pictorial human-interest aspects of the fighting in Bosnia-Herzegovina— old people freezing in unheated nursing homes in Sarajevo, children caught in small-arms fire, children separated from their families, emaciated men behind barbed wire—television has stimulated a more active American (and international) consideration of interventionary policies in the former Yugoslavia.

It is in the light of these successive revelations of the power of television to mobilize the nonpolitical sympathies of the general public for humanitarian purposes—and thus, potentially at least, to manipulate those sympathies for political purposes—that the rumblings of Vietnam and the Gulf War need to be reheard: if the government ever loses its power to manage news coverage in a theater of war, its capacity to use military force for political (rather than "humanitarian") purposes may well be lost. The human costs of war are eminently pictorial; the political imperatives and advantages are not. It would be hard to imagine the successful prosecution of the Civil War had Matthew Brady been replaced by modern television network news.

It seems to me that structural change of this magnitude in the way the media cover foreign affairs has great potential significance for the state of theoretical development in this field. While the media, as I said earlier, have always been able to force a different set of priorities on policy makers from those they themselves would otherwise prefer, in the past that has required a convergence of all the media in pursuit of agreed standards of "news." Now television alone, in pursuit of its own independent and unique norms, can do it. "Elite dissensus," or even "official conflict," will matter less in the shaping of foreign policy news than the fully opened eye of the television camera. With its presumed "objectivity" in capturing "reality" without the mediation of reporters, television even manages to enjoy a substantial immunity to the widespread distrust of the other media that exists among the general public.

Finally, the importance of the changing norms or conventions of news in this circumstance is a strong argument for more and better comparative analysis of the role of media in foreign affairs. Cook's work on France and my own on the Netherlands suggest that different operating norms of journalism are at work in different countries, growing out of the requirements and the norms of different political systems. Real advances in theoretical development with respect to the media and foreign policy will ultimately depend on our looking at more countries, rather than just at more cases.

one

W. Lance Bennett

The News about
Foreign Policy

According to many observers, we have entered a new era of political communications. Even foreign policy, once the private domain of pin-stripe bureaucrats and business elites, that gray world of threats, promises, wars, espionage, and diplomacy, may have become transformed by a combination of new communications technologies and global media systems. Policy-makers have recognized the presence of television cameras at trade negotiations, peace conferences, and in war zones, with the result that foreign policy has taken on a public-relations, or media-diplomacy, dimension of substantial proportions. Elites, interest groups, and foreign governments alike have taken the task of news management as an increasingly important element of the policy process.

Vivid examples are legion. In 1989 the power of grass-roots actors to use the news media was demonstrated as Chinese students in Tiananmen Square turned their protest movement into television drama, playing the goddess of liberty and other symbols of Western democracy back to Western audiences. Although those symbols had little significance in the Chinese political context, they engaged the popular imagination in North America and Europe, inspiring grass-roots and human-rights groups to complicate if not fully change the China policies of various nations, including the United States (Pratt 1989; Shanor 1989). The Gulf Crisis of 1990, leading to the war against Iraq in 1991, saw both Iraqi leader Saddam Hussein and U.S. officials use CNN as something of a diplomatic back channel, sending complex signals to each other and to their respective publics at the same time (Friedland 1991). In 1992, television images of starvation in Somalia helped mobilize an international humanitarian intervention led by a large U.S. military presence. Among the most vivid scenes from that operation was the look of startled Navy Seals in war paint hitting beaches which had already been secured by television news crews to record the landing.

All of this means that policy-makers cannot ignore news management as a key part of the policy process, as they once may have had the luxury of doing. Journalist Marvin Kalb argues that at least since the Iranian hostage crisis of 1979–80—in which President Jimmy Carter was held hostage in the White House by the press for 444 days—decision-makers have been forced to engage in a new dimension of political activity. Kalb calls this new dimension of the policy process *press politics*, reflecting the inseparability of foreign policy from its management in the news.[1]

Although a broad range of foreign policy situations these days are "mass-mediated," it is less clear how the policy process itself is affected by different patterns of coverage. Most generally, what does news coverage contribute to the quality of public communication about, and participation in, foreign policy decisions? Are policy options critically examined? Are informed publics often created? How and when is public opinion mobilized? How are policy-makers and their decisions affected? Are measures of public accountability established to help evaluate the success and failure of policies in the future? These are among the key questions raised in this book. Following a look at controversies about the media and the foreign policy process and an explanation of how the Gulf War figures in these controversies, this chapter provides a framework for analyzing the roles of the media and public opinion across different foreign policy situations.

The Controversy About Mass-Mediated Foreign Policy

Despite the recent explosion of literature on the subject, there is remarkably little consensus on just how the news media affect foreign policy (Cutler 1984; Larson 1988, 1990; O'Heffernan 1990; Serfaty 1991). More than a few scholars and former officials claim that major changes have occurred due to the dominance of the instant electronic forum of television. Some write in nostalgic tones about the passage of an earlier age in which a less publicly examined foreign policy was somehow more deliberate, wise, and coherent. One dire prediction looks toward a global "populist democracy" in the foreign policy arena, with the result that "international discourse will become more complex, more populist and more difficult to manage" (Webster 1991). In contrast to this view, others see the potential for more public participation in foreign policy decisions as a positive development warranted by decades of opinion-poll data indicating a capacity for rational public input (Page and Shapiro 1992; Shapiro and Page 1988; Graham 1992).

Another debate centers around the demise of the old foreign policy establishment. Some observers see the rise of a foreign policy patchwork that looks more like the domestic policy arena, in which the policy agenda is carved up by "narrow lobbies and pressure groups rather than an enlightened citizenry. . . . Worse still, these lobbies and pressure groups represent no underlying consensus but only their own separate interests. American foreign policy, once the realm of the Gods, has become the domain of mere influence peddlers" (Judis 1991, 55). In this view, the intrusions of domestic politics have increased the degree of instability in a once highly managed foreign policy process. Domestic news angles, from jobs to jingoism, increasingly affect how international stories are covered (Judis 1991). Such changes may complicate policy-making in areas as diverse as trade, the environment, arms control, defense projections, and the use of force.[2] Critics of this view cite the continuing reluctance of elites to go public with their foreign policy differences, and the continuing willingness of journalists and publics to accept official ideological definitions of foreign policy situations (Herman and Chomsky 1988).

It is difficult to evaluate these competing views because they are often based on radically different types of observations. For example, the impression of a more intrusive and potentially damaging role for the news media often comes from government officials who have done daily battle with reporters in the officials' efforts to present, defend, and, sometimes, hide aspects of their policy initiatives. In this view, the speed and portability of communications equipment, combined with a public fascination for live events coverage, forces officials to make calculations based on the daily publicity surrounding their actions. Such calculations might result in policies that are hasty, ill-conceived, damaging to future options, or tempered by domestic opinion rather than long-term state interests. In the words of Lloyd Cutler, a former Carter administration official, the media have not only put foreign policy "on deadline" but have changed its substance to fit what may be misleading, yet convincing, television images (Cutler 1984). These kinds of claims need to be examined carefully to see if they have any theoretical standing, or whether they are merely the emotional, if understandable, reactions of harried officials wishfully seeking an easier time in their daily encounters with the press.

A related concern also worth careful investigation is what happens when the unblinking eye of television brings the world into the living rooms of what William Schneider (1984, 19) has called "a vast inadvertent audience." If, as has been suggested, this mass audience also turns out to be skeptical of foreign intrigues since Vietnam, the result may be a change in the methods of promoting domestic consensus by forcing officials to sell almost every policy initiative to the general public (Melanson 1991). If the mass-marketing of foreign policy has become doctrine, it then becomes important to decide whether those sales efforts—which also rely on media imagery—create more demagoguery than democracy in foreign affairs.

This brings us to concerns about the growing sophistication of public-relations and marketing techniques that enable domestic interests and foreign governments alike to intervene directly in shaping both the news and public opinion. As explained by Jarol Manheim in Chapter 6 in this volume, going directly to the public may increase the leverage of various players when lobbying Congress and the bureaucracy. The Gulf War was by no means the first time that foreign governments hired public-relations firms to bypass or supplement traditional diplomatic channels (Manheim and Albritton 1984).

To return to the earlier point, most of these observers agree that mass-media news organizations sit more squarely than ever as mediators of complex policy situations. However, they often disagree on whether mass-mediated foreign policy is more democratic or more demagogic. There is also some evidence to counter the romantic view that the fabled "establishment" once ran foreign policy out of sight of the press and out of mind for most of the public. While the press may have been more co-operative and the establishment more cohesive prior to Vietnam, historical accounts from the Spanish-American War, World Wars I and II, and the various interventions in Latin America and elsewhere all suggest that managing the news images that reach the American people has long been an important concern of policy officials. The stakes may be higher and the margin for error smaller in this era of global media and live coverage, meaning that the most important changes may have occurred in the technologies of political communication and information management without much net gain or loss in the quality of the democratic process. The moral of these important controversies is that we need to be cautious about jumping to conclusions. The jury is still out on the question of how the various relations of power among journalists, publics, and politicians have changed due to the rise of a global media, new information technologies, the emergence of CNN as a video wire service, or shifts in world and domestic politics (Smith 1991).

To frame this debate more sharply, it is worth asking whether modern-day news organizations are any more or less susceptible to being captured by policy-makers and their ideologies than when Walter Lippmann

(1922) warned citizens nearly three-quarters of a century ago about the dangers of taking world news at face value. As Marvin Kalb suggests in his opening provocation, the Gulf War does not stand as a modern-day exemplar of critical journalism. This underscores Manheim's point in Chapter 6 that while the technologies of strategic communication have grown more sophisticated, the political goal of news management is no recent development. Since the dawn of mass advertising and scientific public relations with the pioneering work of Edward L. Bernays and others, both government and private interests have a long tradition of trying to sell images of foreign adventures wholesale to the press and other information brokers, who repackage them for retail distribution to the general public (Immerman 1982).

What about the risk of more demagoguery from the arousal of large, "inadvertent" television audiences? It may actually be more difficult to get the attention of, much less sell policies to, the less informed and less ideological members of the public. As noted by John Zaller in Chapter 9 on elite cues and public responses, the most informed publics are most likely to adopt elite cues in the news to structure their thinking about world events.

Consider, finally, a cautionary word about the political officials who commonly express annoyance with journalists. Official annoyance with the press goes back at least to the bitter foreign policy debates between the Federalists and the Jeffersonians in the early years of the Republic. It was Thomas Jefferson, after all, who championed a critical press in foreign policy, and later condemned its intrusiveness when he became president.

The best way to resolve these questions about the role of the news media in the policy process is to compare different kinds of policy situations in different historical periods with the aim of understanding three broad things: the journalistic and political factors that shape the production of news; the ways in which news content affects public opinion; and how both news images and opinion may constrain the maneuvering room of policy officials. These three broad concerns guide the development of both this chapter and the entire book. By looking to different case studies for the various political factors that drive the news-opinion-policy process, we may better understand the similarities and differences across a range of situations like Tiananmen Square, the Gulf Crisis, the North American trade talks, the Central American policies of the 1980s, and the reasons for the shifts in press criticism, public support, and elite consensus about the Vietnam War before and after 1968 (Hallin 1986). It is in this spirit of drawing on what we have learned from studies of other political situations that we explore the public dimension of policy in the Gulf Crisis.

The Case of the Gulf War

Viewers of the buildup to and eventual war against Iraq witnessed the first large-scale application of the Pentagon's post-Vietnam resolve never again to lose a public-relations war (Woodward 1991). Many policy officials in the Defense Department and the State Department became convinced that the U.S. military defeat and eventual withdrawal from Vietnam resulted, in part, from critical media coverage of battlefield activities and, at home, sympathetic coverage of domestic opposition to government policies.

Within days of the invasion of Kuwait in August, General Colin Powell and chief Pentagon operations officer General Thomas Kelly went to Camp David to meet with President Bush. From that time on, the president's leading policy option appears to have been to go to war if Iraqi leader Saddam Hussein did not withdraw his occupying army from Kuwait. In a talk to our research group, General Kelly said that after meeting with the President, "I never had a doubt in my mind that we were going to war." A key objective in waging that war was winning the home front. As General Kelly put it bluntly, "Anybody who doesn't recognize that the support of the American people is a critical element of combat power is pretty dumb." And as he suggests in his provocation above, a common military view is that once the people have been enlisted, the press should stop carping and get on with reporting the story as people have come to accept it.

From building a policy consensus to launching a war, the case of the Gulf Crisis illustrates the waging of foreign policy on two fronts, as John MacArthur (1992) put it. One front involved the usual balance of military and diplomatic calculations and maneuvers, while the other involved the use of what Jarol Manheim in Chapter 6 calls strategic communications techniques: sophisticated public relations and news management aimed at public diplomacy, or the selling of foreign policy at home. The handling of the Gulf Crisis from the early days of Iraq's invasion of Kuwait through the final decision to break off the ground war after 100 hours demonstrated the ability of the White House, the Pentagon, and the State Department to steer a policy course through months of public scrutiny, and to turn saturation coverage by hundreds of news organizations into a public-relations bonanza. One public-relations expert remarked that:

> "The Department of Defense has done an excellent job of managing the news in an almost classic way. There's plenty of access to some things, and at least one visual a day. If you were going to hire a public relations firm to do the media relations for an international event, it couldn't be done any better than this. . . ."[3]

Indeed, it is hard to overlook the Gulf Crisis as a textbook case in the selling of a foreign policy. But there is much more to this case study than that. As the war itself faded from the news, and public attention turned to other political issues, other aspects and questions lingered on, challenging us to address them. To an important degree, the news became part of the story about the Gulf War, both in terms of what kinds of political information journalists did report and, as some contributors to this volume suggest, what kinds of information could and perhaps should have been reported to the public. The chapters in this book by Gladys and Kurt Lang (Chapter 2), William Dorman and Steven Livingston (Chapter 3), and Robert Entman and Benjamin Page (Chapter 4), provide a detailed analysis of the news record from the rise of Saddam Hussein to power in Iraq in 1979, to the invasion of Kuwait in 1990, and through the outbreak of war in 1991. Readers will note that most of the data in these studies of news coverage are drawn from the leading national newspapers and broadcast organizations. Why use these data sources, particularly the newspapers, when relatively small numbers of the general public actually received their information from them? The simple answer is that the prestige press (particularly the *New York Times*) continues to set the tone and provide much of the content cues for the nation's other mass media outlets. Thus, it is a safe bet that if policy angles are not being emphasized and debated in the prestige national papers, they will not trickle down through the rest of the media system. However, the importance of local, particularly broadcast, media in the Gulf War has not been overlooked in our research. The ways in which the Pentagon courted the local media are documented in several chapters, and the importance of enlisting patriotic support through local television coverage is analyzed by Dan Hallin and Todd Gitlin in Chapter 7.

Understanding the flow of information, opinion, and policy leading up to and following the decision to go to war is a complicated task. Each of the authors in this book has chosen to address different parts of the case. These analyses do not seek to diminish the unique aspects of the

Gulf War which give it so much of its enduring character and interest: the covert press censorship and restricted coverage by escorted press pools, the public-relations techniques employed by a variety of actors, the gripping imagery of smart bombs hitting their targets, the more abstract knowledge that there were no pictures in our minds of the not-so-smart bombs that missed their targets, and perhaps above all, the historic significance of this being the first live, primetime war, complete with color commentary, theme music, network logos, and public-relations briefings from the commanders. However, we note that these features have been dissected and discussed exhaustively in the dozens of other works that have been published on the subject. In addition, throughout this project there has been a general commitment not to become carried away with surface distractions, but to look beneath that surface to see what drove reporters, publics, and policy officials to act as they did. In searching for deeper patterns in the record of events, many members of this group, including this author, became convinced that the enduring story about the Gulf Crisis was not one of press censorship. Nor was it even a question of the propriety of things like setting the news of death and destruction to rock and roll sound tracks. Rather, we looked for the more enduring factors that enable us to locate the Gulf Crisis in the context of other foreign policy events for purposes of comparison.

The challenge of understanding the public dimension of foreign policy is to identify the underlying linkages among reporters, publics, and political elites that enable us to talk about different cases within the same analytical framework. The purpose of the remainder of this chapter is to provide a general framework for studying the public dimension of foreign policy, and to show how that framework can be applied to the case study at hand. The different pieces of this case study trace the flow of information, public opinion, and policy decisions involving Iraq through the decade of the 1980s and through the war itself in 1991. The authors approached this case with an eye to what we have learned from other research about three domains of the mass-mediated policy process: (1) the production of news images by journalists and political actors; (2) the effects of those news images on patterns of public opinion and participation; and (3) the policy effects resulting directly from news coverage and indirectly from the impact of news on opinion and participation. An important goal of this project is to bring these three aspects of the public dimension of foreign policy into the same analytical scheme, rather than leave them isolated as three separate academic concerns, as they often have been in the past.

Thinking About the News, Public Opinion, and Policy

Traditional theories of foreign policy have focused closely on behind-the-scenes politics, isolating such things as: bureaucratic bargaining, elite perceptions of enemies and crises, the workings of the security community, and levels of consensus within the so-called policy establishment (Herman 1990). Attempts to look at more public aspects of the foreign policy process have focused primarily on public opinion and its linkages to elites. These studies have looked at opinion linkages in different ways, including: elite perceptions of publics (Cohen 1973); direct linkages between public opinion and policy (Shapiro and Page, 1988); game theory analyses that view opinion as another piece of information known to both friendly and enemy players in the policy game (Bueno de Mesquita and Laiman 1990); and institutional analyses that see opinion as a power lever along with lobbying and elections (Ninic and Hinckley 1991; Risse-Kappen 1991; Russett 1990–91). In addition, Cohen's (1963) pioneering work on the press suggested that political calculations by reporters and officials affected information flows to publics.

While all of these approaches suggest the importance of a public phase of the policy process, there is no general model that provides an account of why information flows vary from one political situation to another, affecting the ways in which publics become involved and decision-makers are constrained in the policy process. The approach here offers a broad view of how the news record of a policy episode is constructed, how that information record in turn affects opinion formations, and how those formations may enter different institutional arenas and the calculations of policy officials. To begin with, consider a range of imaginable differences across policy situations.

At one extreme, the public exchange of foreign policy information in the news can be relatively rich, with more (and more diverse) voices participating, more views and options being introduced, and continuing for more extended periods of time, with noticeable effects on the course of policy itself. This scenario might be thought of as an *open information flow*, in which different viewpoints are presented in high enough volumes for long enough periods of time that opinion formations respond to information changes, and elites get the sense that they are being held accountable to some standards of popular judgment for their actions. In this scenario, opinion rallies may rise and fall as opposition voices do or do not enter the news (see Brody, Chapter 10 below). In addition, guidelines for evaluating policies may be introduced into the news record so that politicians are called to account for past actions. Perhaps a historical

THE NEWS ABOUT FOREIGN POLICY

context is built up so that it becomes difficult for officials to change course, as often happens in foreign policy, by simply reinventing history. Under these conditions, both the opinion formations in response to news images, and the daily pressures of journalistic scrutiny (including the risks of negative coverage if closely watched policies fail) can affect the course of policy.

At the other extreme are coverage patterns involving less criticism of the leading policy option, with fewer opposition voices and less varied viewpoints making it into the news. In this type of relatively *closed information flow*, there is little ground established for evaluating policies or holding officials accountable. At this end of the news information continuum, there also tends to be a lack of much historical reference, leaving officials relatively free to reinvent history and make untested claims about policies.

Different cases can be located along this continuum. For example, the news information flows surrounding the invasions of Grenada and Panama during the 1980s clearly fall toward the closed end of the continuum, while the news pattern from the post-1967 Vietnam era clearly falls toward the open end. The Gulf War case described in this book falls somewhere in between, although in the view of most of the authors here, more toward the closed end. Recent debates over international trade have been relatively open, reflecting partisan differences between key political players in Washington, and the tendencies of news organizations to key their reporting to elite disagreements.

The beginning point for understanding these and other cases in more detail is to review what we already know about the relations among journalists, publics, and the political actors at the core of the decision process. *First, we need to bring in what we know about the regular patterns of press-government relations, and news organization–audience relations that affect the production of news content.* The goal here is to identify the routine ways in which journalists choose sources, screen angles, and weigh information. Equally important is to understand the news management strategies that politicians use to turn the predictable behavior of journalists to their political advantage. Sometimes officials are successful in structuring information so that journalists are effectively trapped or limited by their own operating procedures. At other times, those political strategies are poorly implemented, or journalists find other sources to help them get around official definitions of policy situations. Finally, we need to pay attention to the ways in which journalists write enduring cultural scripts into the news as events develop in familiar patterns, and audience responses feed back into coverage decisions made by editors and producers. In Chapter 7, Daniel Hallin and Todd Gitlin point out that, following the outbreak of the war against Iraq, enduring cultural themes of community and national prowess became the basis for much of the news, particularly in local television coverage.

These news production factors affect things like the duration and the information diversity of news coverage. By fleshing out the reporting habits of journalists and showing how they interact with the communication strategies used by politicians, we may be able to account for the following kinds of differences in the reporting of foreign policy situations:

- the diversity of actors who make the news (measured by the ratios of official, nonofficial, expert, elite, and nonelite voices in the news, on editorial pages, and on public affairs programs);
- the diversity of policy options reported in the news, and the weight given to those options;
- the degree of historical background established in news coverage;
- the measures of accountability established for decision-makers, both short-term (opinion polls, editorial positions, and experts' judgments), and long-term (standards for measuring the success or failure of policies themselves).

Second, and following from this, we must account for how these characteristics of the news information record affect public opinion, and create opportunities for various forms of popular participation. Of concern here are the relations between the above information-characteristics in the news and patterns of public action, reaction, opinion formation, and change. Among the obvious concerns here are:

- how policy cues (e.g., party opposition, conflict between the White House and Congress, consensus among experts) affect opinion formation among publics with varying degrees of interest and information about an issue;
- how reporting political opposition in the news contributes to the rise and fall of opinion rallies supporting presidents and their policies;
- how the framing of news accounts (e.g., as narratives, around human-interest angles, as ideological choices, or in more abstract economic or political terms) affects popular reasoning and information processing about a policy situation.

Third, we must grapple with the impact of both the news information record and the above opinion and participation effects on the actual policy options chosen, the ones not chosen, and the record of accountability established for the policy itself. In this third public domain of the foreign policy process, officials may find themselves either limited or licensed to take particular actions, depending on factors such as these:

- the persistent coverage of opposition among Washington elites may make policy officials reluctant to pursue risky policy initiatives;
- prominent coverage of divided opinion polls, of demonstrations, or of protest movements may limit officials in their pursuit of particular policy options;
- reporting on the success or failure of past policies may affect the credibility of official claims about new situations;
- reporting that enhances public awareness of historical conditions may affect how officials can define the current situation;
- anticipated negative news coverage of particular policy options may diminish the attractiveness of those options, whatever their other advantages might be.

The inner workings of these three domains of the policy process are specified more fully in the sections that follow.

News Production

We begin with the most obvious aspect of news production, and one of the most established findings in media research: reporters overwhelmingly turn to officials as sources for political stories and for framing the policy content of stories (Cohen 1963; Gans 1979; Sigal 1973; Tuchman 1978). In some of the pioneering research in this field, Bernard Cohen (1963) concluded that journalists and political officials were engaged in a process of symbiosis or mutual dependence, in which each side used the other to promote particular organizational (press or government) goals. More recent research suggests that the dominance of official, particularly executive branch, sources is even more pronounced in national security stories than for the news as a whole (Hallin, Manoff, and Weddle 1990).

OFFICIALIZED NEWS

Some observers argue that for all the complexity of modern-day domestic politics, the press continues to display an underlying pattern of deference to foreign policy elites that results in largely unchallenged reporting of elite definitions of political situations. Thus, the public continues to hear mainly what elites choose to make public, but the range of policy information and debate expands when the elites themselves are in open disagreement or conflict. Those who support this view offer evidence spanning a broad historical range of policy situations from Vietnam, the Central American conflicts of the 1980s, the Gulf War, and other episodes from the 1990s (Bennett 1990; Hallin 1986; Herman 1985).

Even if most foreign policy news is elite-driven, there can be important differences from one policy situation to another in the degree of elite conflict offered up to the press, the duration of resulting news coverage, the play given to different sides of the story, and other information patterns of great consequence to the formation of public opinion and the legitimation of policy. These differences suggest that while journalists may be operating with one norm referring them to official sources, they also operate with an equally important professional norm that discourages taking sides by looking to report different sides of a debate. So strong is this oppositional norm that journalists have been described as going into something of a "feeding frenzy" when conflict and controversy break out within official circles (Sabato 1991).

The operative phrase here remains "within official circles." When a relatively open policy debate occurs along our idealized news information continuum, it most often develops because different officials along news beats have broken with consensus and decided to go public with their policy differences. Elites in open conflict provide journalists with reportable opposition voices and viewpoints. Conversely, when for any reason elite differences are resolved, or attempts at resolution lead officials to retreat behind closed doors, the reportable official conflict disappears, and the policy story often dries up. Thus, for example, U.S. policy toward El Salvador turned from one of the most widely reported and hotly contested stories of the early 1980s, to one of the most neglected. By 1985, a national panel of media critics put El Salvador at the top of the list of ten most (self) censored stories by the press. Although the U.S.-funded war escalated, and El Salvador became the third leading U.S. aid recipient in the world during the period of declining news coverage, journalists complained that Washington officialdom had closed ranks around the administration war policy, leaving the press without much of a policy story. Never mind the presence of an easily accessible war with many domestic and foreign opponents willing to offer themselves as news sources (Bennett 1988, 46–51, 98–99, 137–38).

Differences in the patterns of foreign policy news (diversity of sources, range of viewpoints and policy options) can be explained in large part by this tendency to "index" news coverage to the intensity and duration of official Washington conflicts (Bennett 1990). Indexing has at least two important effects on the information structure of the resulting news. First, journalistic perceptions of divisions among officials open the news gates to contending elite views of policy options, rationales, historical arguments (if there are any), and standards of accountability for evaluating policy successes and failures. Second, when official conflict is sustained, the news gates also tend to open to grass-roots groups, interest groups, opinion polls, and broader social participation in media policy debates because the ongoing story offers news organizations opportunities to follow different angles, opportunities that may enrich news information as journalists look for new ways of reporting the same old story.

Studies of different historical periods and different policy issues confirm the importance of indexing in constructing the information value of the news product. Dan Hallin (1986) attributes much of the news debate during the Vietnam War to the emergence of sustained opposition to administration policies within Congress, and even within the executive branch itself. With the expansion of what Hallin calls the sphere of legitimate controversy, many features of the news policy record began to change, including the frequency of opposition views in the policy debate, and the entry of nonofficial (nongovernment) voices into that debate.

The much more restricted elite debates about the Gulf Crisis help explain the news information patterns found in several of the studies in this book. William Dorman and Steven Livingston note in Chapter 3 that during the important "establishing phase" of public discussion in the months immediately after the invasion of Kuwait, the absence of much elite debate or criticism left the press largely reporting administration views. It was during this phase that the Hitler analogy was applied to Iraqi leader Saddam Hussein with little challenge from the press (see also, MacArthur 1992). Robert Entman and Benjamin Page show in Chapter 4 that the news became more open to opposition views and policy alternatives during the relatively brief periods of congressional debate in November of 1990 and January of 1991. However, these periods of opposition voices in the news were restricted and closed down almost completely after Congress passed a resolution supporting the administration's policy position. Also characteristic of indexing, the narrow margin of passage for the congressional resolution was not as important as the fact that, after its passage, official debate all but ended and so did debate in the leading news media.

What this means in the case of the Gulf War is that the quality of the news information record was affected more by the dynamics of power between high Washington officials than by all the high-tech communications, television's saturation coverage from the front, the slick Pentagon public relations, the overt press censorship, or the press putting policy-makers on deadline. As William Dorman put it, the early stage of the policy debate concerning what to do about Iraq was distinguished by the absence of much opposition from elites in Washington, leading the press to report uncritically on the way the Bush administration framed the issues:

> By accepting the frames offered by Bush, the press helped to limit debate at the time when it would have done the most good— before we got in so deeply that the war became inevitable. Perhaps the most important question of this discussion has to do with why the press behaves as it does. There are a number of reasons, some more significant than others. First, Congress was on vacation, and American journalism is very closely indexed to structured institutional debate. The press didn't know who to turn to for critical reaction to the President's initial policy. In other words, when it comes to foreign policy, if a member of Congress doesn't say it, it isn't as likely to be covered.[4]

Since readers may well remember the televised and often moving congressional debates on the eve of the war, the point must be made clear here: elite policy divisions *were* covered by the media, but: (a) they came relatively late in the policy process, (b) they were contained within a short time-frame, and (c) White House positions generally received the most prominent display in the news record even during the periods of most intense congressional debate. Public opinion responded to points in the information flow when elite opposition voices were raised, but coverage of the opposition was not long enough, prominent enough, or timely enough to seriously affect the leading policy option of war—an option that, as General Kelly noted, was firmly held by the president since the invasion in August.

Routine relations between reporters and officials also yield other insights about news construction. Consider the implications of a seemingly benign fact of daily life for the press: news-gathering in the U.S. is organized around beats. As Timothy Cook explains in Chapter 5, the key foreign policy beats are the "golden triangle" of the White House, the

Pentagon, and the State Department, with Congress also playing a role in many stories. The beat system has obvious bureaucratic and economic advantages for news organizations seeking to schedule reporting assignments, "cover" a large amount of territory, and produce a steady, predictable supply of stories to fill the daily news hole in a cost-effective way. In addition, there is an ideological rationale that in a democracy the news should tell the people what their elected officials say and do, not make independent judgments about where to find a more representative set of political actors for each story covered.

All of these may seem like perfectly good reasons to cover the world from the official viewpoints of Washington, but to many social scientists who study the news they look like the makings of a normative order. Any normative order favors some social values, ideas, and actors over others, and creates certain openings for deception, manipulation, and conflict. As Cook notes in his analysis of bureaucratic routines and Gulf War reporting, U.S. news about the war looked a good deal different than, for example, French news, largely because of differences in the operating routines of news organizations themselves. In the U.S., the beat system has become so routinized that it provides reporters with the ability to anticipate official reactions during crises and breaking events, even when they have not be able to interview their usual sources before filing a story. Cook illustrates this point by contrasting French and U.S. television coverage of the early days of the Gulf Crisis with an example that is developed further in Chapter 5 of this book:

> For [the] French news broadcast, the world was first globally constructed, then ideologically constructed. By contrast, for [the] American broadcast, the world was first domestically constructed, then institutionally constructed. [The American reporters] presented themselves as impartial observers at their newsbeats, but it was clear that none of them had had much opportunity to discuss the breaking news with any sources. Instead, their reactions to [the anchor's] questions largely reflected their understanding of the institution and the individuals in charge. In effect, [they] were almost as much spokespersons for the newsbeats they covered as were the party spokespersons on French television for their parties.

All of which suggests that the bureaucratic interdependence of reporters and officials places some obvious boundaries around policy debates in general. Foreign policy information (and a good deal of domestic politics coverage) is heavily structured by elite cues, official information, and the policy options considered viable by insiders. News information is weighted by the prominence of information sources within the Washington power hierarchy, at least as perceived by the insiders in the national press corps. What these information boundaries mean, among other things, is that even when national debates spill beyond the efforts of officials to define and control the policy situation (often resulting in protests, opinion divisions in society, and lively media debates), the final word in the news is usually reserved for journalists' well-cultivated official sources, led by the president, top administration officials, and key members of Congress.

Grass-roots voices and interest groups do, of course, make the news on the strength of their own public-relations strategies and the dramatic qualities that may surround their political activities. Thus, the protests at Tiananmen Square in 1989 were newsworthy in their own right, but the story eventually became pegged to the reaction in Washington. Moreover, there is reason to suspect that incidents such as Tiananmen, the crisis in Somalia, or the horrors in Bosnia in 1992–94 that brought haunting images into American living rooms, make it easier for journalists to write provocative scripts precisely because those events were not previously established on the policy agendas in Washington.

The dilemma, however, is that sustained news coverage of policy options that originate beyond the beltway is unlikely to occur unless those options eventually find a place on the Washington policy agenda and stimulate official debate.[5] Once the attention of Washington elites is engaged, the common pattern for elite domination of news messages is reasserted, and journalists can once again write world-news scripts from Washington newsbeats even when events and television cameras are "on location." This pattern was taken to extremes in the Gulf Crisis, as noted by a journalist who concluded: "To get at the real story in the Gulf, reporters did not have to travel to the front. They did not even have to travel to Saudi Arabia. Most of the information they needed was available in Washington" (Massing 1991, 24).

All of these patterns help to explain why the opinions of publics and the positions of activist groups may not be incorporated as centrally in news about foreign policy as they are on many domestic issues. Studies of policy debates as different in time and substance as the antiwar movement during Vietnam (Gitlin 1980) and the nuclear freeze movement in the early 1980s (Entman and Rojecki 1993) find that, compared to government officials, grass-roots groups and their spokespeople were portrayed in more negative terms, while being less able to get preferred versions of their messages into the media debate. The bottom line remains that the news gates tend to open or close depending on the levels of conflict among powerful players in the policy situation on Capitol Hill, the White House, the State Department, Defense, and other relevant institutions along the news beat.

PUBLIC RELATIONS AND NEWS MANAGEMENT

Adding to these dynamics of news production, we must now bring in the methods used by various political actors in a situation to try to influence the course of public information. While journalists on their beats are looking for signs of political conflicts, political actors (most often government officials) are trying to feed reporters the daily news line most advantageous to their policy preferences. In short, the same officials who make up the journalist's news index are, themselves, active players in a press management game, applying various techniques of strategic communications (see Manheim 1991) to elevate the volume of their own messages and reduce the credibility of their opponents. The study by Jarol Manheim presented in Chapter 6 suggests something of a public-relations coalition operating between the exiled government of Kuwait and the White House, using similar images based on similar marketing research to advance common policy goals. As Manheim suggests, the images used to sell the war (notably Saddam-as-Hitler) were focus-grouped, test-marketed, and tracked through elaborate polling.

While journalists are aware of, and may try to resist their dependence on officially packaged news, the growing sophistication of press management techniques holds the constant possibility that some officials will be more successful engineering favorable media framings for their positions than others. The textbook example, of course, was the news management strategy of the early Reagan administration, which has by now become legendary. A host of techniques (controlling leaks, putting out a story of the day, setting up computer files scripting the official line of the day for different administration officials), often added up to favorable policy coverage even in many situations where opposition in Congress and in opinion polls might warrant more critical media treatment (Hertsgaard 1988).

News organizations may try to introduce a more independent information flow by turning to experts to assess the claims of officials. However, experts often reinforce the same viewpoints already dominating the news flow. This should not be surprising to the journalists who recruit the experts. In their spare time, experts are establishing their credentials as experts by advising or taking the counsel of the same government officials that journalists seek out in the first place. Thus, the

increasing use of experts in news coverage may create an appearance of
journalistic independence without really adding much to information
diversity in the process.

PRESS-AUDIENCE RELATIONS

Finally, it is important to recognize that news organizations and their
audiences have independent ties that also affect the development of
news stories. To begin with, audiences are consumers in news markets
that can affect how a story is played. In addition, there is an implicit, if
often strained, relationship between journalists and citizens that reflects
and affirms the basic assumptions of the political culture: who "we" are
as a nation, what values are at stake in political conflicts, and what kinds
of actions are appropriate or inappropriate for the government to take
and for the people to support. Since stable public opposition to a war
policy never emerged in response to news information patterns prior to
the war, the media were left in a vulnerable political position vis-à-vis
both public and politicians. Attempts by journalists to introduce independent perspectives on (much less, criticism of) developing government policies were subject to public condemnation as irresponsible
journalism. Such condemnation was easily stirred by administration officials, particularly after the war broke out. The few instances of independent reporting (such as CNN's Peter Arnett filing stories from
Baghdad) were easy prey to charges of biased journalism. As the nation
went to war, the press increasingly played up "yellow ribbon" images,
and featured themes of home, community, and military might: core elements of the political culture. Public condemnation of journalistic de-
partures from these core cultural values (also evidenced by strong public
support for military censorship of the press) no doubt stood as a chilling
reminder to many journalists about the ranking of press freedom in the
value scheme of the American political culture. Crisis and war, of
course, impose added strains on the fragile cultural bond between the
public and its press.

   In Chapter 7, Dan Hallin and Todd Gitlin suggest that ever greater cultural pressures on information flows can occur as public moods change
after a policy decision is made, particularly if that policy is to go to war.
Deeper images of a culture and its communities at war are explored by
the Hallin and Gitlin account of how news organizations dramatized and
scripted the war itself. The link between the news *business* and its role as
a purveyor of *culture* is obvious in this case. Local television news in particular became a showcase for "home front" and "yellow ribbon" stories
about the war. Perhaps in anticipation of this, the Pentagon ran a large-

scale program to fly local journalists to Saudi Arabia before the U.S. attack was launched from there.

To summarize the discussion so far, at least three important theoretical dynamics affect how the mass media construct the news record of policy debates. First, reporters and editors tend to index the voices and viewpoints in stories to the range of official debate available to reporters on the news beats of decision-making institutions of government. Second, government officials try to influence how their voices are played in these debates by implementing public-relations and news management strategies. Third, the press as arbiters of culture (and as protectors of their markets) add important plot elements to news accounts as public moods change and events appear to fit familiar cultural plots. The interaction among these aspects of news production affect the content, duration, and intensity of opposition viewpoints in media policy debates, along with the degree to which grassroots or social voices are included in those debates. The way in which information in these policy debates is structured, in turn, has important effects in the second sphere of the public policy process, the formation of public opinion.

How The News Affects Opinion Formation

The second element of our perspective is based on considerable evidence that the formation of public opinion is cued heavily by information patterns in the news. As Lang and Lang suggest in Chapter 2, there were a number of foreign policy incidents involving Iraq and Saddam Hussein during the 1980s, but because little of that coverage was carried over from one incident to the next, few traces were left of anything that could be called public opinion at the time of Iraq's invasion of Kuwait in 1990. The absence of clear opinion formations about Saddam and Iraq at the time of the invasion made public-relations efforts to equate Saddam with Hitler all the more effective in the early stages of the crisis, as suggested by Dorman and Livingston in Chapter 3 and Manheim in Chapter 6.

In Chapter 8, Iyengar and Simon make it clear that the way an evolving story is framed thematically affects important characteristics of public opinion. The intensity of coverage sets the agenda of issues the public cares most about. The politicians who enter the news picture will be evaluated by the public on the basis of how they handle those important issues. Perhaps most important, how a story is framed (for example, around human interest vs. more analytical themes) affects how people following the debate think about policy options and preferred outcomes. The framing of most of the news about the Gulf Crisis led people to think more clearly about war than about other solutions to the problem. The vivid, personalized framing of Saddam as Hitler made a clean historical break with past administration policies toward Iraq and established a new historical and emotional reference from which opinion formation could begin anew. Iyengar (1992) has demonstrated that the news often frames complex policy situations in personal and emotional terms that appeal to audiences without providing much of a foundation for critical thinking or gathering information.

Framing the Gulf Crisis issues in personalized emotional terms around Saddam-as-enemy made other issues and policy options in the conflict more difficult to grasp. Compared to the option of doing battle against the evil Saddam, the other leading policy alternative—economic sanctions against Iraq—was poorly presented and debated before the public. In large part, this reflected the early consensus in the Bush administration that sanctions would not work and should not be encouraged. In addition, as Entman and Page suggest in Chapter 4, the sanctions option was poorly positioned for public consideration due to the late timing and short duration of the congressional debates. The timing and duration of congressional debate on the policy options are important because, as noted earlier, opinion formations are most influenced by the positions taken by prominent elites.

This pattern of elite cuing does not apply to the inattentive or the uninformed. To the contrary, as people become more informed about the policy issues in a conflict, their opinions become more responsive to cues from elites as those cues are reported in the news. As John Zaller describes it in Chapter 9:

> Evidence from half a century of polling in the United States firmly supports the proposition that the more citizens know about politics and public affairs, the more firmly they are wedded to elite and media perspectives on foreign policy issues. When elites are united in support of a foreign policy, politically aware Americans support that policy more strongly than any other part of the public. When elites divide along partisan or ideological lines, politically attentive citizens are more likely than the inattentive to align their opinions with that segment of the elite which shares their party or ideology. And when elite opinion changes, political awareness is a major determinant of which members of the public follow the elite lead.

This iron law of opinion and foreign policy offers one reason why indexing opposing viewpoints in news stories to divisions among Washington power brokers becomes so important in a foreign policy debate. The news index of elite opposition in a given situation becomes the best predictor of opinion formation, particularly among the informed publics who are looked to by both elites and journalists for signs of support and legitimation in the policy process.

Patterns of elite opposition in news reports also contribute to the rise and fall of opinion rallies. In foreign policy crises, great upwellings of public support for presidential actions can make policy courses appear to be on solid and politically safe ground, only to crash suddenly, leaving publics and policy-makers to start building consensus all over again. As Chapter 10 by Richard Brody shows, the initial rally of support following President Bush's decision to send the troops to Saudi Arabia crashed dramatically when news reports began telling of increasing elite opposition to the president. (It is especially interesting that much of this opposition was aimed at domestic economic policies, while the opinion rally was clearly triggered by the Gulf Crisis.) Brody's findings about the Gulf War are consistent with his studies of a number of other policy episodes (Brody and Shapiro 1989a, 1989b). The sensitivity of public rallies to elite policy debates in the news marks an important departure from the traditional view that rallying publics are solidly bound together by patriotism, often following leaders blindly through crises (Mueller 1973; Kernell 1978).

The analysis of poll data and news content reported here by Brody suggests that while crisis and uncertainty may trigger a rally, particularly in the absence of initial elite opposition, the subsequent outbreak of elite criticism and more general opposition in the news will almost certainly end it. Brody elaborates on the rally phenomenon with this explanation:

> political elites frame the public's response to uncertain international events. If and when opinion leaders publicly interpret a crisis as a result of policy failure, a rally will not take place. If the elite is silent or openly supportive of the administration's position, the public will respond to the administration's generally positive one-sided view of the events—to the administration's "spin"—and rally behind the president. A rally will last as long as the president's tacit or explicit support-coalition persists. (Brody, in this volume, Chapter 10)

When the initial rally behind sending troops to Saudi Arabia finally crashed in October, opinion became fairly evenly divided between support for military and nonmilitary solutions for the crisis. This might have created an opening for a public debate exploring policy options in more critical ways, even turning public opinion against the war option. This policy scenario did not develop, however, for reasons explained in the next section.

The Policy Domain

Variations in news information flows help resolve some of the puzzles about the impact of the news and public opinion on elite decisions. In the traditional view, it was hard to imagine that public opinion directly shaped elite policy preferences, in part because much opinion is uninformed and subject to volatile mood swings (at least in the eyes of many elites). At best, there was a tendency described by Bernard Cohen (1973) as elite "responsiveness," in which decision-makers tried to present their chosen courses of action in ways that appeared to fit public expectations.

More recently, observers have noted stable opinion formations on major policy issues, suggesting the possibility that elites may take opinion on foreign policy into account, or at least have a reasonable basis for doing so (Graham 1992; Page and Shapiro 1992; Shapiro and Page 1988). The tricky question, of course, is whether elite cuing is predominant, making public opinion largely a dependent variable in the policy process, or whether opinion is at least somewhat independent of propaganda and elite influence, making publics more like democratically idealized initiators of policy. Studies suggest that both of these patterns may occur under different circumstances (Bartells 1991; Bennett 1990).

As General Kelly suggested in his meeting with our group, the support of the public is essential to policy success, particularly if the policy is to go to war. This suggests that it is probably too simple to think of opinion as either an input or an output in some mechanical policy process. Rather, opinion formations simply become part of the decision calculus, creating obstacles for some policies and requiring public-relations and news management efforts to overcome those obstacles. From interviews with decision-makers, Patrick O'Heffernan concludes in Chapter 11 that government policy officials pay considerable attention to news information flows and the opinion formations that take shape around them. O'Heffernan adds that surrounding these relations between press, government, and public today are more complex communications flows and political pressures than existed a decade and more ago. At the very least, this means that news management has become more complex, and the potential for damage to policies may have become greater due to the effects of instant global coverage of foreign and domestic political players and their public-relations campaigns. This highlights the importance of strategic communications techniques aimed at putting the best news "spin" on contested policy options. Had congressional opposition during the Gulf Crisis emerged earlier, lasted longer, or become more of a party issue for the Democrats, the viability of the war option might have rested even more than it did on the battle for public opinion waged through the news media.

What emerges here is the idea that mutual adjustments occur between elites, journalists, and publics in the process of constructing news policy coverage. In an information system so heavily indexed to official opposition, the timing of official debates and the strategic communications practices of officials become particularly important aspects of the policy process. To put it bluntly, administration officials may not have to worry so much about explaining the logic or establishing enduring rationales for their policy options as they must worry about becoming trapped by news accounts of opposition to their decisions. Patterns of opposition voices in the news produce opinion dynamics that may constrain policy options. Earlier and more protracted congressional debates and other displays of elite opposition might have significantly altered the structure of public opinion and the political calculations about going to war against Iraq. As it was, General Kelly informed our group, Congress never became a worry for administration policy, and the undivided attention of the policy circle was focused on mobilizing public support through the media.

Even if a less advantageous flow of news and opinion would not have altered President Bush's resolve to go to war, it might well have raised more questions about the reasons for going to war, while establishing clearer measures for evaluating the success or failure of the policy. In short, other patterns of coverage might have left the president less free to establish his own policy goals (liberating Kuwait but stopping short of invading Iraq and destroying Saddam's army), and more accountable for failing to depose Saddam Hussein, who was, after all, central to the entire framing of the original policy problem.

As Chapter 12 by John Zaller makes clear, it would be a mistake to think that elites go public with their policy options without first considering the personal and party politics surrounding those options. Among the factors that shape positions taken in the news are calculations about "worst case" news scenarios that might develop around various options. The image of Jimmy Carter held prisoner in the Oval Office by 444 days of news about the Iranian hostage crisis in 1979 must stand as an icon for

future presidents to consider in structuring their public communications. For President Bush, it is clear that the decision to wait for sanctions
to force Saddam Hussein out of Iraq was fraught with news pitfalls: hundreds of thousands of troops sitting on the ground in sweltering heat,
doing nothing, while Saddam had a media bonanza pointing out the
helplessness of that Great Satan, the United States. Such coverage
would be all the more intolerable politically to Bush if, as his advisors
apparently calculated, there was no way to enforce an economic block-
ade of Iraq effectively enough to make it work quickly. This scenario
would have pushed an eventual war into an election year. As Zaller
notes, presidents do not start wars during elections, but they do start
them during periods of economic distress of the sort faced by Bush.

At the other end of Pennsylvania Avenue, leaders of the Democratic
opposition in Congress were faced with their own news-politics calculations. According to Zaller's sources, the Democratic leadership opposed
the war on moral grounds, but they faced the political risk of being portrayed in the news as contributing to a constitutional crisis if they tried to
block the war option. In addition, a party vote might have created other
unpleasant news scenarios, including the identification of the Democrats as opponents of a possibly victorious war. Going to war is, as Hallin
and Gitlin suggest, more than just another foreign policy option; it is also
an embodiment of cultural themes of prowess and community. Would
the Democrats risk opposing what could (and eventually did) turn out to
be a grand celebration of cultural values? The short answer was no, particularly when the leading alternative was the possibly unworkable option of economic sanctions. To top it all off, the Democrats at the time
were giving President Bush a political trouncing in the 1990 mid-term
elections and in a budget agreement that forced him to move his lips and
retract that famous 1988 campaign promise: "Read my lips. No new
taxes." Politically speaking, the Democrats minimized their political
losses and preserved their political gains by backing the option least
likely to produce lasting political damage in the news. The war issue was
presented to members of the party by their leaders as a vote of individual
conscience, meaning that the potential was removed for introducing the
kind of sustained party and institutional opposition that can turn news
coverage and public opinion formations into forces that change the
course of policy in the minds of key decision-makers inside an administration. The result was that the nation went to war without substantial
challenge to the policy preference reportedly staked out by the president
within days of the original invasion of Kuwait.

Conclusion

As we survey the panoply of foreign policy challenges from Somalia to Bosnia and from Tiananmen Square to the Gulf War, the inescapable conclusion is that the media can construct a range of different policy scenarios. Rather than tending toward either a more democratic or demagogic direction, the potential for both popular initiative and public manipulation in the policy process may be broader than ever before.

As the old cold-war policy consensus gives way to an increasingly chaotic world abroad and indications of growing isolationist opinion at home, elites are likely to make policy based on short-term, case-by-case political calculations. If this trend continues, the public record of news information will reflect an increasingly broad range of situational dynamics. When elite political calculations produce open and extended policy clashes in public, stable divisions of opinion are likely to emerge and policy alternatives are likely to receive more careful examination and to acquire clearer standards of accountability on the media record. In contrast, when political calculations result in little sustained elite opposition, startling policy initiatives may be undertaken with little popular grasp of their rationale or the measures against which to judge their success. The latter is closer to the policy scenario in the Gulf War.

All of this suggests that the presence of live, "saturation" media coverage is not a force that, in and of itself, is likely to result in more or less democratic foreign policy, a more or less enlightened public, or more or less constrained elites. As the Gulf War indicated, the daily clamoring of thousands of journalists for information simply created a strategic communication challenge that the Pentagon, the White House, and even the Kuwaiti royal family were more than equipped to handle. At no point in the Gulf Crisis did the "foreign policy on deadline" syndrome appear to derail or even substantially alter the chosen policy course of the administration. Perhaps the origins of that syndrome during Vietnam, and later in the Carter administration hostage crisis, merely reflect the experiences of policy-makers who did not prepare themselves to incorporate public diplomacy and media management into their policy schemes.

What is clear about the contemporary world of foreign policy is that the policy process includes public information management as an integral political calculation. Depending on how those calculations are played out against the background of political opposition and resulting public opinion formations, the range of policy scenarios can be very broad indeed. However, as the Gulf War indicates vividly, the immediacy and intensity of press coverage, alone, by no means increases the diversity of policy information on the public record or the degree of public influence in the policy process.

Notes

The author would like to thank the Social Science Research Council for providing opportunities to think about these issues. The comments of Brigitte Nacos, Ellen Hume, Robert Entman, and the other contributors to this book on earlier versions of this argument were very helpful. Thanks, in addition, to Regina Lawrence for the valuable research assistance.

1. Marvin Kalb, personal communication.
2. For various perspectives on this point, see the collection of articles in the special issue on "Democracy and Foreign Policy: Community and Constraint," *The Journal of Conflict Resolution* 35, no. 2 (June 1991).
3. Michael Deaver, quoted in the *New York Times*, February 15, 1991, p. A9.
4. *The Media and The Gulf: A Closer Look*, Proceedings of the Conference held on May 3–4, 1991, at the Graduate School of Journalism, University of California, Berkeley, pp. 15–16.
5. Variations on this journalistic pattern hold true even for domestic policy issues, and all the way down to local politics, as shown in Edie Goldenberg, *Making the Papers* (Lexington: Heath-Lexington Books, 1975). See also, Protess et al., *The Journalism of Outrage* (Guilford Press, 1992).

References

Bartells, L. M. 1991. "Constituency Opinion and Congressional Policy Making: The Reagan Defense Buildup." *American Political Science Review* 85:457–74.
Bennett, W. L. 1988. *News: The Politics of Illusion*. 2d ed. New York: Longman.
———. 1990. "Toward a Theory of Press-State Relations in the United States." *Journal of Communication* 40:103–25.
Brody, R. A., and C. R. Shapiro. 1989a. "A Reconsideration of the Rally Phenomenon in Public Opinion." In *Political Behavior Annual*, ed. Samuel Long. Vol. 2. Boulder: Westview Press.
———. 1989b. "Policy Failure and Public Support: The Iran-Contra Affair and Public Assessments of President Reagan." *Political Behavior* 11:353–69.
Bueno de Mesquita, B., and D. Laiman. 1990. "Domestic Opposition and Foreign War." *American Political Science Review* 84:747–65.
Cohen, B. C. 1963. *The Press and Foreign Policy*. Princeton: Princeton University Press.
———. 1973. *The Public's Impact on Foreign Policy*. Boston: Little, Brown.
Cutler, L. 1984. "Foreign Policy on Deadline." *Foreign Policy* 56:113–28.

Entman, M., and A. Rojecki. 1993. "Freezing Out the Public: Elite and Media Framing of the U.S. Anti-Nuclear Movement." *Political Communication* 10:155–74.

Friedland, L. A. 1991. "Democracy, Diversity, and Cable: The Case of CNN." Manuscript, University of Wisconsin.

Gans, H. J. 1979. *Deciding What's News.* New York: Pantheon.

Gitlin, T. 1980. *The Whole World Is Watching: Mass Media in the Making and Unmaking of the New Left.* Berkeley: University of California Press.

Graham, T. W. 1992. "Public Opinion's Influence on American Foreign Policy." Presented at the Thomas P. O'Neill, Jr., Symposium on the Politics of American Foreign Policy, Boston College, April 3–4.

Hallin, D. C. 1986. *The "Uncensored War": The Media and Vietnam.* Berkeley: University of California Press.

Hallin, D. C., R. K. Manoff, and J. K. Weddle. 1990. "Sourcing Patterns of National Security Reporters." Presented at the annual meeting of the American Political Science Association, San Francisco, August 30–September 2.

Herman, C. F. 1990. "Changing Course: When Governments Choose to Redirect Foreign Policy." *International Studies Quarterly* 34:3–21.

Herman, E. S. 1985. "Diversity of News: Marginalizing the Opposition." *Journal of Communication* 35:135–46.

Herman, E. S., and N. Chomsky. 1988. *The Manufacture of Consent: The Political Economy of the Mass Media.* New York: Pantheon.

Hertsgaard, M. 1988. *On Bended Knee: The Press and the Reagan Presidency.* New York: Farrar, Strauss and Giroux.

Immerman, R. 1982. *The CIA in Guatemala.* Austin: University of Texas Press.

Iyengar, S. 1992. *Is Anyone Responsible? How Television Frames Political Issues.* Chicago: University of Chicago Press.

Judis, J. B. 1991. "Twilight of the Gods." *Wilson Quarterly.* Autumn.

Kernell, S. 1978. "Explaining Presidential Popularity." *American Political Science Review* 72:506–22.

Larson, J. F. 1988. "Global Television and Foreign Policy." *Headline Series* no. 283. New York: Foreign Policy Association.

———. 1990. "Quiet Diplomacy in a Television Era: The Media and U.S. Policy Toward the Republic of Korea." *Political Communication and Persuasion* 7:73–95.

Lippmann, W. 1922. *Public Opinion.* New York: The Free Press.

MacArthur, J. R. 1992. *The Second Front: Censorship and Propaganda in the Gulf War.* New York: Hill and Wang.

Manheim, J. B. 1991. *All of the People, All the Time: Strategic Communication and American Politics.* Armonk: M. E. Sharp.

Manheim, J. B., and R. B. Albritton. 1984. "Changing National Images: International Public Relations and Media Agenda Setting." *American Political Science Review* 78:641–54.

Massing, M. 1991. "Debriefings: What We Saw, What We Learned." *Columbia Journalism Review* 30:23–24.

Melanson, R. A. 1991. *Reconstructing Consensus: American Foreign Policy Since the Vietnam War.* New York: St. Martin's Press.

Mueller, J. 1973. *War, Presidents and Public Opinion.* New York: Wiley.

Ninic, M., and B. Hinckley. 1991. "Foreign Policy and the Evaluation of Presidential Candidates." *Journal of Conflict Resolution* 35:333–55.

O'Heffernan, P. 1990. "Mass Media and U.S. Foreign Policy: An Inside-Outside Model of Media Influence in U.S. Foreign Policy." Presented at the annual meeting of the American Political Science Association, San Francisco, August 30–September 2.

Page, B. I. and R. Y. Shapiro. 1992. *The Rational Public.* Chicago: University of Chicago Press.

Pratt, L. 1989. "The Circuitry of Protest." *Gannett Center Journal* 3:105–15.

Risse-Kappen, T. 1991. "Public Opinion, Domestic Structure, and Foreign Policy in Liberal Democracies." *World Politics* 43:479–512.

Russett, B. 1990–91. "Doves, Hawks, and U.S. Public Opinion." *Political Science Quarterly* 105:516–38.

Sabato, L. 1991. *Feeding Frenzy: How Attack Journalism Has Transformed American Politics.* New York: The Free Press.

Schneider, W. 1984. "Public Opinion." In *The Making of America's Soviet Policy,* ed. Joseph Nye, Jr. New Haven: Yale University Press.

Serfaty, S., ed. 1991. *The Media and Foreign Policy.* New York: St. Martin's Press.

Shanor, D. R. 1989. "The 'Hundred Flowers' of Tiananmen." *Gannett Center Journal* 3:128–36.

Shapiro, R. Y., and B. I. Page. 1988. "Foreign Policy and the Rational Public." *Journal of Conflict Resolution* 32:211–47.

Sigal, L. 1973. *Reporters and Officials.* Lexington: D. C. Heath.

Smith, A. 1991. *The Age of Behemoths: The Globalization of Mass Media Firms.* New York: Priority Press.

Tuchman, G. 1978. *Making News: A Study in the Construction of Reality.* New York: The Free Press.

Wallis, R., and S. Baran. 1990. *The Known World of Broadcast News: International News and the Electronic Media.* London: Routledge.

Webster, D. 1991. "New Communications Technology and the International Political Process." In *The Media and Foreign Policy,* ed. S. Serfaty. New York: St. Martin's Press.

Woodward, B. 1991. *The Commanders.* New York: Simon and Schuster.

part two

The News as Political Information

two

Gladys Engel Lang and Kurt Lang

The Press as Prologue

*Media Coverage of Saddam's Iraq,
1979–1990*

Not until August 2, 1990, when Iraq invaded Kuwait, did the news media depict either Saddam Hussein or the regime he had headed since 1979 as a major player on the world stage or as a potential disturber of world peace. Public opinion, according to what little polling data were available, had been equally oblivious to this threat. Nor, so it appears, had the foreign policy establishment been much concerned with gauging how the public might react to a confrontation with Iraq. The crisis, when it came, was a near-total surprise. People in general, even habitual followers of foreign affairs, had no ready-made framework from which to derive a reaction. To fill this void and so guide the debate, the political leadership resurrected two haunting memories: that of Hitler (linked by an improvised analogy with Saddam Hussein) and that of Vietnam.[1]

In this chapter we consider how the news media reflected and/or affected the substance of American policy toward Iraq in the decade before its invasion of Kuwait. We do so on the understanding that the media connection to foreign policy is a two-way street but with many detours. Much of the influence in either direction is indirect and has to be inferred.

Directly, the media are a major input. Officials in Washington and in embassies all over the world receive daily press summaries. They pay attention to editorials and to some news columns, while a small staff in the State Department has for some years collected information from public polls, largely conducted for and by media organizations, to keep abreast of public attitudes on foreign policy questions. On the other hands, knowledgeable reporters (as well as some editors) have been cultivated both for whatever esoteric information they can convey and as conduits for putting the official view across. There exists, as in other branches of government, an exchange relationship between reporters and officials who often have different understandings of what is appropriate behavior (Blumler and Gurevitch 1981). Although the relationship becomes strained whenever policy-makers attempt to exploit the insatiable need of the press for usable copy, the members of the fourth

43

estate do function on occasion, perhaps unwittingly, as tools of an establishment whose influence, according to their own professional code,
they are supposed to balance.

Indirectly, the media exert influence through their effects on third parties: first and foremost, on the public in their own country. When there
is no well-informed public opinion, as in the case of Saddam's Iraq, the
hands of policy-makers are freed—at least until such opinion crystal-
lizes (Cohen 1963). At the same time, other governments, friendly or
hostile to the U.S., make the press reaction part of their own policy
moves. It is at least possible that the Iraqi ruler, in invading Kuwait, convinced himself there was no reason to fear that an outraged press would
put pressure on the Bush administration to deviate from its past policy of
appeasement.

Whether such a calculation figured into Saddam's decision we are
unlikely ever to know. Nor is it the central concern of this chapter, in
which we take a look at the press and video coverage of some events
assumed critical in shaping public and elite imagery of Iraq and, to this
extent, a factor in the decisions of American policy-makers. We try to
shed some light on how the media coverage framed these events and to
supplement this with information gleaned from polls about the public
response.

Public Awareness

Despite huge amounts of polling, some of it sponsored by government
agencies, questions bearing even remotely on Iraq in the 1980s are few
and far between. We begin with two polls of American attitudes toward
leaders in the Middle East, the first by Louis Harris and Associates in July
1980, just a year after Saddam secured his power base by killing off all
potential rivals, the second by a private firm (for the American Jewish
Congress) in 1988 when Iraq was being accused of using chemical
weapons in its war with Iran. So far down in the ranking of world villains was Saddam that neither survey included his name in the list of
leaders whom respondents were asked to judge.[2] This absence is symp-
tomatic. Polls are largely driven by journalistic criteria, and the media
community obviously did not perceive an imminent threat from Iraq;
nor had they reason to think that the public felt otherwise.

In fact, the same 1980 poll by Harris asked a national sample to name
which of fifteen countries "could be a threat to the security of the United
States." Iraq, which appeared on this list, was mentioned by 17
percent—far behind the USSR (84 percent), Iran (56 percent), and

China (41 percent) and only a bit ahead of Saudi Arabia (14 percent).[3] In October that year, only a few weeks after Iraq attacked Iran, a preelection poll for *Time* found a mere 8 percent of 1,622 registered voters who, in response to an open-ended question, named the conflict as one of the "main issues or problems facing the country (that particularly) worried or concerned" them.[4] Relative threat perceptions established in the earlier survey suggest that concern was directed more at Iran than Iraq.

Perceptions did change a bit in response to the Israeli raid that destroyed Iraq's nuclear reactor in 1981, but, apparently, not for very long. A month after the successful Israeli attack, 57 percent of 2,000 adults queried by Roper thought that, despite categorical denials by Iraq, it had indeed been planning to use the facility to make bombs. Other evidence of a low concern comes from a survey five months later: asked to look back on the year's events, only 4 percent of a national sample remembered the bombing as one of the year's main developments.[5]

Images of Iraq were hardly well thought-out nor did they have any great stability. Much depended on how questions were posed and in what context. A survey conducted in October 1987 asked respondents to select from a list of countries the ones they thought had a nuclear capability and then to pinpoint which gave them the "greatest concern—I mean which one or two you feel would be the most likely to explode a nuclear weapon." This time Iraq, mentioned by 64 percent, topped the list, with the Soviet Union, named by 36 percent, coming in a poor second.[6]

Whatever unease people may have felt over Iraq's nuclear capability, it seems not to have spilled over into antipathy against the brutally repressive Baath regime and its dictator. Thus, we note that, prior to the Iraqi invasion of Kuwait, not a single public poll had asked about the size of the Iraqi military machine and its growing arsenal of advanced weapons which, according to some experts, included significant chemical and biological warfare capability in addition to A-bombs. Nor, for that matter, had they asked about Iraq's belligerent stance toward Israel and other neighbors. In this atmosphere, few Americans would have considered Senator D'Amato's post-invasion denunciation of the Iraqi president as "a butcher, a killer, a bully"[7] as anything but familiar extravagant Cold War rhetoric applied to a new country.

What did change, as measured by a Harris poll question first asked in January 1982 and repeated five years later, was the number who ticked off Iraq (from a list) as an "unfriendly" country. The number rose from just over one-half of all respondents to about two-thirds.[8] This trend toward greater hostility ran contrary to U.S. policy, which had, in the intervening period, taken Iraq off the list of countries accused of practicing terrorism and had normalized diplomatic relations. The official tilt toward Iraq seems reflected in a CBS/*NYT* poll in April 1986. Asked whether any other country in the Middle East besides Libya was responsible for international terrorism, a mere 1 percent named Iraq.[9]

It is indeed remarkable how little news about Iraq and its ruler had stirred Americans. But there was an almost instantaneous change following the invasion. Once Saddam Hussein's prior actions and pronouncements became common knowledge, he was catapulted into the pantheon of world villains.

The Study

Our review of the role of the media focuses on five periods, ranging from two to seven weeks in length. Each period brackets a critical event with implications for American policy and presumably worth some media attention. These are (1) the elevation of Saddam in July 1979 as the official leader of Iraq, simultaneously holding the position of president, chairman of the Revolutionary Command Council, and commander-in-chief of the Iraqi armed forces; (2) the 1981 Israeli raid on Osirak, the Iraqi nuclear reactor; (3) chemical warfare against Iranian troops in 1984; (4) further employment of chemical weapons against Iraqi Kurds in March 1988 and again in August immediately after the signing of the armistice ending the Iran-Iraq war; and (5) the execution in 1990 of an Iranian-born journalist reporting on Iraq for the *London Observer* along with the successful seizure of American-made nuclear triggers being shipped to Iraq.[10]

We began analysis of each period the day news of the event "broke" and continued until the story was pretty much exhausted in the *New York Times* (*NYT*) and the *Seattle Times* (*ST*), the first as an example of an elite paper, the second of a regional paper. We also looked at the coverage in *Time* and used the Vanderbilt *Television News Index and Abstracts* to gauge the play Saddam and Iraq received on network news.

The total yield of relevant items from the two newspapers and network news for each event is summarized in Table 1.[11] By this measure, the preemptive strike by Israel on the Osirak reactor was by far the biggest news story, much of it on the front page or a lead item on evening newscasts.

As a preliminary step towards more detailed examination, we looked at each news item to see if one or more of the following topics received significant treatment (major theme) or came in for at least some contex-

TABLE 1.   Number of Items Relevant to Iran-Iraq War

Medium	1979	1981	1984	1988	1990	Total
NYT	8	120	35	53	20	236
ST	2	37	24	17	3	83
Network TV*	7	50	16	11	10	94
Total	17	207	75	81	33	413

*Number of days on which a network carried an item on Iraq regardless of position or length.

tual discussion (minor theme): (1) the personality or political role of Saddam Hussein; (2) the Iraqi military buildup; (3) Iraq's commitment to the development of unconventional weapons (nuclear, chemical, and biological) and/or their actual use in warfare; (4) the human rights record of the Baath regime; (5) Iraq as the sponsor of terrorism; (6) the illicit export of contraband material of potential military use; and (7) U.S. foreign policy considerations related to any of the above.

Table 2 gives an overview. The development or the employment of unconventional weapons—nuclear, chemical, and biological—appear to have been the most newsworthy stories; they were the major focus of 42 percent of all stories in the two newspapers. Their less frequent introduction as a subtheme suggests that this topic was not as a rule discussed within the context of U.S. foreign policy. Most striking is Saddam Hussein's low news profile throughout these years; in only 4 percent of all items examined was the man himself, his pursuit of military superiority, or his sponsorship of terrorism a main or even a subsidiary topic. But these are only crude quantitative measures of media content. To assess

TABLE 2.   Number of Occurrences of Major and Minor Themes
in Relevant Stories

	New York Times		Seattle Times		TOTAL*	
	Main	Minor	Main	Minor	Main	Minor
Unconventional weapons	95	51	45	1	140	52
Foreign policy	58	27	16	3	74	30
Human rights	22	11	11	2	33	13
Military buildup	6	11	7	5	13	16
Weapons exports	22	3	22	5	44	8
Saddam Hussein	6	1	7	1	13	2
Public opinion	7	0	7	0	14	0
Sponsor of terrorism	1	1	2	0	3	1

*The totals for major and minor themes come to more than 319 because of some double-coding.

more meaningfully the probable effect of media treatment of Saddam's Iraq as prologue to the Gulf War, the rest of this chapter offers a more detailed assessment of the coverage of each of these events and their cumulative consequences.

Saddam Seizes the Helm: 1979

In her 1991 book, Elaine Sciolino, who had covered the Middle East for the *New York Times*, called Saddam Hussein "an outlaw who built an outlaw state" (Sciolino 1991, 16). Already as a twenty-one-year-old, he had been actively involved in the 1958 Baathist plot to assassinate pro-Soviet Iraqi leader General Qassem. The failure of that attempt forced him to flee first to Damascus, then to Cairo, where he rose steadily in the ranks of the clandestine Baath party, which finally seized power in 1968. Ahmed al-Bakir became president but shared power with Saddam, his cousin, who was made vice-president.

While al-Bakir made rabble-rousing speeches against Jews, Zionists, and foreign plots, it fell to Saddam to purge the enemy. He had become, in the words of one observer, "the apparatchik who forged the Baath into a powerful subversive tool capable of . . . holding power. His tactics were a mixture of Trotsky and Goebbels" (Timmerman 1991, 6). Terror played a big role. There were frequent public executions. Saddam's effort to transform Iraq into a great military power began long before he formally succeeded al-Bakir as president. He had gone to Moscow and France to acquire nuclear capability and biological weapons, had been the prime mover in the formation of a "rejection front," and had openly encouraged terrorists intent on punishing Egypt's Sadat for making peace with Israel and Western leaders and for siding so openly with his old enemies (al-Kalil 1989).

Given Saddam's record, one might have assumed that his formal rise to power would concern Washington and attract attention in the American media. Yet conventional wisdom has it that President Carter was too preoccupied with Iran after the 1978 revolution to pay attention to a threat from Iraq. Besides, Saddam's touting of his opposition to Soviet foreign policy goals made his considerable purchases of arms and technology less worrisome.

How much attention did the media pay to the new Iraqi leader and his background? For the most part, news of Saddam's rise to power became the story of a routine succession in leadership. Only on CBS did this story, on July 16, make the evening news. In the three weeks that followed, the three networks carried a total of seven news items amounting to two and a half minutes of air time. The new ruler's attendance at the execution of his old friends received but a single mention. There were no Western camera crews there to portray the full horror of a purge in which some 500 Baathists may have been murdered.

Journalists, especially photojournalists, had little or no direct access to independent sources. Of six items in the *NYT*, only one (from Reuters) carried a Baghdad dateline and even this story, from all appearances, relied entirely on the official Iraqi press agency. In Baghdad nothing had been published about the "tens and perhaps more than a hundred" arrests high in the Baath party, so Flora Lewis reported from Paris, attributing this guesstimate to Western diplomatic and intelligence sources.[12] But not many Western journalists, if any, were pursuing the confidential reports appearing in the opposition (underground) press outside the country.[13]

Not until July 30 did the report of a major purge make the front page of the *NYT*. Yet this dispatch from Beirut had little to say about the actions of an autocrat, speaking instead about a crisis of leadership and what this might portend for the Arab world.[14] The tone did not change until the announcement, also on the front page but more than a week later, of the harsh verdict by the court. Quoting "Arab sources," the *NYT* described President Hussein as "a man who . . . could not 'tolerate a reformist movement' within the regime" and reported that he had used an "alleged conspiracy to consolidate his control . . . by eliminating any critics or rivals."[15]

Still, in all three print sources examined, the new Iraqi president's bid for power was not viewed with much alarm: under his direction economic and diplomatic ties with the West were expected to improve and counter the influence of the Soviet Union, Iraq's long-time backer.[16] Nor was this basically "upbeat" tone in any way challenged by images carried over network news. *Time*, which first mentioned the changeover on August 20, three weeks after it occurred, was most upbeat about the new "anti-Communist ruler of Iraq," describing him as acutely worried about the risks of terrorism and "particularly anxious to reduce the chances of P.L.O.-inspired violence."[17]

The Israeli Raid on Iraq's Nuclear Facility: 1981

Until the overthrow of the Shah of Iran, U.S. arms exports to its once reliable ally "had far outpaced European and Soviet arms sales to Iraq" (Timmerman 1991, 73). But the circumstances that had made this seem a viable policy changed very quickly with the proclamation of Iran as an

Islamic republic; by the seizure of the American embassy in Teheran, in which fifty-three persons were taken as hostages; and by Iraqi troops crossing the border into Iran. Soon, the U.S. was looking at Iraq in a new light. Although the Senate in late August had failed to approve the sale of commercial aircraft to Iraq, the secretary of state was prepared to support Saddam's arming as a means of stopping Soviet expansionism. Possibly reflecting this policy tilt, a *NYT* editorial indulged in cautious speculation that the "chances are that Iraq's President, Saddam Hussein, is less a holy warrior than a cautious opportunist."[18] And the paper, in one of the few media profiles of Saddam, described him as "a wary Iraqi in a hostile world" intent on enhancing his power and moving his nation into a larger role in the Gulf, yet also intent on projecting a more benign image, stressing the modernization of his society and economy.[19]

Iran and Iraq had been at war for nearly nine months when on June 7, 1981, Israeli jets attacked and destroyed Iraq's nuclear reactor. No event between 1979 and July 1990 generated more coverage of Iraq. The *NYT* averaged four stories per day over the three weeks following. *Time* featured the raid on the cover of its June 22 issue together with an assessment of world reaction by the magazine's correspondents in all the major capitals. For three days the story also led the news on all three network evening broadcasts; on three more days, it led the news on two networks. Fifty of the sixty-three newscasts taped by Vanderbilt during this period had at least one item dealing, however briefly, with the Israeli raid.

No less important a question is how the event was framed. The raid could be presented in three different ways: as a sign of Saddam's military and political objectives, as an Israeli violation of international law,[20] as a problem for U.S. policy-makers in maintaining the delicate balance of military power in the Middle East. The question of Iraq's progress toward becoming a nuclear power could hardly be avoided; as the days passed, however, the dilemma the raid had created for U.S. policy, namely, maintaining friendly ties to Israel without jeopardizing improving relations with conservative Arab states, came to dominate the news. Overall, just about twice as many items dwelled on the foreign policy problems posed by the raid as on the danger of nuclear proliferation it signaled. Attention quickly turned toward the United Nations, as it maneuvered to reach a compromise that would condemn Israel while withholding sanctions.

Meanwhile, Saddam remained surprisingly invisible through the entire episode. Although his name appeared in 41 of the 157 news items about the destruction of Osirak, he was the main subject in only one.

Nearly all the rest did no more than refer to him by name. Did Saddam deliberately avoid all contact with the Western press? Not completely. He actually solicited a televised interview from Barbara Walters, of ABC, to deliver his own message to the world. Since Israel possessed the bomb, he told Walters, Arabs also had a right to have one. The raid on Osirak, conducted with sophisticated American weapons, had shown "all Arabs that they had to have the means to protect their vital projects from attack."[21]

Save for this starring role on American TV, Saddam maintained a low profile by keeping the press at arm's length. Hardly any American news stories were datelined Iraq; they came from Washington, New York, the United Nations, and Paris. (France had been the supplier of the reactor plant.) But less benign characterizations of the Iraqi leader by Israeli leaders and their friends in Congress also received full play. Menachem Begin, the Israeli prime minister, called him "evil" and "meshugge"—a colorful yiddish word for a lunatic.[22] Other labels ran the gamut from irresponsible, crazy, evil, murderer, to "butcher," by now a familiar epithet that appeared in the *NYT* only once on June 11.

Two national polls taken soon after the raid found an unusually high level of public awareness for an event that did not *directly* involve the U.S.: 86 percent of those responding to a Gallup poll and 88 percent responding to a CBS/*NYT* poll a few days later had heard or read about the attack. Gallup respondents, by 45 to 38 percent, thought the raid *not* justified, and a majority supported suspension of a shipment of four fighter planes to Israel. The CBS/*NYT* poll showed an even split of 39 and 39. Asked generally whether the U.S. should punish Israel in some way, only 18 percent agreed; a much higher proportion favored "no action" of any kind.[23]

Another poll, taken a month after the raid, revealed lingering suspicions about Iraq. Asked to look back at the raid, a clear majority agreed that Iraq had been planning to make a nuclear bomb, over a third just "did not know," and only 9 percent did not think so.[24] The same suspicion was articulated in letters from readers of *Time*. One questioned why "an oil-rich country like Iraq [should] need a nuclear reactor. Certainly not to produce electricity." Another hailed Israel, which "[i]n just a few minutes . . . did more for nonproliferation . . . than all the treaties have done in all these years."[25]

It seems that even while most Americans at the time did not consider the raid justified, they did believe Iraq had indeed been seeking A-bomb technology. But once this chapter in history was closed, there was little more to depict Iraq as a nuclear threat. Its next image problem stemmed from the use of chemical weapons in the war against Iran and against the Kurdish minority within its own borders. These clear violations of the Geneva Protocol, to which Iraq was a signatory, moved that country back onto the front page.

Chemical Warfare Against Iran: 1984

By the fourth year of its war with Iran, things had evidently not been going well for Iraq; it could hardly expect to achieve victory on its own. An overture by Baghdad, some two months before the Israeli strike, to restore normal diplomatic relations with the U.S., had been rebuffed (Sciolino 1991, 63). As the situation deteriorated, Iraq's open courtship of Washington began to have some success. On February 26, 1982, the U.S. took Iraq off the list of countries practicing terrorism, thereby opening the door for American subsidies and loan guarantees. The Reagan administration showed itself, if not eager to help, then at least willing to look the other way as other countries helped Iraq build its military arsenal and, especially with help from West Germany, its chemical warfare capability.

The charge by Iran, on March 4, 1984, that Iraq had turned to poison gas to halt attacks by masses of Iranian troops blew away this veil of secrecy. American spokespersons quickly acknowledged that they had information supporting the Iranian charges. When the U.N. sent in an investigating team, the U.S. responded even before any report was delivered, by placing new restrictions on the export to Iraq of five chemical compounds that could be used to make poison gas. But this step was less than a full policy reversal. It did not keep the U.S. from resuming full diplomatic relations with Iraq the following November.

Both the horrors of chemical warfare and the international reaction to it put Saddam's Iraq in the spotlight. Television dealt mostly with the effects on troops, occasionally mentioning how the components of these weapons, supposedly embargoed, had gotten through. The print media provided more background on the U.S. policy of evenhanded neutrality, as expressed in official statements that balanced criticism of Iraq with criticism of Iran for its refusal to end the war short of an overthrow of the Iraqi government as "inconsistent with the accepted norms of behavior among nations."[26] Inasmuch as Washington was said to have become increasingly concerned in recent months over a possible Iranian victory and its costs in lives and property as well as its repercussions in the Gulf region, this was the first report for some time of American criticism, though tempered, of Iraqi actions.

In its entirety the *NYT* coverage—including editorials—gives a picture of what a policy of neutrality in the Iran-Iraq conflict meant in 1984. In the last two days of March, with Iraq's use of gas making headlines and leading the evening telecasts, chemical weapons were again front-page news. Reacting to a *NYT* report, the State Department confirmed that it had evidence that Iraq had employed nerve gas. Its ban on exports to Iraq of five chemical compounds was coupled with an announcement that the same curbs applied to Iran. In fact, these curbs were far more inclusive and, to one journalist with expertise in the Middle East, "provided one more clue to the diplomatic enigma that became a virtual American alliance with Saddam Hussein"; they were meant to show that the U.S. would carry out its pledge to bring the ayatollah to his knees and was therefore willing to help Iraq in a variety of discreet ways, some of which have as yet to be uncovered (Timmerman 1991, 142).

Though less detailed than the *NYT,* the coverage in the *ST* and on the networks fell roughly into the same mold. After the *NYT* forced into the open what was known by U.S. intelligence about the Iraqi arsenal of chemical weapons, this became a lead story on all three networks, and they also highlighted the announced ban on the export of chemical agents. Yet one can hardly ignore the fact that Saddam was, if anything, even less in evidence than he had been in 1981. Nor did the media seek to establish a link between his failure, due to the Israeli raid, to join the club of nuclear powers and his stepped-up search for alternative weapons of destruction. Chemical warfare in a distant part of the world was simply one foreign story among many other newsworthy developments. It never even reached a level of controversy sufficient for pollsters to take the public pulse.

Gassing the Kurds: 1988

The news value of the bogged-down Iran-Iraq war decreased progressively over time, even for journalists covering it. Until Iraq dropped chemical bombs on its rebellious Kurds, threats to shipping were the only events causing Americans to take notice, as they did in May 1987, at least for a few days, after the U.S. navy frigate *Stark*, on patrol in the Gulf, was struck by missiles fired from an Iraqi jet. Just before the *Stark* was hit, 32 percent of the American public had described themselves as either paying "no attention" or "not too much attention" to events in the Gulf. But almost everybody had read or heard about this tragedy— treated as an "accident"—that resulted in the deaths of thirty-seven American sailors and caused some criticism of President Reagan, whose handling of the situation was approved by a modest plurality of only 49, with 41 percent disapproving.[27]

But whatever anger against Iraq the attack on the *Stark* may have aroused, it was soon to dissipate. After a few months, only 29 percent remembered that the missiles had come from an Iraqi plane, while 25 percent thought, mistakenly, that they came from Iran and 43 percent could not remember which country was responsible.[28]

More significant perhaps was the initial reluctance of most Americans to take sides in the Iran-Iraq conflict. In December 1986, those willing to express a preference, which most were not, favored Iraq by 19 to 10 percent. A paltry 1 percent thought that it was U.S. foreign policy to support Iraq in its war. But after the presumed "accident," people began to tilt toward Iraq, with some 30 percent preferring an Iraq victory and only 5 percent pulling for Iran. By September 1987, 43 percent preferred that Iraq win, 8 percent that Iran win, and the rest not prepared to state an opinion or not caring.[29] But most hoped for an end to hostilities that would relieve the U.S. of responsibility for assuring the flow of oil through the Gulf. Seventy-seven percent favored ending the war through a UN resolution, with sanctions on countries for noncompliance. In the same survey, 90 percent did not believe that sanctions would put a stop to the flow of arms for the war.[30]

Nothing should have alerted the world more to the brutality of the Iraqi regime than the indiscriminate gassing of Kurds at Halabja in March 1988. Never before had nerve gas been used on such a scale and against civilians. But in this instance, also, the first response from the international community was restrained. Many governments were reluctant to do anything that might upset the peace process underway in the UN. It was not until August that its Security Council acted to condemn Iraq for its heinous and brutal conduct.

We have no readings of public reaction in America. What people most often remember today are the pictures of massacred civilians shown on eleven network evening newscasts between March 22 and April 2. Looking back, it comes nevertheless as a surprise that no newscast made Halabja the lead story. Neither then nor later in September, when Iraq resumed its attacks on its Kurdish minority for having sided with Iran during the conflict, did the networks give the atrocities or the subsequent effort to outlaw chemical warfare as much play as they had given the earlier raid on the Osirak reactor.

We also suspect that the shock value of the video of this latest Iraqi atrocity against its enemies was diffused by questions repeatedly raised about culpability, including allegations, from the Pentagon among others, that both sides had resorted to chemical bombs and that Iran had promised it would cease if Iraq would. Both houses of Congress, reacting to the reports of Iraq's use of chemical weapons against civilians, voted repeatedly to impose limited sanctions, which the State Department opposed, on Iraq. This legislation died because of last-minute problems in the days before adjournment (*Congressional Quarterly* 1988, 20).

In late August 1988 when Saddam Hussein, with a cease-fire in the Iran-Iraq war in place, once again launched poison-gas attacks against the Kurds, the networks carried much of the story. ABC was most persistent, with three video reports by Barrie Dunsmore on the plight of Iraqi Kurdish refugees who had crossed into Turkey. He had some victims tell their own story on camera and cited information from Amnesty International and the U.S. State Department in support of the Kurdish version of the events.[31] CBS fielded a similarly well-crafted piece by Tom Fenton, using clips of interviews with the American secretary of state, the Iraqi foreign minister, a State Department spokesman, a Kurdish gas casualty, and a Kurdish journalist.[32]

Yet Saddam himself did not appear in any of the six items on Iraq featured on TV news throughout September, all dealing with chemical warfare. Anyone relying on TV for most of their foreign news could hardly have learned very much of his larger ambitions, whereas newspaper readers—especially if they read the editorials—may have found more reason to wonder just how far beyond the pale Iraq's president was prepared to go.

In March the *Seattle Times* had compared the gas attacks to Nazi experiments while the *New York Times,* in its writeups on the need to control the arms trade in the Middle East, was raising questions about "war crimes."[33] Coverage in the *NYT* was, as expected, heavier than in the *ST* and contained references to, as well as captions about, Saddam's responsibility and to the possibility of American complicity in the profitable arms trade, which none of the trade partners wanted to give up. One story early in September alluded to relations between Reagan and Saddam to explain why, despite the Senate vote to embargo arms to Iraq, the administration remained officially unconvinced that there had been any misuse;[34] another suggested that its "inexcusable dithering" could become a campaign issue.[35]

Thus, the outline of what only years later emerged as a calculated strategy on the part of the administration to keep Saddam Hussein on our side, to bring him into the circle of democratic nations by turning a blind eye to his ambition and brutal behavior, was available to the attentive reader. But coverage was hardly prominent enough to put U.S. policy toward Iraq on the agenda of important problems facing the country. Nor was it much of an issue in the presidential campaign of 1988. As for Saddam, he remained a faraway unknown who, despite his acts of terrorism vividly recorded for television, was not yet a leading focus of public hostility.

March 1990: Death of a Journalist/A Successful Sting

Two dramatic events in March were signals of things to come but never got the message across. First, on March 15 there was Iraq's summary execution of the British journalist Bazoft, which should have driven home the true nature of human rights under the Saddam regime. Rather, the central issue in the news columns became the Iranian-born journalist's guilt: had he, as charged, truly been a spy? The second event, later in the month, was the foiling of a plot to smuggle contraband krypton devices, of potential utility as nuclear detonators, into Iraq. The end result of an eighteen-month undercover operation by the U.S. Customs Service, the discovery became a story about a successful sting operation with overtones of a spy thriller. The implications for American policy of Iraq's drive to become a nuclear power were no more than a sidebar.

Neither event generated the kind of newspaper coverage likely to have created anything like a wave of indignation: between March 8 and March 31 the two newspapers we examined carried just twenty-three items on Iraq. To be sure, the execution was more of a British story. Margaret Thatcher had called it "an act of barbarism deeply repugnant to all civilized people." On the other hand, since it involved a freedom-of-the-press issue, close to the raw nerves of journalists, one might have expected it to be a big story. Yet the seizure of the nuclear triggers at Heathrow Airport got bigger play in the papers, in *Time*, and on TV.

Time devoted just 130 words to Bazoft's murder, along with a picture of the journalist and another of protestors in England.[36] Then, two issues later, *Time* used 1,538 words on the "Middle East: The Big Sting."[37] On March 29 all three networks led with the sting and carried follow-up items the next evening. In the *NYT* the seizure of the nuclear triggers was front-page news, with eye-catching graphics, headlined "Atom Bomb Parts Seized in Britain En Route to Iraq."[38] For a change, here was a success story featuring the U.S. government in a spy thriller not to be missed, even by television. By prearrangement, NBC had a camera crew at the airport to record the successful completion of the eighteen-month "sting." It should be noted, however, that ABC's *Nightline* had devoted one of its half-hour reports to the Bazoft execution.

In addition, the policy messages to be drawn from these events, about the nature of Saddam's Iraq and U.S. policy, came through loud and clear on the op-ed page. William Safire, the *NYT* columnist, charged the president with ignoring an atrocity. In an explicit "j'accuse," he asked, "What hold does the Butcher of Baghdad have on the President of the United States?" Saddam had declared a school holiday to swell the crowds he ordered to demonstrate in front of the British Embassy in Baghdad but none, for good reason, were ordered to demonstrate against the Americans: The Bush administration had refused to join the worldwide appeals for clemency. And after the hanging, the presidential press secretary expressed regret that all appeals had gone unheeded but, when asked what the government meant to do about it, said he had not thought to ask.[39]

In similar vein, Flora Lewis wondered how Saddam could have escaped opprobrium for all his gross misdeeds. There are, she wrote, "outbursts of indignation when something becomes too obvious"—like killing a newsman, gassing large numbers of Kurds, wiping out villages—but then the spotlight shifts. The State Department issues reports with no consequences. And when the Middle East Watch put out a thick dossier on Iraq recently, it attracted little notice in the press.[40] Editorially, the *NYT* was more reticent. Characterizing Saddam's killing of a journalist as self-defeating behavior, it nevertheless did not explicitly challenge the policy of maintaining cordial relations with a regime hell-bent on becoming a nuclear power, as its columnists had.[41]

Saddam's name also surfaced in television reports on the smuggling operation. At least one professor called him a "megalomaniac"[42] while other experts reminded viewers of his past chemical warfare against Iran and the Kurds. Apart from these harsh words and the frontal attack by two respected columnists on U.S. policy toward Iraq, there was very little in the coverage of the two events by the two papers or on network television to drive home the true nature of the Saddam regime or to call into question the way the administration continued to court his favor. It would have taken an avid news consumer to spot the danger signals.

Conclusion

The analysis of the media coverage highlights the limits of personal experience as a basis for our opinions on matters of public concern, opinions which "inevitably cover a bigger space, a longer reach of time, a greater number of things, than we can directly observe. They have, therefore, to be pieced together out of what others have reported and what we can imagine" (Lippmann 1922, 79). Our dependence on the providers of information is especially great for events which, like many that are in the focus of foreign policy, lie outside the orbits in which most of us habitually move. To what extent, then, can one hold the media coverage of the Gulf prior to the invasion of Kuwait responsible for the lack of an articulate and effective public opinion on the Iraqi regime as a threat to peace?

We have shown that there was enough information for an attentive news reader to have a sense of what the Saddam regime was all about. But media attention was sporadic. It rose and ebbed with the flow of events. There is some evidence, based on experiments, that an "episodic" form of coverage geared to spot news generates less understanding than coverage that can be described as issue-oriented insofar as it highlights an underlying condition or problem (Iyengar 1991). But experiments have their limitations, and the reactions to Saddam's military attack dramatize the circumstances under which public opinion can be mobilized to respond to events defined as a crisis (see Brody, Chapter 10 of this volume; Mueller 1973). The five events that could have served as an alert to the impending danger from Saddam's Iraq obviously failed to do so. What caused the failure? We advance the following reasons in explanation.

Conditions or problems remote from personal experience will break through only if media coverage approaches a saturation point, that is, when it intrudes into the focus of attention of nearly everyone and begins to crowd out other issues. This is how Watergate, to cite just one example, finally made it onto the issue agenda (Lang and Lang 1983). The Israeli raid on Osirak was the only one of the earlier events to attract, even if only for a short period, this level of coverage but at a time when the public was at least equally preoccupied by the economic problems that the Reagan administration had to cope with during its first term.

No matter how heavy (or light) the coverage was, the potential threat to world peace never provided the organizing frame under which the particular events were subsumed. While the destruction of the Iraqi reactor could have served as a peg for discussions of nuclear proliferation, few journalists availed themselves of this opportunity. Instead the main issue to emerge in the aftermath was how to deal with Israel for its violation of international law. As to the other events, Saddam's rise to power was treated as a routine succession in leadership; the mustard-gas attack evoked a quarrel about whether Iraq had or had not actually resorted to chemical warfare in its cruel war with Iran; the attack on the Kurds evolved into a UN debate; the summary execution of a journalist, which could have galvanized the journalistic community, remained little more than just another spy story.[43]

To what extent those responsible for the coverage felt constrained by an American policy of clandestine collaboration with the Saddam regime behind a posture of official neutrality is hard to say. Coverage of these events in "matched" publications in Britain and Germany—not presented here for want of space—did not reveal any differences attributable to the policies of their governments toward Iraq.[44] What is clear is that the Reagan/Bush administration went to some length to shield its policies from public scrutiny, and reporters have always been dependent, more than most are willing to admit, on what official sources are prepared to feed them (Sigal 1973; see also, Rühl 1971; Tuchman 1973; Fishman 1980).

One has also to understand that news-gathering is organized according to certain assumptions. Iraq did not fit into the journalistic map of a Near East dominated by Israel, to which the U.S. had close connections, and by Egypt as the most important among the Arab nations (Gans 1979). Besides, Iraq was a closed society and a dangerous place for inquisitive journalists. This made the Western press highly dependent on Iraqi sources controlled by Saddam Hussein for its coverage of that country while many of the domestic experts called upon for interpretation had themselves had a hand in the formulation of policy.

But the system is hardly leak-proof. How much reporters with expertise in the Near East or with long experience on the foreign-policy or security beat suspected, failed to find out, actually knew without drawing the full conclusions, or simply held back, on a story not easily verified yet damaging to the government, are open questions. Some obviously knew more than they wrote about and many more must have had at least some idea of what was going on.

Still, for all the above reasons, the public did not know what it needed to know to judge foreign policy performance in relation to vital national interests. Thus, it behooves us to repeat a question raised by A. M. Rosenthal in November 1992: "Would the gulf war have taken place if American citizens had known from the beginning that Saddam Hussein was the beneficiary of a Western buildup, military and political? Since Washington knew, and Saddam knew, and foreign offices friend and foe knew, why was the policy kept secret from the American public?"[45] For whatever reason, the press did not, and perhaps could not, fulfill its ad-

versary function against a government intent on exercising its preroga-
tive of classifying and withholding information necessary to the
formation of an informed public opinion.

Notes

1. Schuman and Rieger (1992) have shown how analogies can affect opinion.

2. Louis Harris and Associates (hereafter Harris), July 11–23, 1980; Martilla
and Kiley, Inc. (1988), April 18–24, 1988. Information on polls with no source
indicated comes from the archives of the Roper Center, University of Connecticut. Other information was provided by Bernard Roshco and Alvin Richman,
U.S. Department of State, whose generous assistance the authors gratefully acknowledge.

3. Harris, July 11–23, 1980.

4. *Time*/Yankelovich, Clancy, Shulman (hereafter Yankelovich), October
14–16, 1980.

5. The Roper Organization (hereafter Roper), July 11–18 and December 5–
12, 1981.

6. Martilla and Kiley (1988), "Americans Talk Security," October 15–19,
1987.

7. *NYT*, August 24, 1990, p. A29.

8. Harris, January 8–12, 1982, and February 20–24, 1987.

9. CBS News/*New York Times* (hereafter CBS/*NYT*), April 15, 1986.

10. This is a subsample of a larger list of events selected for comparison with
Britain and Germany because they were expected to have attracted significant
coverage in those countries.

11. We defined as "relevant" all items referring either to Iraq or Saddam Hussein except for routine reports of military operations or those without any political relevance, such as an item on archaeological finds in Iraq.

12. *NYT*, July 28, 1979, p. A-3.

13. See al-Khalil (1989, 70), who notes that no two accounts of the purge
match but that the general sense of the scale of the purge was more or less common knowledge.

14. *NYT*, July 30, 1979, p. A-8.

15. *NYT*, August 8, 1979, p. A-1+.

16. *NYT*, July 22, 1979, sec. iv, p. 5.

17. "Putting on the Pressure." *Time*, August 20, 1979, p. 25.

18. *NYT*, September 23, 1980, p. A-22.

19. *NYT*, September 24, 1980, p. A-12.

20. This was the main theme in British and German papers examined.

21. Barbara Walters, ABC, June 23, 1981, as cited in Timmerman (1991,
104).

22. *NYT*, June 14, 1981, sec. iv, p. 1.

23. Gallup, June 19–21, 1981; CBS/*NYT*, June 22–27, 1981.

24. Roper, July 11–18, 1981.

25. *Time,* July 13, 1981, p. 4.

26. *NYT,* March 6, 1984, p. A-1.

27. See polls by *Los Angeles Times,* December 6–9, 1986, and May 29–June 1, 1987; ABC/*Washington Post,* May 8–June 6, 1987; Harris, June 25–30, 1987; Yankelovich, August 17–19, 1987.

28. CBS/*NYT,* September 21–22, 1987.

29. Questions were not identical. *Los Angeles Times,* December 6–9, 1986: "If you have a preference, which side would you like to see win the Iran-Iraq war?" Roper, May 16–30, 1987, presented a list of countries, including Iraq, and asked respondents to "tell me if you believe that the country has acted as a close ally of the US, has acted as a friend but not a close ally, has been more or less neutral toward the US, has been mainly unfriendly toward the US but not an enemy, or has acted as an enemy of the US?" CBS/*NYT,* September 21–22, 1987: "In the war between Iran and Iraq, which country do you want to win?"

30. Harris, June 22–30, 1987.

31. ABC, September 8, 13, and 18, 1988.

32. CBS, September 8, 1988.

33. *ST,* March 24, 1988, and *NYT,* March 23 and March 26, 1988.

34. William Safire, "Nobody Is Perfect," *NYT,* September 12, 1988, p. 21.

35. *NYT,* September 12, 1988, p. A-21.

36. "A Shocking Execution," *Time,* March 26, 1990, p. 148.

37. Jill Smolowe, "The Big Sting," *Time,* April 9, 1990, p. 44.

38. *NYT,* March 29, 1990, p. A-1.

39. William Safire, "Bush Again Ignores Atrocity," *NYT,* March 11, 1990, p. A-19.

40. *NYT,* March 24, 1990, p. A-27.

41. *NYT,* March 16, 1990, p. A-34.

42. Joseph Alpher of the Center for Strategic Studies, as quoted on ABC, March 31, 1990.

43. On framing and how news stories can be used to dramatize issues, see Molotch and Lester 1975; Roshco 1975.

44. The publications were: *The Times,* the *Western Mail,* and *The Economist* (in Britain); the *Frankfurter Allgemeine Zeitung, Ruhr Nachrichten,* and *Der Spiegel* (Germany).

45. *NYT,* November 12, 1992.

References

al-Kalil, S. 1989. *Republic of Fear,* London: Hutchinson Radius.

Blumler, J. G., and M. Gurevitch. 1981. "Politicians and the Press: An Essay in Role Relationships." In D. D. Nimmo and K. R. Sanders, eds., *Handbook of Political Communication.* Newbury Park: Sage, pp. 467–93.

Cohen, B. C. 1963. *The Press and Foreign Policy.* Princeton: Princeton University Press.

Congressional Quarterly. 1988. *Congressional Quarterly Almanac.* Vol. 44. Washington, D.C.

Gans, H. J. 1979. *Deciding What's News*. New York: Pantheon.

Iyengar, S. 1991. *Is Anyone Responsible? How Television Frames Political Issues*. Chicago: University of Chicago Press.

Lang, G. E., and K. Lang. 1983. *The Battle for Public Opinion: The President, the Press, and the Polls During Watergate*. New York: Columbia University Press.

Lippmann, W. 1922. *Public Opinion*. New York: Harcourt, Brace.

Martilla and Kiley, Inc. 1988. "National Survey of American Voters: Attitudes Toward the Middle East." Highlights and Key Findings Prepared for the American Jewish Committee (mimeo).

Molotch, H., and M. Lester. 1975. "Accidental News: The Great Oil Spill as a Local Occurrence and National Event." *American Journal of Sociology* 81:235–60.

Mueller, J. E. 1973. *War, Presidents and Public Opinion*. New York: Wiley.

Roshco, B. 1975. *Newsmaking*. Chicago: University of Chicago Press.

Rühl, M. 1971. *Die Zeitungsredaktion als organisiertes soziales System*. Duesseldorf: Bertelsmann.

Schuman, H., and C. Rieger. 1992. "Historical Analogies, Generational Effects, and Attitudes Toward War." *American Sociological Review* 57:315–26.

Sciolino, E. 1991. *The Outlaw State*. New York: Wiley.

Sigal, L. V. 1973. *Reporters and Officials: The Organization and Politics of Newsmaking*. Lexington: Heath.

Timmerman, K. R. 1991. *The Death Lobby*. Boston: Houghton Mifflin.

Tuchman, G. 1973. "Making News by Doing Work: Routinizing the Unexpected." *American Journal of Sociology* 77:110–31.

three

William A. Dorman and
Steven Livingston

News and Historical Content

*The Establishing Phase of the Persian
Gulf Policy Debate*

I'm reading a book, and it's a book of history, a great big history about World War II, and
there's a parallel between what Hitler did to Poland and what Saddam Hussein has done
to Kuwait.
                                                          President Bush[1]

Background and context get skipped. The past comes in, if at all, in the form of analogy,
with someone speaking of the current situation as like some other. That may be to put a
familiar face on something strange. It may be for advocacy—because the analogue's supposed lesson supports the speaker's preference as to what to do.
                                                          Neustadt and May (1986, 4)

Introduction

The quality of news coverage is never more important than when a society is pondering whether to wage war. In judging the quality of news
coverage of the conflict with Iraq it is useful to divide the confrontation
into at least three chronological phases: (1) The *establishing phase* lasted
from Iraq's August 2, 1990, invasion of Kuwait to President Bush's November 8 announcement that 150,000 additional troops would be sent
to the Persian Gulf area to provide an "adequate offensive military option." (2) The *nominal debate phase* lasted from November 9, 1990, to
January 15, 1991. (3) The *war phase* lasted for the duration of armed
conflict, beginning on January 16 and ending February 28, 1991. Of
these three phases, we are most interested in the first.

The point of this chapter is to raise questions regarding the quality of
national debate at the inception of the Persian Gulf Crisis. Central to
public debate in a democracy is relatively free, open, and accessible information pertinent to the situation at hand. In American society the
news media have a constitutionally guaranteed right and, therefore, we
would argue, responsibility to provide information that goes beyond
government publicity campaigns. As Entman and Page point out in
Chapter 4 of this volume, "reporting that circulates information and

opinion at odds with the administration is vital to the possibility of democracy in the foreign policy process."

What interests us, then, is how—and whether—information reported by the news media encouraged or undermined vigorous democratic debate. Our argument here is not that journalists somehow should or could have prevented the war in the Gulf. Rather, our concern is with whether the news media performed according to the tenets of democratic theory and the professed values of American journalism itself (Rivers and Schramm 1969).

The Establishing Phase

This phase (August 2–November 8) takes its name from our belief that it was during this early period that the news media and political elites first accepted what came to be the dominant rhetorical frame for understanding the Gulf conflict and, secondly, first rallied behind the Bush administration's policy of military confrontation. When people say they remember a vigorous debate over the president's Gulf policy, invariably it is the nominal debate phase that they have in mind. When pressed for examples, they will cite press coverage of the Senate Armed Services Committee hearings and the debate in both houses over a resolution approving the use of force should Iraq ignore the U.N.'s January 15 deadline. Yet, one should recall that the Armed Service Committee hearings did not begin until November 28, 1990, or almost four months after the confrontation began. Likewise, the congressional debate over the force resolution did not begin until January 10, 1991, or only five days before the U.N. deadline, with the final vote coming but three days before the deadline.[2] What interests us, then, is the question of how the debate was framed in the four months prior to these events.

What is sometimes forgotten is the degree of consensus which marked Bush's Gulf policy during the establishment phase.[3] In fact, endorsements during the establishment phase came from some of Congress's most liberal members. "You've got to weigh what's strategically important," said Connecticut senator Christopher Dodd. President Bush's opponent in the 1988 election, Michael Dukakis of Massachusetts, was among those endorsing the president's handling of the invasion. "I think he's doing exactly the right thing."[4] The Reverend Jesse Jackson, the other major Democratic contender for the presidency in 1988, also endorsed Bush's actions. "He [Saddam Hussein] must be driven back to the borders, and the United States," said Jackson, must be prepared to "use military force, either multilaterally or unilaterally."[5]

Not surprising in such a political environment, strong support was also evident in the editorial pages of some of the country's leading newspapers. According to Bennett, there is a tendency for the media in foreign policy crisis to "index" their coverage to the range of opinions that exist within the government (Bennett 1990). With mainstream elites inside and outside the government in virtual agreement with Bush's handling of the early crisis, it is thus no surprise that the media carried scarcely a whisper of criticism of the president. As the *New York Times* editorialized on the day after Bush announced that he was deploying U.S. ground troops to the region: "President Bush has drawn a line in the sand, committing U.S. forces to face down Saddam Hussein. The costs and risks are enormous . . . (but) on balance, he has made the right choice in the right way."[6] Similarly, the *Washington Post* described the crisis situation in these terms: "Forces are gathered under many flags, and President Bush is leading this gigantic enterprise with skill. . . . This extraordinary array of forces is drawn together from many countries by one central conviction: that it would be very bad for each of them, and for the world in general, if Iraq's invasion succeeded."[7]

The extraordinary support for the president's Gulf policy among elites during the establishing phase induced most of the American public to rally as well, as described later in this volume by Brody (Chapter 10) and Zaller (Chapter 9). Public support for administration policy, once it began to register in public opinion polls, quickly became a major asset to President Bush in the crisis. It deterred potential critics in Congress from opposing Bush while also helping to convince foreign leaders, particularly in the Arab world, that Bush would be able to deliver on the promises of military action that he was making. This, in turn, enhanced Bush's ability to create an international coalition against Iraq. In short, by the time the country got around to debating Bush's Gulf policy, it was largely an established fact.

The basic point made in this chapter is that the debate which took place after November 8 reflected the framing of the issue during the establishing phase. Central to the framing of the Persian Gulf Crisis during the establishing phase was a selective attention to information by the news media, *particularly information regarding the historical root causes of the crisis.*

For instance, with important exceptions discussed below, during the crucial first few weeks of the Gulf conflict, the mainstream press virtually ignored a central contradiction of the Bush administration's emerging policy toward Iraq: How was it that an Iraq constantly at war with its own people, or for eight years with Iran, did not pose a clear and present danger to world peace, while an Iraq at war with Kuwait suddenly did? Similarly, why was Saddam Hussein not only tolerated by the Bush and Reagan administrations but even given vital economic and military support by them for a decade if he was a character as evil as Adolf Hitler? Like one of the sudden and socially unacknowledged transformations of friend to foe in Orwell's *1984*, Saddam the ally became Hitler incarnate virtually overnight.

This contradiction convinced us that a useful focus for our investigation would be an examination of the ways early news accounts of the Gulf Crisis provided context—or "framed"—key political actors and events. Specifically, we are interested in determining the degree to which the press provided historical context for unfolding events in the Gulf as Americans were making up their minds about whether or how to defend Kuwait. It seemed to us that no other type of news during the establishing phase—whether of military deployments, diplomatic maneuvering, presidential proclamations, and so on—had quite the same potential to influence public debate as would a detailed and sustained examination of our past relations with Iraq (Bennett 1988, 188).

Questions regarding the recent history of relations between Iraq and the United States were largely ignored by the press. By and large, the press failed to *systematically* inform the American people of the U.S. role in helping Saddam Hussein throughout the eight-year Iran-Iraq war and beyond. While it is true that some of the details regarding the support given to Saddam Hussein by the Reagan and Bush administrations were not fully realized until well after the war (largely as a result of Congressman Henry Gonzalez's House Banking Committee investigation and the reporting of Douglas Franz and Murray Waas of the *Los Angeles Times* in the spring of 1992), the general contours of the relationship *were* publicly available in the summer of 1990. Yet this history was generally missing from reporting during the establishing phase. A brief review makes the point.

There was little mention in the major news media, for instance, of the fact that the Reagan and Bush administrations had looked the other way for some six years while Iraq used chemical weapons against Iran. Moreover, there was scant mention that it was the Bush administration which had convinced the U.S. Senate not to cut off all aid to Iraq when it used chemical weapons against the Kurds in the spring of 1988.

Nor was there much light shed on U.S. counterterrorism policy toward Iraq in the 1980s. In the spring of 1982, the Reagan administration dropped Iraq from the State Department's list of terror-sponsoring nations. This action had little to do with any changes in Iraq's support of terrorism; Saddam continued to support and play host to the same terrorists groups he always had.[8] Rather, because trading with a country on the list was prohibited by law, the listing of Iraq had made the Reagan administration's desire to support Saddam in his war against Iran difficult. Once Iraq was dropped from the list, Reagan and Bush were free to assist Saddam in the creation of one of the largest and most well-equipped armies in the world.

It wasn't until the establishing phase that Saddam's ties to international terrorism were once again a popular topic for the Bush administration and journalists. Newspaper columnists and the administration issued dire warnings that Iraq was "cultivating terrorists ties" and that terrorism was Saddam's "ultimate fifth column."[9] The ties had been there all along, though ignored.

Our analysis indicates that two of the most resourceful and competent newspapers in the United States (the *New York Times* and the *Washington Post*)[10] devoted what at best could be called modest attention to the historical context most directly relevant to the unfolding events in the Gulf in 1990: the near decade-long relationship between Saddam Hussein and the Reagan and Bush administrations.[11]

Between August 2 and November 8, 1990, some ninety-eight days, the *New York Times* and the *Washington Post* published a combined total of 4,214 stories, editorials, or columns concerning Kuwait, Iraq, or Saudi Arabia.[12] The *Post* published 1,742 pieces (averaging 18 per day) while the *Times* published 2,472 (averaging 25 per day). Despite this remarkable devotion of time and resources to the Gulf conflict, we found that both papers devoted quite modest attention to the policies and events relating to U.S.-Iraqi relations in the ten years prior to events in August 1992. On the other hand, the news was rich with references to an alternative historical context: Adolf Hitler and Nazi Germany, a news frame which tended to limit the range of alternative policy options in the public debate preceding the war. Why we believe this is true will be discussed in a moment.

Relevant historical context was not, of course, completely absent from the *Times* and *Post* coverage during the opening weeks of the conflict. During the establishing phase, each newspaper published several articles[13] and columns[14] which, to varying degrees of depth, outlined the historical relationship between the Reagan and Bush administrations and Iraq. Though a generous count would put the total at twenty articles and columns, references to U.S. collaboration with Saddam's regime were often only in passing, such as when Rachel Ehrenfeld remarked in her October 28 *New York Times* column that "We are courting

Syria like we courted Iraq until it invaded Kuwait—because we regard it as the lesser of two evils." All in all, out of the 4,214 *Times* and *Post* stories, columns or editorials published during the establishment phase, we have found that approximately one in every two hundred of the published pieces provided readers with information regarding the history of Reagan and Bush administration policy in the Persian Gulf.

On September 20, late in the establishing phase, congressional sources quoted in the *Times* raised concerns that Reagan-Bush administration policies toward Iraq prior to the August 2 invasion did little to discourage it. Congressman Tom Lantos is quoted as saying that the United States "obsequious treatment" of Hussein encouraged him to invade Kuwait.[15] The day before, President Bush had claimed to regret the overtures made to President Hussein in previous months, though at the same time he insisted they had nothing to do with the subsequent invasion.

Late in the second month of the crisis, the press had a second opportunity to open the question of the Bush administration's record, when Iraq released a transcript of the July 25 meeting between Saddam Hussein and U.S. ambassador April C. Glaspie. According to the transcript, Ambassador Glaspie appears to have been considerably less than forceful in warning Hussein about the consequences of belligerent actions toward Kuwait. She reportedly informed the Iraqi leader that the United States had "no opinion" regarding Iraq's oil and border dispute with Kuwait. Again, the *Times* published a promising article only to let the matter drop.[16]

The *Times* also published two important articles during the opening days of the conflict which could have pointed the way toward a more critical discourse. On the tenth day of the crisis, a front-page analysis by Thomas J. Friedman questioned President Bush's assertion that the defense of Saudi Arabia was a priori in the vital interest of the U.S.[17] Following on the heels of the Friedman piece was a particularly strong front-page analysis by Michael Wines, the tone of which was clearly set in the lead: "For 10 years, as Iraq developed a vast army, chemical weapons, nuclear ambitions and a long record of brutality, the Reagan and Bush Administrations quietly courted President Saddam Hussein as a counterweight to Iran's revolutionary fervor. Now, critics say, Washington is paying the price for that policy."[18] According to Wines, Iraq had achieved its power "with American acquiescence and sometimes its help," and he went on to detail the forms of assistance provided to Iraq by Washington.

The story at the *Washington Post* is much the same. As early as August

8th, the *Post* published an article which outlined the Bush administration's timid handling of Saddam prior to the invasion. On September 13, 1990, the *Post* carried a news-analysis piece by Jim Hoagland which provided extensive quotations from the Iraqi transcripts of Ambassador Glaspie's July 25 meeting with Saddam Hussein.[19] Here, too, the story was not sustained.

On August 26, *Post* published what was perhaps to that point the single most comprehensive review of U.S.-Iraqi relations during the previous decade.[20] On September 16, the *Post* again noted the relationship between Iraq and U.S. businesses. Finally, on November 1, the *Post* noted that between 1985 and 1990 the U.S. approved $1.5 billion worth of computers, machine tools, and electronic equipment for sale to Iraq, all of which could be used to produce nuclear weapons.[21]

When these twenty articles and columns, taken from what are often regarded as the two leading newspapers in the country, are reviewed seriatim, as we have done here, one is left with the impression that there actually *was* considerable attention paid to the very issues we claim were most relevant. However, a handful of published pieces, when balanced against more than 4,200 total news articles, columns, and editorials, simply failed to stretch the limits of discourse. Given the sheer numbers involved, it would have been a rare newspaper reader who could have kept in mind these handful of stories for help in making the connection between Reagan and Bush's decade-old policies and the situation in the summer of 1990. If nothing else, the noise from competing historical frames would have presented readers with formidable obstacles.

Rather than clear and reoccurring references to the relationship between Saddam Hussein's Iraq and the West, mythological references to Hitler and Nazi Germany dominated the news.[22] Framed in this way, policy debates were limited. It is to an analysis of this mythological context that we turn next.

Creating Enemies: The Origins of the Hitler Analogy

Even under the best of circumstances, trying to make sense of any international conflict is difficult. It may have been particularly difficult for Americans to understand the complexities of Middle East politics. Nightly tracking surveys of American attitudes on the Persian Gulf Crisis conducted by the Wirthlin Group found that during the establishing phase, only a modest 27 percent of the public could correctly identify Kuwait as a monarchy (Wilcox, Ferrara, Allsop 1991).[23] Most respondents were simply unable to proffer a response of any kind. As Clyde

Wilcox, Joe Ferrara, and Dee Allsop remark: "Most Americans did not enter this crisis with much information about or interest in Middle East politics, *and this provided political elites with substantial potential for persuasion*" (Wilcox, Ferrara, Allsop 1991, 4; emphasis added).

Though the potential for persuasion may have been great, the means for doing so were not so obvious. As the *Washington Post's* Charles Paul Freund remarked, when President Bush "went to the oratorical cupboard" for his August 8, 1990, speech intended to explain the United States military commitment to Saudi Arabia, "it was bare."[24] With the end of the cold war went the prime rhetorical frame for U.S. foreign policy. Bush eventually relied on images predating the cold war, images served up by terms such as blitzkreig, Munich, and Adolf Hitler. But the analogy did not originate with President Bush.

The practice of comparing Saddam Hussein to Adolf Hitler actually preceded the invasion of Kuwait by several weeks. On April 5, after Saddam threatened to "scorch half of Israel" if it attacked Iraq, the *New York Times* columnist A. M. Rosenthal compared Saddam Hussein to Hitler.[25] Most of the Hitler comparisons did not appear until later, during the month preceding the invasion of Kuwait. The *Washington Post's* Jim Hoagland hinted at it on July 5, when he described Saddam's threat against Israel as an "airborne version of Hitler's ovens."[26]

Political figures also began to use the Hitler analogy in July. Israel's defense minister, Moshe Arens, told the U.S. secretary of defense, Richard Cheney, during a trip to the United States that Saddam Hussein was "another Hitler." Arens repeated the comparison on July 22 before members of the Conference of Presidents of Major Jewish Organizations.[27] A few days later, on July 25, *USA Today* quoted Congressman Tom Lantos as saying that Saddam Hussein reminded him of Hitler "in his blatant arrogance, his bloodthirsty brutality."[28]

During this same week, the Senate and House debated the suspension of Commodity Credit Corporation credits to Iraq. In the course of the debate on July 26 and 27, Senators Alfonse D'Amato of New York, Claiborne Pell of Rhode Island, and William Cohen of Maine also used the Hitler analogy.[29] Yet what is interesting about the Senate debate is the degree to which the Nazi Germany analogy, and World War II more generally, were used to describe and criticize Reagan and Bush administration policy, not Saddam Hussein, though that was certainly there too. Senator Cohen, for example, offered this somewhat tortured remark "(A)t one point in our history we heard the tap-tap-tap of Neville Chamberlain's umbrella on the cobblestones of Munich. Now we are about to hear the rumble of the farm tractor on the bricks of Baghdad. Make no mistake about it, we are following a policy of appeasement."[30] This is interesting, for it suggests that later, when the Bush administration used the Hitler analogy to frame its policy toward Iraq, the potential was always there for it to explode in the administration's face. Simply put, if Saddam Hussein was Adolf Hitler, up until August 2 George Bush had played the role of Neville Chamberlain, not Winston Churchhill. As we will see below, though, the press rarely made the connection.

Also on July 27, columnist Charles Krauthammer made the rhetorical connection between Saddam and Hitler. In an interview with the authors, Krauthammer said that at the time he used the Hitler analogy he was unaware of Moshe Arens' or any other political figure's use of the comparison. Instead, what he had in mind was the similarity he saw between Saddam's threatening remarks—directed at Kuwait—and Hitler's threats directed against Czechoslovakia and Poland.[31] Whatever the inspiration, Krauthammer's column was important, for it was often specifically mentioned in debate in the Senate that day, and was even entered into the *Congressional Record* by Senator D'Amato and Representative Tom Lantos. In short, the Saddam-Hitler analogy was quite well established before the invasion of Kuwait.

After the August 2 invasion, use of the Hitler analogy exploded. Between August 2 and January 15 the *Washington Post* and the *New York Times* published 228 stories, editorials, or columns on Iraq and/or Kuwait which invoked the Saddam Hussein–Adolf Hitler analogy (*Times*, N = 107, *Post*, N = 121).[32] Well over half of the articles (140) came during the establishing phase.

Though Charles Krauthammer was the first columnist to repeat the Hitler analogy (on the day after the August 2 invasion),[33] President Bush was the single greatest source for the Hitler analogy in this period. According to press accounts, Bush first made the comparison on August 8, the day he announced the first deployment of American combat personnel to the Persian Gulf.[34] Invoking the image of Hitler quickly became a near daily occurrence for him. The analogy was, as the *Washington Post's* E. J. Dionne remarked, "everywhere."[35] After a brief mid-phase lull, Bush once again invoked the analogy on a regular basis in speeches and remarks he made just prior to the November elections.[36] In fact, Bush's use of the Hitler analogy became so common at one point, his *failure* to use it was considered newsworthy by the *New York Times* and the *Washington Post*.[37]

The Hitler Analogy, Public Debate, and Foreign Policy

In the absence of an alternative, a majority of the public latched onto the analogy very early in the conflict. According to a survey conducted on August 9 and 10 for the *New York Times*, 60 percent of the public "accepted Mr. Bush's comparison of Saddam Hussein of Iraq to Hitler."[38] As Jarol Manheim in Chapter 6 points out, Hill and Knowlton's focus-group data indicated that the critical factor in American public support for the president's policy was not sympathy or identification with Kuwait but antipathy toward Saddam Hussein.[39] Of the initial fifty prospective message strategies considered by Hill and Knowlton, the campaign was narrowed to a single message designed to reinforce the Saddam-as-enemy sentiment.

The demonization of Saddam Hussein by the administration was clearly recognized by several journalists writing in the *Post*. On at least two occasions during the initial days of the confrontation, the *Post* ran articles which spoke of Saddam Hussein's demonization, then in its initial stages.[40] On August 9, for example, Marjorie Williams remarked: "He (Saddam Hussein) has undergone a striking transformation, over the past week, in the American media and the American imagination. Once a dictator whom most Americans could not identify, but with whom the United States has sided for most of the past decade, Saddam Hussein is now suddenly revealed as a fiend in human form." Later she remarked that "The administration and the American media have done a brilliant job, as the imagemakers might say, of driving up his negatives."

Though the Hitler-Saddam analogy was challenged on occasion, it simply overwhelmed the alternatives. The authoritative status of the president makes his "definition of the issue more readily acceptable for an ambivalent public called upon to react to an ambiguous situation" (Edelman 1977, 25). This is why the president's references to Hitler and Nazi Germany became the dominant context for evaluating events and policy options in the Gulf during the establishing phase. Because this was the case, public debate during the establishing phase was restricted.

In and of themselves, the relative presence or absence of particular historical contexts may not seem important. What make historical analogies important are the policy implications inherent in any commonly accepted description of distant and poorly understood places and events. Competing descriptions—including suggested problem origins—of often ambiguous and poorly understood events carry with them key assumptions regarding, among other things, which policy responses are most appropriate and which options are open to debate.[41] As Murray Edelman has noted, "How the problem is named," how it is described, "involves alternative scenarios, each with its own facts, value judgments, and emotions" (Edelman 1977, 23, 29). Human relations, identities, responsibilities, and "what is necessary," are all established in the definition process (Edelman 1988, 12; 1977, 26).

Similarly, Bennett has remarked that "To a remarkable extent, the actor who controls the selection and symbolization of critical information in a political conflict may possess a decisive measure of control over key political considerations" (Bennett 1982, 187). *By focusing on specific problem origins, public consideration of other possible explanations and solutions is discouraged or eliminated.* In this way much of the ambiguity and complexity that is often endemic to politics is removed. The situation is sharpened and clarified through the elimination of complicating alternative interpretations and policy implications.

The analogies with Hitler certainly seemed to accomplish that. The alternative, to have defined Saddam Hussein as the creation of the Reagan and Bush administrations and European allies over the previous decade, would have been to raise serious questions about not only the appropriateness of past policies regarding Iraq but also more vigorous debate on the appropriateness of the direction Bush administration policies were taking at the time. This would have been accomplished by raising the central contradictions of the Bush administration's policies discussed earlier in this chapter: Why was Iraq not a clear and present danger to the United States and the world during its long period of hostility to its neighbors and its own citizens during much of the 1980s, while an Iraq at war with Kuwait suddenly was such a danger? Similarly, why was Saddam Hussein provided intelligence and military aid by the Reagan and Bush administrations if he was a character as evil or even more evil than Adolf Hitler?

On the other hand, in personalizing the conflict, by casting Saddam Hussein as Adolph Hitler, the Bush administration was able to successfully specify the origins of the conflict in the simple villainy of a lone individual, rather than as the logical outcome of the foreign policy of the Reagan and Bush administrations. The situation was indeed sharpened and clarified, but the certainties that were created tended to exclude from consideration the role played by two successive administrations in the creation of the threat Iraq posed in the fall of 1990.

Secondly, awareness of the policy implications of the Hitler analogy would have also lent insight, in the late summer of 1990, into the likely outcome of the Gulf conflict. Given the dominance of the Hitler analogy as the frame of reference, one could reasonably assume from the start that the Bush administration had limited the United States to but one policy option: war. Indeed, this was apparent to a handful of veteran journalists. Mary McGrory put it most succinctly, "Appeasement is . . . out of the question. He [President Bush] has cast Saddam as Hitler."[42] Or, as Stephan Rosenthal, writing in the *Post* on October 19, put it: "It is not simply that Saddam has committed terrible human rights crimes and set himself on a path of aggression. *With Hitler, you cannot compromise;* the only acceptable result in a confrontation with him is his unconditional surrender" (emphasis added).

And this is really the point: With Saddam-as-Hitler, "compromise," or any other alternative policy option, was effectively eliminated from debate well before the actual debate got under way. This was the case because the news media tended to accept the compelling, though rather facile, Hitler analogy, rather than expanding the debate by focusing on the fundamentally flawed realpolitik policies that led to the creation of a militarily threatening Iraq in the first place. Again, it was not the press's responsibility to stop the war. It *was* the press's responsibility to present the widest possible array of explanations regarding the origins (and therefore the solutions) for the problem at hand. Instead, the press merely replayed the highly personalized Saddam-as-Hitler analogy that was so thoroughly tested and refined by Hill and Knowlton research. After all, the premise behind strategic public diplomacy is that the news media were accessible conduits for focus-group-generated message strategies. It seems to have been a sound premise.

There is, of course, the question of what alternative frames the press might have adopted instead of "Saddam-as-Hitler." Communications scholar Elihu Katz has suggested the "feuding neighbors" frame, which is the way journalists encouraged Americans to view Iraq's eight-year war with Iran. That war, after all, also involved an invasion of one Persian Gulf country by another, and with far more casualties. If it "were not for the rhetoric of World War II—as proposed by the President and the media," says Katz, "the Iraqi invasion of Kuwait might also have been construed as holding little interest" (Katz 1992, 6).

And, of course, as we have suggested throughout this chapter, the press might well have adopted a "this is what you get when you encourage someone like Saddam" frame. More succinctly stated, this might be referred to as the Neville Chamberlain frame, with George Bush in the lead role. This frame would have had the effect of expanding the debate to include consideration of American support for highly autocratic regimes (such as Saudi Arabia, Kuwait, and Iran before the overthrow of the Shah, and Iraq before the invasion of Kuwait). In addition, consideration of U.S. Middle East policy might well have focused more attention on the United States continued dependence on Middle East oil, Reagan and Bush administration energy policies, and the human and moral costs of maintaining access to relatively cheap oil reserves. Instead, debate centered on when to attack Saddam and at what potential cost.

Conclusion

For the Bush administration to have explicitly advocated a policy solely in the name of oil would have been to concede the point of its foreign policy critics, that American interests in "liberating" Kuwait were motivated not by a sense of moral justice, love of liberty, disdain for dictators, or desire to see a truly democratic and free Kuwait. After all, reinstating the emir was about as much of a blow for democracy as was the reinstatement of the Shah by the CIA in 1953. But reliance on the oil rationale alone presented additional problems. Why should a near-bankrupt Iraq, whose only source of revenue is oil, seek to cut off its supply to its most lucrative customer, the West? We could find no satisfactory editorial or reportorial inquiry into this question.

A second concern was raised by Bob Woodward's book *The Commanders.* How early in the crisis was it possible for journalists such as Woodward to raise the possibility that Bush, almost from the beginning, was set on the war option? At least two reviewers wonder what Woodward knew, when he knew it, and why he did not tell what he knew in a more timely fashion (Massing 1991; Weiner 1991).

And what of other journalists? In his review of Woodward's book, Michael Massing pointed out that the *New York Times* ran a front-page analysis, "From the First, U.S. Resolve to Fight," on March 3, 1991, which informed readers that planning for the war option had begun early in the fall of 1990. According to Massing (1991, 10): "The article went on at great length, chronicling the administration's relentless march toward war. Appearing a week after the end of the conflict, the story attracted little attention. Had it appeared last fall under a different headline—say, 'President Approves Secret Timetable for War'—a public uproar might have ensued."

Throughout the 1990–91 Persian Gulf crisis U.S. policy can be said to possess all of the characteristics suggested by the social psychologist Ralph K. White which distort reality during times of international confrontation: a diabolical enemy-image; a virile self-image; a moral self-image; and selective inattention (White 1970). The selective inattention of the *New York Times* and the *Washington Post* reveals that, during the establishing phase, the news media fell short of helping to create a robust culture of debate, one sufficient to counteract these characteristics.

By and large, journalists failed to examine U.S. policy claims, moral or otherwise, within the context of alternative historical settings. As a result, popular discourse was dominated during the crucial defining moments of the confrontation with Iraq by themes offered by the Bush administration. In this regard, journalists tended to perform as passive "chroniclers" rather than active "examiners," to use categories suggested by Pollock (1981, 29).

There were important exceptions, of course, *Newsday* among them. The work of Pentagon correspondent Knut Royce and his colleagues Patrick J. Sloyan, Timothy M. Phelps, and Saul Friedman, among others, produced a consistent body of work that challenged the administration's assumptions from the beginning—and that proved to be on the mark as time passed.[44]

Given that efforts such as those of *Newsday* were the journalistic exception rather than the rule, what are the implications for future coverage of conflict involving U.S. interests? First, if the Gulf experience offers any evidence, the end of the cold war has not made much difference in the performance of mainstream journalism. What continues is a journalism of deference to the national security state, the sources of which are beyond the scope of this chapter (Dorman and Farhang 1987). It suffices to say that in public discourse a statist sensibility still predominates that favors the official perspective, assumptions, and boundaries of thought and vocabulary. A second concern centers on the reality that conflict between the West and Middle Eastern nations over oil resources is likely to continue long after Saddam Hussein has left the scene. The problem is compounded when considered in light of the undeniable U.S. interventionist impulse to project power in the region.

Under the circumstances, the lessons to be learned in the long run by journalism from the confrontation with Iraq may be at least as significant as those that went unlearned in Vietnam.

Notes

1. Thomas L. Friedman, "No Compromise on Kuwait," *New York Times* (hereafter *NYT*), October 24, 1990, p. A10.
2. And as Entman and Page argue, even then debate was restricted.
3. The authors would like to thank John Zaller for his valuable contributions to the development of this portion of the argument.

4. "Dukakis Supports Actions by Bush," *Washington Post* (hereafter *WP*), November 9, 1990, p. A33.

5. E. J. Dionne, "Post–Cold War Consensus Backs U.S. Intervention," *WP,* August 8, 1990, p. A12.

6. "The U.S. Stands Up. Who Else?" *NYT,* August 9, 1990, p. A22.

7. "To Rescue Kuwait," *WP,* August 8, 1990, p. A20.

8. See Steven Livingston, *The Terrorism Spectacle: Domestic and Foreign Policy Implications of the Portrayal of Terrorism* (Boulder: Westview Press, 1993), chap. 2.

9. See Bruce Hoffman, "Saddam Hussein's Ultimate Fifth Column—Terrorists," *Los Angeles Times* (hereafter *LAT*), August 26, 1990; Ronald J. Ostrow and Robin Wright, "U.S. Fears Iraq Is Cultivating Terrorists Ties," *LAT,* September 2, 1990. For a review of what was known about Iraqi support of international terrorism well before August 2, see Steven Emerson and Cristina Del Sesto, *Terrorist* (New York: Villard Books, 1991).

10. Both authors independently examined news stories, editorials, and commentaries concerning the Middle East published between August 2, 1990, and January 20, 1991, in the *Times* and the *Post. The Washington Post* and *The New York Times* were selected for review because of their reputation for excellence, independence, and thoroughness. If the *Times* and the *Post* failed to provide sufficient historical context during what we refer to as the establishing phase, it is unlikely other news sources did. Several other publications in the United States, England, and Israel were less systematically reviewed, usually with the aid of Mead Data Central research services.

11. Of course, a potential criticism of our assumptions and concerns might be this: We cannot realistically expect journalists to serve as historians, too. Readers must instead turn to books and other publications to gain historical perspective. This is an important and cogent consideration, one we wish to thank Leon Sigal for pointing out to us. We believe, however, that this criticism misses an important point. The news implicitly and/or explicitly utilizes historical content regardless of whether journalists consciously provide it. If journalists do not place the events they report in the most relevant historical context, those with a stake in the adoption of a particular description of the event will.

12. A Mead Data Central Nexis search was designed to count *only once* any story which mentioned any one country, two of them, or all three countries. In other words, this number does not reflect any given story being counted more than once. It does reflect, however, all articles, columns, and editorials from each newspaper.

The frequency of such stories during this time period was so high we quite frankly did not believe the count to be accurate. After running the search a second time, consulting with Mead Data Central and speaking with editors at *The Washington Post* and *The New York Times*, we came to the conclusion that these frequencies accurately reflect the coverage.

13. Thomas L. Friedman, "U.S. Gulf Policy: Vague 'Vital Interests,'" *NYT,* August 12, 1990, p. A1; Michael Wines, "U.S. Aid Helped Hussein's Climb; Now, Critics Say, the Bill is Due," *NYT,* August 13, 1990, p. A1; Clifford Krauss, "Rights-Group Report Asserts Syria Tortures and Kills Political Foes," *NYT,* September 14, 1990, p. A10; Andrew Rosenthal "Did U.S. Overtures Give Wrong Idea to Hussein?" *NYT,* September 19, 1990, p. A12; R. W. Apple, "Criti-

cism of U.S. Gulf Policy Growing Louder in Congress," *NYT,* September 20, 1990, p. A10; Elaine Sciolino with Michael R. Gordon, "U.S. Gave Iraq Little Reason Not to Mount Kuwait Assault," *NYT,* September 23, 1990, p. A1.

R. Jeffery Smith, "Some Nations Now Condemning Saddam Had Helped Arm Him," *WP,* August 7, 1990, p. A1; David Hoffman, "U.S. Misjudgment of Saddam Seen: Early Evidence of Bellicosity, Drive for Dominance Noted," *WP,* August 8, 1990, p. A1; Nora Boustany, "Doctrine, Dreams Drive Saddam Hussein," *WP,* August 12, 1990, p. A1; R. Jeffery Smith and Benjamin Weiser, "Commerce Dept. Urged Sale to Iraq: Furnaces Useful In Making A-Arms," *WP,* September 13, 1990, p. A1; Guy Gugliotta, Charles R. Babcock, and Benjamin Weir, "At War, Iraq Courted U.S. Into Economic Embrace," *WP,* September 16, 1990; Glenn Frankel, "How Saddam Built His War Machine: West Provided Much of the Necessary Technology, Expertise," *WP,* September 17, 1990, p. A1; John M. Goshko and R. Jeffery Smith, "State Department Assailed on Iraq Policy: Democrats Cite Failure to Avert Invasion; Sale to Saudis Is Criticized," *WP,* September 19, 1990, p. 1; David Hoffman, "Bush Cabled Iraq's Saddam Before Attack: U.S. Officials Say Note Sought Better Relations," *WP,* October 21, 1990, p. A25.

14. Tom Wicker, "Not the Only Crisis," *NYT,* September 12, 1990, p. A.31; Anthony Lewis, "Paying for Reagan," *NYT,* October 5, 1990, p. A37; Rachel Ehrenfeld, "With Friends Like Syria," *NYT,* October 28, 1990.

Charles Krauthammer, "A Festival of Appeasement," *WP,* August 3, 1990, p. A23; Lally Weymouth, "In Backing Saddam Hussein Against the Ayatollah, Our Policymakers Failed to See Iraq's Intentions," *WP,* August 26, 1990, p. C2; Amos Perlmutter and Benjamin Frankel, "Soviet Secrets in the Gulf," *WP,* September 16, 1990, p. B1; Richard Cohen, "Secretary of Stealth," *WP,* September 28, 1990, p. A27.

15. R. W. Apple, Jr., "Criticism of U.S. Gulf Policy Growing Louder in Congress," *NYT,* September 20, 1990, p. 10.

16. Elaine Sciolino with Michael R. Gordon, "U.S. Gave Iraq Little Reason Not to Mount Kuwait Assault," *NYT,* September 23, 1990, A1.

17. Thomas Friedman, "U.S. Gulf Policy: Vague 'Vital Interests,'" *NYT,* August 12, 1990, p. A1.

18. Michael Wines, "U.S. Aid Helped Hussein's Climb; Now, Critics Say, the Bill Is Due," *NYT,* August 13, 1990, A1.

19. Jim Hoagland, "Transcripts Shows Muted U.S. Response to Threat by Saddam in Late July," *WP,* September 13, 1990, p. A33.

20. Lally Weymouth, "In Backing Saddam Hussein Against the Ayatollah, Our Policymakers Failed to See Iraq's Intentions," *WP,* August 26, 1990, p. C2.

21. Unsigned, "American Sales to Iraq Totaled $1.5 Billion," *WP,* November 1, 1990, p. C1.

22. Research has shown that among the basic components of any effective message strategy is the repetition of a relatively unambiguous message (Bennett 1988, 75).

23. Tracking surveys were conducted by the Wirthlin Group from August 22 to December 30, 1990. The survey included a total of 16,903 respondents from all forty-eight continental states. This figure includes a 1,000 respondent benchmark survey. Such data place into perspective the contradictions involved

in the popular wartime slogan "Free Kuwait," as if it had been or was likely to be free of despotic rule if Iraq were removed. One of the authors interviewed Dee Allsop of the Wirthlin Group on August 20, 1991.

24. Charles Paul Freund, "In Search of a Post-Postwar Rhetoric: When President Bush Went to the Oratorical Cupboard, It Was Bare," *WP,* August 12, 1990.

25. A. M. Rosenthal, "We Are Warned," *NYT,* April 5, 1990, p. A29.

26. Jim Hoagland, "Turning a Blind Eye to Baghdad," *WP,* July 5, 1990.

27. Gail Fitzer, "Arens Said Concerned About Iraqi Threats, Possibility of War," Reuters, July 22, 1990. See also Jonathan Schachter, "Arens: Strategic U.S. Ties Vital," *Jerusalem Post,* July 24, 1990.

28. Johanna Neuman, "Mixing Politics and Oil in the Mideast; Oil Fuels Iraq Bid for Role as Leader," *USA Today,* July 25, 1990.

29. See *Congressional Record,* Senator D'Amato's floor statement of July 27, 1990. See also Michael Ross, "U.S. Lawmakers Vote to Punish Iraq," *LAT,* July 28, 1990, p. 7.

30. U.S. Congress. Senate, 101st Cong., 2d sess. 136 *Cong. Rec.,* S10902, vol. 136, no. 99; continuation of Senate proceedings of July 26, 1990, no. 98; and proceedings of July 27, 1990, no. 99.

31. Telephone interview in Washington, D.C., June 3, 1993.

32. These numbers were obtained with the assistance of Mead Data Central's Nexis on-line service, a full-text data base. It should be noted that although the vast majority of the references to the Saddam-Hitler analogy were articles which simply repeated the assertion, several argued *against* the appropriateness of the analogy. But even here, it should be noted, the debate is limited to the Hitler-Saddam context.

33. William Safire claimed on August 24 that Saddam Hussein was rightly compared to Hitler. Walter Laqueur also made the comparison in a column published in the *Post* on August 27.

34. Andrew Rosenthal, "Bush Sends U.S. Forces to Saudi Arabia as Kingdom Agrees to Confront Iraq," *NYT,* August 7, 1990, p. A1.

35. E. J. Dionne, "Mainstream Reporting and Middle East Extremities: What Is Fair Reporting When It Comes to a Saddam Hussein?" *WP,* September 1, 1990, p. C1.

36. For examples, see Maureen Dowd, "President Seeks to Clarify Stand," *NYT,* November 2, 1990, p. A9; Unsigned A.P wire story, "Crude Oil Prices Show Strength, Then Fall," *NYT,* November 2, 1990, p. D15; Thomas L. Friedman, "No Compromise on Kuwait, Bush Says," *NYT,* October 24, 1990, p. A10; Dan Balz, "Near Site of Japanese Attack, Bush Issues Warning to Saddam," *WP,* October 29, 1990, p. A19. Ann Devroy, "Bush: Saudis Back Hard Line on Iraq: Powell Weighs Need to Augment Gulf Force," *WP,* October 24, 1990, p. A15; Edward Cody, "Dangerous Impasse Seen In Gulf Crisis Diplomacy; With No Substantive Contacts, Sides Harden," *WP,* October 16, 1990, p. A16. Dan Balz, "President Warns Iraq of War Crimes Trials; Bush Calls Invader's Acts 'Hitler Revisited'," *WP,* October 16, 1990, p. A19. Dale Russakoff, Washington Journal feature, "When Words are Held Hostage," *WP,* August 16, 1990, p. A21.

37. David Hoffman, "Gulf Crisis Tests Baker as Diplomat, Politician," *WP,* November 2, 1990, p. A1; Ann Devroy, "Bush Shifts Theme—Again; GOP Fortunes

Ignite White House Feuding," *WP,* November 5, 1990, p. A1. Maureen Dowd, "In Switch in Campaign Tactics, the Kinder Gentler Bush Emerges," *NYT,* November 3, 1990, p. A10.

38. Unsigned, "Poll on Troop Move Shows Support (and Anxiety)," *NYT,* August 12, 1990, p. A13.

39. Hill and Knowlton is the powerful Washington lobbying and public relations organization that landed the contract to present the Kuwaiti case to the U.S. Congress, news media, and public. See Manheim (chap. 6, below) for a more complete description.

40. Marjorie Williams, "Monster in the Making," *WP,* August 9, 1990, p. D1; Charles Paul Freund, "In Search of a Post-Postwar Rhetoric," *WP,* August 12, p. C2.

41. See Livingston (1993, chap. 1).

42. Mary McGrory, "Incoherent Mideast Policy," *WP,* November 6, 1990, p. A2.

43. Stephan S. Rosenfeld, "Gorbachev and the Gulf," *WP,* October 19, 1990, p. A23. See also Richard Cohen, "Heads They Win, Tails We Lose," *WP,* September 7, 1990, p. A15.

44. See for example Knute Royce and Saul Friedman, "Invasion of Kuwait: CIA Warned Bush of Invasion," *Newsday,* August 4, 1990, p. 4; Knute Royce and Patrick J. Sloyan, "Bush's Message in Show of Force," *Newsday,* August 16, 1990, p. 4; Timothy Phelps, "Middle East Crisis," *Newsday,* August 20, 1990, p. 7; Knute Royce, "Iraq Sent Pull-out Deal to U.S.," *Newsday,* August 29, 1990, p. 3; Knute Royce and Saul Friedman, "U.S. Prepares for Offensive," *Newsday,* August 31, 1990, p. 5.

References

al-Khalil, S. 1989. *Republic of Fear.* Berkeley: University of California Press.

Albright, D., and M. Hibbs. 1991. "Hyping the Iraqi Bomb." *The Bulletin of the Atomic Scientists* 47:26–28.

Bennett, W. L. 1982. "Rethinking Political Perception and Cognition." *Micropolitics* 2:175–202.

———. 1988. *News: The Politics of Illusion.* New York: Longman.

———. 1990. "Toward a Theory of Press-State Relations in the United States." *Journal of Communication* 40 (Spring): 103–25.

Dorman, W. A. 1986. "Peripheral Vision: U.S. Journalism and the Third World." *World Policy Journal* 3:419–45.

Dorman, W. A., and M. Farhang. 1987. *U.S. Press and Iran: Foreign Policy and the Journalism of Deference.* Berkeley: University of California Press.

Edelman, M. 1977. *Political Language: Words That Succeed and Policies That Fail.* New York: Academic Press.

———. 1988. *Constructing the Political Spectacle.* Chicago: University of Chicago Press.

Emerson, S. A., and C. Del Sesto. 1991. *Terrorist.* New York: Villard Books.

Fund for Free Expression. 1991. *Managed News, Stifled Views: U.S. Freedom of Expression and the War—an Update.* Special Report. February 27, 1991.

Katz, E. 1992. "The End of Journalism? Notes on Watching the War." *Journal of Communication* 42 (Summer):5–13.

Livingston, S. 1993. *The Terrorism Spectacle: Domestic and Foreign Policy Implications of the Portrayal of Terrorism.* Boulder: Westview Press.

Massing, M. 1991. "Sitting on Top of the News." *New York Review of Books,* June 27, 1991.

Neustadt, R. E., and E. R. May. 1986. *Thinking in Time: The Uses of History for Decision Makers.* New York: The Free Press.

Pollock, J. C. 1981. *The Politics of Crisis Reporting.* New York: Praeger.

Rivers, W. L., and W. Schramm. 1969. *Responsibility in Mass Communications.* New York: Harper and Row.

Weiner, J. 1991. "Why We Fought: The Commanders." *The Nation,* June 10, 781–84.

White, R. K. 1970. *Nobody Wanted War: Misperception in Vietnam and Other Wars.* Garden City: Anchor Books.

Wilcox, C., J. Ferrara, D. Alsop. 1991. "Before the Rally: The Dynamics of Attitudes toward the Gulf Crisis before the War." Paper presented at the 1991 meeting of the American Political Science Association, Washington, D.C.

four

Robert M. Entman and
Benjamin I. Page

The News before
the Storm

*The Iraq War Debate and the Limits
to Media Independence*

The preceding two chapters show the limited, selective nature of the information on which the American public had to rely when thinking
about Iraq before and immediately after its invasion of Kuwait. Lang and
Lang (Chapter 2) reveal that prior to the invasion Iraq was simply not
very visible in the news, whatever it did, while Dorman and Livingston
(Chapter 3) show that the period following the Iraqi invasion saw little
elite dissent from the administration's interpretive frame. This chapter
explores media coverage of the debate over U.S. policy toward Iraq after
the Bush administration announced its installation of an offensive capacity in the Persian Gulf on November 8, 1990, but before the war began. The theoretical interest of this period arises from the occurrence
then of unusually vigorous elite contention over the new Bush policy.
This circumstance provides the opportunity for research on one of the
central issues in the study of the media and foreign policy: how much
critical distance the news *can* develop from the position taken by the
president and his administration.

Bennett's (1990) indexing hypothesis and other work (Entman
1991) suggests that when most elites publicly support the administration line, news coverage will thoroughly favor the White House, sometimes verging on propaganda. However, when elites dispute an
administration's foreign policy, the news will to some still unknown degree "index" or reflect the amount of dissent and offer critical information. The prewar debate on Iraq presented nearly ideal conditions for
such reporting: unusually fractured elites engaged in relatively lengthy
and public dispute. Using that ideal case, this chapter traces the nature
and boundaries of media independence, assessing the extent to which
the administration line influenced media coverage even during intense
elite debate.

Given the president's constitutional and traditional power over the

foreign policy apparatus, reporting that circulates information and opinion at odds with the administration is vital to the possibility of democracy in foreign policy. Such coverage offers the potential for the public to
assess administration policy critically and to participate in genuine policy deliberation. Reporting independent of the administration can also
catalyze and embolden elite opposition, further bolstering democratic
debate. Thus an understanding of the limits to journalistic distance from
the administration is important for the construction of any theory on
the media, foreign policy, and democracy.

Careful public deliberation is especially important when it comes to
decisions on going to war. Research has established that the media developed only sporadic and limited challenges to the U.S. administration
during the Vietnam War (Hallin 1986), but there are reasons to expect
greater independence since. Chief among them: the diminution in
elites' foreign policy consensus since Vietnam; the rise in public and
journalistic cynicism toward politicians; improvements in communication and information technologies; and the decline and final disap-
pearance of the cold war as an ideology and cognitive frame. Moreover,
the public and the elites evidenced much more initial skepticism about
administration policy toward Iraq than they did in the preliminary
stages of Vietnam (Mueller 1993).

Factors that make the elite debate over war versus sanctions that was
joined on November 8, 1990, a best-case scenario for research on media
independence include the following:

• The decision to go to war was not carried out immediately, in an ur-
gent crisis atmosphere, as with Grenada or Panama. There was time for
elites to debate and for journalists to investigate.

• Legitimate, prestigious figures in Congress and among the foreign
policy establishment strongly and publicly disagreed with the administration's apparent direction after November 8. Thus if media coverage
reflects elite dissensus, this was a period when reporting should have
been as diverse and distant from the administration line as it ever gets in
reporting about the use of American military force.

• The mass public also seemed divided. There was no overwhelming
audience position that might have pressured media managers to curb
critical analysis of government policy. Three CBS/*New York Times* surveys in December and early January, for example, found the public divided almost exactly in half on whether, if Iraq failed to withdraw from
Kuwait by January 15, the U.S. should start military action.[1]

Our analysis focuses on two crucial nine-day periods when critical
voices would be expected to be at especially high levels: Period 1, No-

vember 8–16, when opponents reacted to President Bush's announcement of the massive troop increase, and Period 2, November 27–December 5, when Congress held hearings on Iraq policy that featured prominent (and often unexpected) critics.

In harmony with our best-case approach, we emphasize results from the *New York Times* and *Washington Post*, papers with large foreign news staffs, high prestige and sophistication, and a proven record of willingness to take on the government. One might expect these outlets to be particularly scrupulous in reporting the many criticisms of administration policy that were voiced during the periods analyzed. We coded hundreds of assertions from their stories, using a quantitative analytical protocol. For data from an outlet of wider circulation among nonelites, we used the same protocol to code transcripts of ABC's nightly "World News" programs. But traditional quantitative content analysis cannot fully reveal many message properties that affect the cognitive accessibility of information, and thus the public's ability to deliberate independently of the administration. Hence we employ qualitative evidence as well. For illustrations and a broader context we also draw upon a careful reading of all *New York Times* editorials and op-ed columns during the full November 8–January 15 period.

Findings

Our findings can be summarized in four main observations:

1. Criticism of Bush administration policy was indeed reported frequently, although support was also heavily represented.

2. The most pertinent critical information tended to be displayed less saliently than supportive information, and much of the reported criticism was procedural rather than substantive.

3. The prominence of media attention to critics and supporters was calibrated according to the degree of power over war policy they exerted.

4. Few fundamental criticisms of administration policy appeared.

HIGH VOLUME OF CRITICISM

We found that during both periods studied, a substantial amount of news criticizing administration policy and behavior appeared. During both periods, in both newspapers, assertions that were critical substantially outnumbered the supportive; ABC, though tending more toward support, also offered considerable criticism.

We coded all assertions that explicitly or implicitly assessed the Bush

TABLE 1. Administration Criticism and Support, All Stories

	Critical Assertions		Supportive Assertions		TOTAL	
Period 1						
N.Y. Times	63.2%	(299)	36.8%	(174)	100%	(473)
Post	53.6%	(237)	46.4%	(205)	100%	(442)
ABC	36.7%	(40)	63.3%	(69)	100%	(109)
TOTAL	56.2%	(576)	43.8%	(448)	100%	(1024)
Period 2						
N.Y. Times	54.3%	(153)	45.7%	(129)	100%	(282)
Post	54.3%	(133)	45.7%	(112)	100%	(245)
ABC	43.9%	(36)	56.1%	(46)	100%	(82)
TOTAL	52.9%	(322)	47.1%	(287)	100%	(609)
TOTAL						
N.Y. Times	59.9%	(452)	40.1%	(303)	100%	(755)
Post	53.9%	(370)	46.1%	(317)	100%	(687)
ABC	39.8%	(76)	60.2%	(115)	100%	(191)
TOTAL	55.0%	(898)	45.0%	(735)	100%	(1,633)
N = 1,633						

administration policy or policy-making behavior. The codes were for (1) explicitly critical, (2) implicitly critical, (3) mixed or ambivalent, (4) implicitly supportive, and (5) explicitly supportive assertions. Table 1 displays the aggregated results.[2] Of the total of 1,633 assertions coded, 55 percent were critical and 45 percent supportive of the Bush administration. As table 2 shows, however, support very nearly equalled criticism in the news stories.

The more mass-oriented ABC was considerably more supportive than critical of administration policy. Combined with other features of the video coverage and the fact that citizens rely most heavily on TV for news, this result suggests that television may have bolstered mass support of the president's policy, while these two newspapers, serving generally upscale and attentive audiences, more accurately reflected the roiling debate among elites.[3]

Indeed, the newspapers' editorial pages were heavily skewed against the administration, especially in the *Times*. During the first period, for example, critical assertions in *Times* editorials and op-ed pieces outnumbered supportive by almost four to one (124 to 34). If *Times* editorial expressions have special significance for officialdom, the nation's "paper of record" may have encouraged elite dissent (more on *Times* editorials below).

TABLE 2.   Administration Criticism and Support, News Stories Only

	Critical Assertions		Supportive Assertions		TOTAL	
Period 1						
N.Y. Times	55.6%	(175)	44.4%	(140)	100%	(315)
Post	48.4%	(156)	51.6%	(166)	100%	(322)
ABC*	36.7%	(40)	63.3%	(69)	100%	(109)
TOTAL	49.8%	(371)	50.2%	(375)	100%	(746)
Period 2						
N.Y. Times	49.8%	(109)	50.2%	(110)	100%	(219)
Post	52.7%	(109)	47.3%	(98)	100%	(207)
ABC	43.9%	(36)	56.1%	(46)	100%	(82)
TOTAL	50.0%	(254)	50.0%	(254)	100%	(508)
TOTAL						
N.Y. Times	53.2%	(284)	46.8%	(250)	100%	(534)
Post	61.8%	(265)	38.2%	(164)	100%	(429)
ABC	39.8%	(76)	60.2%	(115)	100%	(191)
TOTAL	49.8%	(625)	50.2%	(629)	100%	(1,254)
N = 1,254						

*ABC figures same as in table 1—all items are news.

Breaking down all the news data to focus only on assertions on the central dispute, war vs. sanctions, we found the following:

	Period 1			Period 2		
	Crit.	Supp.	N	Crit.	Supp.	N
NYT	41%	59%	102	56%	44%	124
Post	49	51	81	55	45	109
ABC	42	58	26	47	53	36

In the first period, information suggesting support for Bush's move toward war appeared more frequently than that for continued reliance on sanctions, in reporting of both the *Times* and ABC. *Post* news was evenly divided. The second period, probably the peak of newsworthy elite criticism of the military option (because of the congressional hearings), still provided frequent support for the Bush policy. We suspect these data on Period 2 establish the outer boundaries of media independence from an administration. Circumstances were ideal: respected elites were actively using the media to publicize and mobilize opposition. Even under these optimum conditions, and even though editorial policy slanted clearly against the administration in the two papers, the news provided heavy representation to the administration.

CRITICISM LESS SALIENT AND FREQUENTLY PROCEDURAL

Although criticism predominated in overall frequency, on the more-noticed news pages it was equaled by support. More importantly, much of the most relevant, substantive criticism was obscured by its placement in the news. Quantitative counts aside, the administration dominated the narrative flow.

First, coded assertions tended to be relatively sparse on page 1, the most prominent spot. In the *Times,* there were 755 relevant assertions, of which 112 appeared on page 1; 89 of 687 in the *Post* were similarly placed—no more than one in six. While this is in part an artifact of the reality that most material in newspapers is not printed on page 1, it does have theoretical significance because information printed on inside pages tends to receive much lower readership. Most of the discourse on policy during these times of dramatic dissensus was relegated to less-noticed portions of the newspapers.

Table 3 shows data for page one assertions—presumably the most salient—only.[4] It also divides the assertions into two categories, substantive and procedural.[5] Substantive information concerned policy options: specifically, whether war or sanctions should be preferred and the costs and justifiability of the policy. In many media studies, only such assertions concerning the merits of the policy are coded. In keeping with our generous test for media independence from the administration, we also included the procedural category, which covers evaluative information on the *process* and *politics* of decision-making: Bush's leadership behavior (especially his explaining the policy and consulting Congress and foreign leaders), and the state of public and foreign opinion.[6] It turns out that omitting this category of the news would have led to underestimating the degree and misstating the dimensions of media independence.

There was a considerable change across the time periods in the substantive or procedural nature of critical assertions. During Period 1, criticism in each medium focused more on the procedural than the substantive, especially for the *Times* and ABC. There were many attacks on the president and hardly any support, for example, on his failure to explain the policy clearly and his duty to consult Congress. Support, on the other hand, was heavily substantive; there was much justification of the war policy.

The data in Table 3 show that the administration maintained a healthy flow of highly visible claims supportive of its substantive policy.

TABLE 3. Procedural and Substantive Criticism, Page One Stories Only

	N. Y. Times			Washington Post			ABC*		
	Substantive	Procedural	N	Substantive	Procedural	N	Substantive	Procedural	N
Period 1									
Critical	29%	71%		47%	53%		34%	66%	
(N)	(10)	(24)	34	(16)	(18)	34	(11)	(21)	32
Supportive	79%	21%		75%	25%		64%	36%	
(N)	(27)	(7)	34	(9)	(3)	12	(24)	(15)	42
Total									
(N)	(37)	(31)	68	(25)	(21)	46	(38)	(36)	74
Period 2									
Critical	83%	17%		75%	25%		54%	46%	
(N)	(19)	(4)	23	(15)	(5)	20	(13)	(11)	24
Supportive	91%	9%		87%	13%		63%	37%	
(N)	(10)	(1)	11	(20)	(3)	23	(25)	(15)	40
Total									
(N)	(29)	(5)	34	(35)	(8)	43	(38)	(26)	64

*For ABC, lead story only.

During Period 1, the critical juncture immediately after the troop aug-mentation, the most salient reporting in the *Times* and on ABC empha-sized substantive support of the administration by a better than 2-to-1 ratio. The *Post* alone was more critical on substantive grounds in Period 1. Across the three media, the total substantive support-to-criticism ra-tio in the most prominent news coverage was 60:37 in Period 1, 55:47 in Period 2.

The administration could act to reduce procedural criticism without altering the policy that was receiving so much supportive press during Period 1. By attempting more vigorously to explain the policy, by con-sulting Congress and obtaining U.N. approval—all of which happened during Period 2—the administration could reduce the overall volume of criticism. The bottom half of table 3 shows that total criticism in each medium did decline considerably by Period 2, despite the congressional hearings. If one assumes that early coverage is the most important be-cause it frames audience reactions to succeeding information, the heavy predominance of substantive support in the elite paper of record and on the most watched network during Period 1 was a critical achievement for the administration.

With procedural objections answered, the focus of the remaining cri-tique shifted to the substantive during Period 2, especially in the news-papers. Yet measured quantitatively, Period 2 criticism was far from overwhelming. In the nation's two leading newspapers, table 3 reveals, substantive criticisms barely outnumbered plaudits (34 to 30), meaning each paper averaged not quite two negative substantive assertions per day on page one. And ABC favored the administration on substantive matters by a 2:1 ratio during Period 2 just as it had during Period 1.

The network offered just thirteen substantive criticisms in lead stories during the second period. Thus, for example, when two former military chiefs endorsed sanctions on November 28, ABC found room for only one sound bite:

ADMIRAL WILLIAM CROWE: War's not a need, it's not tidy and once you resort to it, it's uncertain and it's a mess.

After two equally spare prosanction sound bites from Democratic leaders, the story provided longer quotations from two pro-Bush sources (his press secretary and Henry Kissinger) and concluded with the White House's cynical interpretation of the dissent:

BRIT HUME: The Administration sees political mischief in Demo-cratic advice that would keep U.S. forces in the desert through

summer while the standoff keeps fuel prices up and the US economy down. The hope here is that if the UN authorizes force, the US
Congress will too. Brit Hume, ABC News, the White House.

To emphasize the importance of substantive discourse does not deny
the significance of procedural criticisms. Such complaints place pressure
on administrations—ever tempted by the twin lures of secrecy and unchallenged control of policy—to consult Congress. Consultation, if public, requires the president to share his thinking and intentions, thereby
heightening the possibility of democratic dialogue. But fulfilling this potential demands a press that pays sustained attention to the substance of
the ensuing debate, making information highly accessible to an easily-
distracted public.

By focusing the most salient criticism during the crucial issue-framing
Period 1 on procedure, media coverage, we believe, tended to soften the
edge of opposition and obscure the major issue before the public: was
the policy itself wise? Procedural reproaches, even if decoded by the
mass audience as disguised attacks on the policy itself, provide the public
little cognitive basis for participating in deliberation. The paucity of well-
supported substantive criticism may help explain why most of those initially opposed to the Bush policy converted as war approached and began. They had little foundation for continued opposition once proper
procedures had apparently been followed (the U.N. and Congress gave
their blessing).[7]

Procedural criticism was especially notable in the unsigned editorials
of the *New York Times* (cf. LaMay 1991, 63–64). During the entire November 8–January 15 prewar phase of the Gulf Crisis, the *Times* ran a
total of twenty-five editorials concerning Iraq. Of those, five focused on
the theme that Congress should be consulted on any decision to go to
war (11/16, 12/15, 1/3, 1/7, and 1/13). This left the newspaper's opposition to war somewhat limp after Congress voted to authorize force. Indeed, the *Times* devoted its harshest language, concerning President
Bush's "Double Insult" (11/16) and "unconscionable" dodging of the
issue (1/3 and 1/7) by Congress, to procedural issues rather than to the
necessity or horrors of war. The theme that Bush should better "explain"
or "give reasons" for his policies was featured in four editorials (11/14,
12/2, 1/1, and 1/2), and the idea that allies should get a bigger voice in
policy took up one editorial (12/11). Thus, though the *Times* editorials
were the most strongly and consistently critical voice we found, fully ten
of the twenty-five editorials, or *40 percent*, were devoted to procedural
matters.

A CLOSER LOOK AT COVERAGE OF THE HEARINGS

Closer examination (both quantitative and qualitative) of the specifics of media coverage reveals more clearly the ways the administration maintained considerable control over the news and reduced the salience of substantive criticism. We focus here on Period 2 (November 27–December 5), when the congressional opposition mounted an organized effort to publicize dissent and mobilize public opposition.[8]

In his hearings, Senator Sam Nunn (D.–Ga.) brought together a series of former military officers and other experts who testified that sanctions should be given time to work. Admiral William J. Crowe, for example, the former chairman of the Joint Chiefs of Staff (JCS) under Reagan and Bush, pointed out the many problems that would remain in the Middle East after Saddam's departure. Crowe noted the sacrifices and uncertainties of hostilities and casualties, and argued that "we should give the sanctions a chance before we discard them" (Sifry and Cerf 1991, 234). Former JCS chairman General David C. Jones said the deployment of more forces could lead inexorably to war and that sanctions should be given time (ibid.).

Consider the *Post*'s reporting of these hearings. On November 28, it featured a front-page story headlined "Democrats Urge Caution on Gulf." Only in the continuation, back on page 31, did the story quote Nunn's statement noting the "fundamental shift" in policy represented by Bush's doubling of American troops in the Gulf. That point was buried beneath a story on U.N. wrangling over the Palestine Liberation Organization and dwarfed by a Christmas tree ad. Such treatment suggests how the administration's emphasis on gaining approval from the U.N., where it had more clout than in Congress, helped it steer the news focus away from the hearings. It also suggests how the news routine of focusing attention on the administration's actions and pronouncements frequently operates to deemphasize key anti-administration arguments. The continuation page was also where the *Post* printed the surprising assessment of the hawkish former defense secretary and CIA head, James Schlesinger, that sanctions were very likely to be successful within about a year.

The next day (November 29) the lead *Post* headline was, "Ex-Chiefs Chairmen Urge Reliance on Sanctions." Despite this headline and two other front-page stories on Iraq, page 1 discussed nothing but processes: partisan and institutional wrangling over control of policy and public opinion, predictions of likely events relevant to that control, and assessments of likely Iraqi reactions. Again, page 1 did not detail what might be seen as the key and most surprising news: military leaders Crowe and Jones expressing opposition. Quotations from the witnesses, words illustrating the substantive themes mentioned in the page 1 headline, were obscurely displayed near the end of the story, back on page 46. Such treatment heightened readers' information costs, making it more difficult to find and store oppositional arguments, and perhaps creating a cognitive and emotional vacuum that the administration could fill.

On the third day, November 30, the hearings were pushed aside by the banner-headlined story, "UN Vote Authorizes Use of Force Against Iraq." Only on page 30, in the middle of a story headed "No Plans for Recalling Congress," did the *Post* note that Ronald Reagan's former secretary of the navy, James H. Webb, had joined the "parade" of military witnesses criticizing administration policy. Far more prominent— headlined on page 1, continued and extensively excerpted (with a photo) on page 21—was "Quayle Cites 'Moral Costs' of Waiting." Vice President Dan Quayle had not previously been considered an authoritative voice on American foreign policy, yet the *Post* gave his speech the sort of prominent display usually reserved for presidential addresses. The paper granted about as much attention to his remarks alone as it accorded Crowe, Jones, Schlesinger, and Webb combined (22 coded assertions for them, 21 for Quayle).

From there on it was downhill for coverage of critical testimony in Nunn's hearings. The *Post* of December 1 recorded the launch of a diplomatic effort that functioned—whatever its intentions—as a major public relations counterattack. It headlined, top-right on page 1: "Bush Proposes Mission to Iraq As Final Bid to Preserve Peace," subheaded "Legislators Hail Decision to Seek Talks." Later events indicated that the administration had no interest in negotiations and only reluctantly scheduled the token Baker-Aziz meeting in Geneva (Woodward 1991); some of the coverage suggested journalists thought as much, but this did not prevent them from allowing the initiative to push the hearings into obscurity. A front-page box headed "Bush Speaks Out" contained a photo of a determined president accompanied by lengthy quotations. Inside were long continuations of the stories and voluminous excerpts from Bush's news conference. The headlines treated the action as if it were unambiguously a peace mission, though Bush did not propose to negotiate but merely to reiterate his demand for unconditional withdrawal, repeatedly rejected by the Iraqis. The hearings were discussed on pages 21 and 24.

One of the key tools of presidential influence over media coverage is the ability to generate newsworthy events that distract journalists and elites alike from a suddenly old or less compelling controversy.[9] The institutional power of the presidency can help an administration reduce critical media coverage even when elites are in thorough dissensus.

Throughout Period 2, the *Times* handled matters quite similarly to the *Post*. For example, on December 4, the *Times* (like the *Post*) put the congressional testimony by defense secretary Richard Cheney and secretary of state Baker in its most prominent page 1 position ("Cheney Sees Need to Act Militarily Against the Iraqis"), and devoted almost the entirety of page 12 to extensive excerpts from their testimony. This honor was not granted *any* of the critical witnesses.

For Period 2 as a whole, our overall impression—even more than the various counts—is that the administration had very much the best of it in the contest to control coverage of the elite debate in the *Post* and *Times*. And ABC provided even skimpier coverage of the elite dissent: the one sound bite from the Jones and Crowe appearance, for example, in a story providing no reasoned basis for audiences to believe sanctions might actually work. While most scholars would expect little else from network news, that two of the nation's most distinguished newspapers diminished the hearings in comparison to the pronouncements of the administration is more surprising. They did this despite the hearings' extraordinary newsworthiness: not only were they the chief forum for the nation's solemn debate, but they featured the "man bites dog" appeal of well-known hawks taking a dovish stand. Some significant aspects of the hearings went virtually or entirely unreported, including the testimony of peace researcher Gary Milhollin, former navy secretary Webb, historian Phebe Marr, consultants James Placke and Christine Helms, and hawkish military expert Edward Luttwak.

Yet, making their news decisions all the more intriguing, the two papers did not promote the administration line on their editorial pages. Editorials in the *Times*, for example, said (November 11) that the administration was going "Too Far Too Fast in the Gulf" or asked "What's the Rush?" (November 29). In the *Post*, a November 30 Haynes Johnson column called the hearings "vital" as a "national forum." Yet, the *Post* itself that day virtually ignored the testimony in its news columns.

ATTENTION CALIBRATED TO POWER OVER POLICY

A systematic analysis of the Iraq news, after November 8, including not just reports of the hearings but all other Iraq-related events and pronouncements, shows that administration officials' action and talk received highest attention. This may result from a definition of news in terms of helping audiences predict future events by focusing on actions, plans, and statements of the powerful. The assertions of those who have less power to affect future events are given secondary status even when what they say is substantively important. So, during the Armed Services Committee hearings, the criticisms and other remarks of congressional Democrats were given more prominent attention than statements of Schlesinger, Crowe, Jones, et al., but all were given much less fanfare than the rebuttals of Bush, Cheney, Baker, or even Quayle. And experts completely outside officialdom, like Milhollin, were essentially ignored. Even Henry Kissinger on November 28 obtained just seven lines of text in the *Post* (plus one line in the photo caption) at the very end of the hearings story. The fact that Kissinger's remarks favored Bush supports the notion that calibration to power rather than ideological bias explains the lower prominence accorded administration critics.

The predominance of administration figures is especially striking when we look at simple counts of how often their names appeared, either as subjects or sources of news. Such a count for all Iraq stories in the *Times* and the *Post* taken together, during Period 2—covering the Nunn hearings and administration counterattack—reveals that President Bush's name was by far the most frequently invoked—1,086 mentions, over half (54 percent) of the 2,012 total. The next most cited were James Baker (17 percent), Richard Cheney (5.8 percent), and Colin Powell (4.3 percent). Together with Dan Quayle and Brent Scowcroft, the administration's six top leaders accounted for *84.8 percent* of all names mentioned.[10] All the critics who testified before the Nunn committee were named a total of 129 times, or 6.4 percent. Aside from Nunn himself (71 mentions), most members of the Armed Services Committee were rarely or never cited; he and the other members accounted for 138 mentions, 6.9 percent of the total. Bush-supporter Kissinger, with 38 citations, rounds out the list of most-cited figures.

More generally, although journalists called editorially for public debate and congressional participation, the coverage of the hearings ironically undermined debate by diminishing attention to critics, as compared to Cheney, Powell, Quayle, and Bush. Such coverage increased the information costs to citizens seeking independent data on the administration's policy, while dampening the pressure that perceived public awareness might have applied to Congress.

FEW FUNDAMENTAL CRITICISMS

Few of the reported criticisms challenged fundamental aspects of the administration's policy. For example, only 13.4 percent of the coded assertions (N = 73) for the *Times* and *Post* in Period 2 focused even implicitly on the wisdom and justice of the underlying policy goal of forcing Iraq out of Kuwait, and 81 percent (59) of these were supportive, only 19 percent (14) critical. Virtually all reported voices in the autumn 1990 "great debate" over peace or war with Iraq shared certain basic assumptions with the Bush administration (cf. Chapter 3 by Dorman and Livingston and Chapter 7 by Hallin and Gitlin).

In particular, nearly all reported critics as well as supporters agreed that *Iraq must be unconditionally dislodged from Kuwait by force, if necessary.* The arguments put forward by Nunn, Crowe, Jones, and others did not contest the goal of dislodgement, or the means of force, but merely the question of immediate necessity. Thus the gaps in argumentation were not entirely the responsibility of the media. Senator Nunn's hearings were carefully orchestrated to showcase "moderate" and conservative views. The otherwise hawkish Sam Nunn's emergence as chief congressional critic of administration policy suggests not only the numerical breadth of opposition to immediate war but also the intellectual narrowness of the deliberation.

The limited scope of media criticism can be clearly seen by analyzing the 118 Iraq-related *New York Times* op-ed pieces and editorials that appeared during the November 8–January 15 prewar phase of debate. The 81 op-eds that dealt explicitly with U.S. policy fell into three general camps: those favoring negotiations and/or substantive compromise with Iraq (N = 21); those favoring continued reliance on sanctions, at least for a time (N = 40); and those favoring the use of force (N = 20).

Three aspects of this distribution are especially interesting. First, the bulk of editorials and op-eds—49 percent of them, including all eighteen relevant unsigned *Times* editorials—favored the "centrist" position of "patience" with sanctions. As the *Times* repeatedly put it (11/18, 11/29), "What's the Rush?" about going to war. And this position was balanced on both sides by virtually equal numbers of hawkish and dovish signed columns.

Second, the "centrist" position, though strongly critical of Bush's offensive troop buildup and deadline, did not actually disagree much about the policy goal: it favored unconditional Iraqi withdrawal from Kuwait, no "linkage" with the Palestinians or disputed islands or oil fields or anything else ("No Booty for Iraq. None," 12/24); and it explicitly called for the use of force if and when sanctions failed to work.

Third, the more dovish of the *Times* op-ed pieces, constituting 26 percent of the total, were themselves rather tame. Anthony Lewis, by far the most frequent voice for serious negotiations (author of ten of the twenty-one dovish columns), never specified terms of compromise and never ruled out the use of force. Only Rashid Khalidi (12/26) and Roger Morris (1/9) outlined comprehensive peace strategies that took seriously some of Iraq's grievances. Not a single op-ed voice in the *Times* clearly took Iraq's side against Kuwait or argued against U.S. involvement in the matter. But it is true that a few voices for negotiation were at least present on the op-ed page; they were all but absent from the news pages, where the administration-sanctioned options defined the field of discursive play.[11]

Conclusion

In this "best case" test of media independence from the administration line there was a substantial amount of critical reporting. We did not observe hegemonic media operating entirely at the disposal of the state. However, even at this time, a period of unusually vocal and lengthy elite dissent over application of military force, support was reported as frequently as criticism in the news columns, and, on ABC television, more frequently. Support, as documented especially in our closer look at Period 2, received more prominent treatment, meaning that audience members tending to oppose the administration had a harder time finding concrete bases for counterarguments against the administration than those tending toward support. Furthering the difficulty of opponents, a significant part of the criticism reported was procedural rather than substantive, and administration officials received much more attention in the news than those outside the executive branch. Moreover, few fundamental criticisms were aired. That is to say, even under these nearly ideal conditions, media distance from the administration had definite boundaries.

What forces restricted the media's criticism of administration policy? A number of interrelated factors pushed in the same direction. It is a familiar story, for example, that the media tend to rely heavily on official sources and tend to report them favorably (Sigal 1973; Gans 1979). They do so, in part, because of the ease of regular access to officials, the dependable supply of news the officials provide, the need to cultivate such sources over time, and the usefulness of citing legitimate, authoritative sources, all of which serve important commercial needs to these for-profit businesses (cf. Entman 1989). In particular, as Timothy Cook in Chapter 5 proposes, the existence of regular beats encourages the over-representation of administration views. The beat system also probably reinforces the procedural element in the coverage, since reporters share a career interest with sources on the beat in making sure the process includes an influential role for the institution covered.

The findings suggest a refinement to the established finding that journalists rely upon government officials and elites: even at the highest level, all elite sources are not equal. It appears that the media calibrate news judgments rather precisely to the clout of the powerful actors whose remarks or actions are covered: the higher their power to shape newsworthy events, the more attention they receive. The lower the power, the less attention, even if the substantive information offered might be of great value to a deliberating citizen.

If they had defined their roles more self-consciously as stimulators of public participation and debate, the media might have deliberately given opposition voices, no matter what their institutional roles or power, equal play with administration leaders. Perhaps they hesitated to do so for fear of seeming to editorialize. But they did emphasize Cheney's testimony and Bush's announcements and even Quayle's speech without worrying about editorializing, most likely because they defined news in terms of helping audiences predict future events, which meant focusing on the most powerful officials. The failure to recognize that slight alterations in news practices could have promoted more informed public participation is suggested by the contradiction between the clearly anti-administration editorial stands of the two papers, which urged vigorous public debate, and treatment of opposition claims on their news pages, which in some ways discouraged it.

Finally, we must bear in mind that the degree of media distance found in this case, in the putatively independent-minded *Times* and *Post*, depended crucially upon the existence of divisions among elites—particularly of articulated opposition to administration policy among members of Congress. We cannot expect even this much debate to appear in the media on the more frequent occasions when "bipartisanship" prevails and elites are relatively monolithic (cf. Dorman and Farhang, 1988).

Notes

We thank Northwestern University's Center for Urban Affairs and Policy Research for providing research funds, Bea Chestnut, Michael Hostetler, Limor Peer, and Hiram Sachs for research assistance, and participants in the SSRC Working Group on the Media and U.S. Foreign Policy for their helpful comments.

1. *New York Times*, December 14, 1990, p. A8; January 9, 1991, p. A6; January 15, 1991, p. A13. Other polling data, however, tapping other dimensions of public thinking, indicate that the public started lining up with the Bush administration by November (see Mueller 1993). Thus news organizations might have found the signals about mass opinion to be ambiguous, if not leaning toward the administration, as early as November.

2. Coding protocols were slightly different during the two periods, because the major issues of the policy debate altered somewhat. The coding procedure also differed in that, for Period 2, only one coder was employed for most of the text, while for Period 1 two coders were employed for the *Washington Post* and *New York Times*. For Period 2, there was much discussion among the authors and the coders to ensure consistent coding decisions, and coders resolved uncertainties by consulting with each other or with the authors. For the Period 1 stories from the *Post* and *Times*, initial intercoder reliability as to codable assertions was .80, with the final data used reflecting only those assertions whose coding could be reconciled by the coders. "Reliability" was relatively low, reflecting the considerable ambiguity of real-world news and policy discourse. The key area of ambiguity tended to be whether an assertion that on its face was simply declarative would be read *in the context of the ongoing news text and policy debate* as a potentially evaluative claim. Often we found news messages to be suffused with implicit though sometimes ambiguous evaluation, and rather than throw out the many implicit assertions—which could predispose the analysis toward finding more administration dominance of the news, since criticism is more likely to be implicit—we counted them when both coders agreed on their relevance.

An example of explicit opposition would be: "The chairman of the Senate Armed Services Committee today criticized the Bush Administration's decision to drop its plan to station troops in Saudi Arabia, saying that it puts the United States on too fast a track toward war." Implicit opposition: "Senator Nunn and Representative Aspin agreed that the Administration should seek Congressional approval if it decided to wage war against Iraq."

Implicit support: "The reason is that every month Iraq goes unbombed brings it a step closer to producing nuclear weapons." Explicit support: "His [Bush's] purpose is surely justifiable; Saddam Hussein's aggression cannot be allowed to stand."

3. Most important, research in progress, to be reported in detail in Entman's *Projections of Power: Media and American Foreign Policy Since Vietnam*

(University of Chicago Press, forthcoming), suggests that the administration receives heavy preference on the visual dimensions of the TV message. For example, administration figures are shown much more frequently smiling, in settings they control, and in juxtaposition with flags or other authority-enhancing symbols.

4. An assertion counts here as page 1 if it appeared on the first page of the first section of the paper or on page 1 of the "Outlook" or "News of the Week in Review" Sunday summary sections of the *Post* or *Times*, respectively. (An assertion that appeared on page 7 of the Sunday summary sections counts the same as a page 7 assertion in the first section, and so forth.)

5. For Period 1, we coded nine dimensions of evaluative information. The following three were considered substantive: war vs. sanctions; degree of danger to U.S. forces if war comes; justification of the ultimate policy objective of ejecting Hussein. The other six were counted as procedural: state of foreign opinion; state of domestic public opinion; Bush's need or failure to explain his policy; attribution of political motives to Bush or his opponents; Bush's need or failure to consult Congress; and evaluation of Bush's leadership skills as exhibited in this crisis. For Period 2, somewhat different dimensions were coded, reflecting the slight differences in discourse at that time. The categories were: merits of the goal (is the policy goal of forcing Iraq from Kuwait justified or not?); danger of war (is Bush's path leading to war or peace?); timing (is Bush rushing into action? should sanctions have more time to work?); motives (are the administration's motives selfish and political, or not?); external support (are the public or elites supporting or opposing Bush?); articulateness (is Bush explaining his policies well enough?); and consultation with Congress (is Bush consulting with Congress sufficiently or not?). We consider the first three of these to be solidly substantive and the last four to be procedural. In coding Period 2 assertions, we found not all critical or supportive comments fit these categories. Most omissions were of supportive assertions, for example, praise of Bush's diplomatic skill in garnering U.N. support. A few critical claims were omitted, largely those involving wrangles over the specific date when Congress should go into session to vote on commencement of military action.

6. Assertions were coded in these latter categories when they generally characterized the state of external support, *not* when they included a substantive evaluation of the policy. Thus a sentence saying "Polls show most Americans back Bush's policy" would be coded as favorable to the administration, in the external support category. But a sentence "Most Americans support Bush's Jan. 15 deadline as a necessary response to

Saddam's aggression" contains a substantively-grounded evaluation of the policy and would be coded as favoring Bush in the war vs. sanctions category. In any case, references to public opinion were often reported in the context of Bush's actions or strategies in achieving congressional or U.N. approval, and thus they concerned procedural matters.

7. Hinckley (1992, 111; and Brody chapter, fig. 6) indicates, though the matter is highly complicated (cf. Mueller 1993), that the bulk of Bush's Iraq policy support dropped off before November 8, as the typical postcrisis rally faded. Approval declined from 78 percent on September 9 to 64 percent on October 14 and 59 percent on November 15. Then it stabilized during the very period of most intense elite debate covered here, so that by December 9 it went up slightly, to 62 percent. Approval reached 69 percent by January 9, and 83 percent on January 20, after the war had started.

8. Members of Congress were just recovering from the 1990 elections during Period 1, indeed most were back in their districts, so that opposition was less organized than in Period 2, which should offer the best case.

9. Woodward (1991, 335–36) argues that public relations concerns were a paramount cause of the initiative (cf. MacArthur 1992).

10. The count assessed the administration officials listed in the text plus the names of all testifiers at the Senate Armed Services Committee hearings and all members of the committee.

11. Since events following the war suggest Hussein's regime and Iraqi society can survive sanctions for a long term, one might argue the sanctions advocates were indeed wrong. Arguably, that makes the narrowness of the debate and especially the exclusion of the negotiation option even more significant.

References

Bennett, W. L. 1990. "Toward a Theory of Press-State Relations in the United States." *Journal of Communication* 40 (2): 103–25.

Dorman, W., and M. Farhang. 1988. *The U.S. Press and Iran.* Berkeley: University of California Press.

Entman, R. M. 1989. *Democracy Without Citizens: Media and the Decay of American Politics.* New York: Oxford University Press.

———. 1991. "Framing U.S. Coverage of International Affairs: Contrasts in Narratives of the KAL and Iran Air Incidents." *Journal of Communication* 51 (4): 6–27.

Gans, H. J. 1979. *Deciding What's News.* New York: Pantheon.

Hallin, D. C. 1986. *The "Uncensored War."* New York: Oxford University Press.

Hinckley, R. H. 1992. *People, Polls, and Policymakers: American Public Opinion and National Security.* New York: Lexington Books.

LaMay, C. 1991. "The Goals of War: Newspaper Editorial Coverage at Defining Moments of the Crisis." In *The Media at War: The Press and the Persian Gulf Conflict.* New York: Gannett Foundation.

MacArthur, J. R. 1992. *The Second Front: Censorship and Propaganda in the Gulf War.* New York: Hill and Wang.

Mueller, J. 1993. *Policy and Opinion in the Gulf War.* Chicago: University of Chicago Press.

Page, B. I., and R. Y. Shapiro. 1992. *The Rational Public.* Chicago: University of Chicago Press.

Sifry, M. L., and C. Cerf. 1991. *The Gulf War Reader: History, Documents, Opinions.* New York: Random House.

Sigal, L. 1973. *Reporters and Officials.* Lexington: D. C. Heath.

Woodward, B. 1991. *The Commanders.* New York: Simon and Schuster.

part three

Constructing the News

five

Timothy E. Cook

Domesticating a Crisis

Washington Newsbeats and
Network News after the
Iraqi Invasion of Kuwait

On January 10, 1991, the U.S. secretary of state, James Baker, and Iraq's foreign minister, Tariq Aziz, met in Geneva for talks that would prove to be one of the last chances to avert an air war in the Persian Gulf. The talks went on longer than anticipated, raising hopes for a settlement. Then Baker appeared before the television cameras at 8:00 P.M. Geneva time to announce that they had failed, just in time to be at the top of the hour of the nightly French television news broadcast. After announcing the breaking news and after consulting with reporters in Moscow and Geneva, the French news was faced with the task of how best to comprehend and fill out the implications of this new development. The French journalists did what they habitually do; they turned to reactions from notables and spokespersons from each of the various parties, from the Communists on the left to the National Front on the right.[1]

On February 21, 1991, ABC's Moscow correspondent, Jim Laurie, was the first television broadcast network reporter to announce a preliminary agreement between Aziz and the Soviet president, Mikhail Gorbachev, one of the last chances to head off a ground war. As with so much of the war, this news broke in prime time, interrupting Peter Jennings' 6:30 (EST) nightly news broadcast. Once the details of this agreement were in, the ABC news team was faced with a task similar to that of its French counterparts. The American journalists did what they habitually do: they declared a "Special Report" and toured the "Golden Triangle" (Hess 1983) of key newsbeats in Washington with Brit Hume at the White House, John McWethy at the State Department, and Bob Zelnick at the Pentagon.[2]

For this French news broadcast, the world was first globally constructed, then ideologically constructed. By contrast, for this American broadcast, the world was first domestically constructed, then institutionally constructed.[3] Hume, McWethy, and Zelnick presented themselves as impartial observers at their newsbeats, but it was clear that none of them had had much opportunity to discuss the breaking news with any sources. Instead, their reactions to Jennings' questions largely reflected their understanding of the institution and the individuals in charge. In effect, Hume, McWethy, and Zelnick were almost as much spokespersons for the newsbeats they covered as were the spokespersons on French television for their parties.

This paper explores the domestic processes that produced American television news coverage of the Persian Gulf Crisis in the initial weeks after the Iraqi invasion of Kuwait. This coverage provided opportunities for those political actors who were better placed to frame the unexpected event to provide support for their policy response—in particular, officials in pivotal positions at the most heavily reported newsbeats. In so doing, they could set the agenda, define alternatives, and represent a public mood that was beneficial to their preferences and interests.[4]

It is now widely recognized that the Iraqi invasion of Kuwait was a failure of the American policy—which had been clearly expressed by the president, at the State Department, and by the U.S. ambassador to Iraq, April Glaspie—stressing Iraq as a crucial counterweight to Iran and misgauging the seriousness of the threats by the Iraqi president, Saddam Hussein, against Kuwait. Immediately after the invasion, the Bush administration did not initially perceive a crisis; in an early morning meeting on August 2, "the prevailing attitude among the group, according to one participant, was 'Hey, too bad about Kuwait, but it's just a gas station, and who cares whether the sign says Sinclair or Exxon?'" (Smith 1992, 17).

But the news media, as early as the night of the invasion, saw it as more ominous. ABC's *Nightline* cancelled its originally scheduled program on August 1 in order to assess the invasion,[5] and it led all three major nightly news broadcasts the following evening. Yet in spite of the president's initial indifference, and the awareness on the part of journalists of the government's previous policy missteps,[6] the administration was ultimately able to turn the situation around to its advantage and put into place a military option that was largely unquestioned.

I focus here upon the first two months of coverage by the three major commercial broadcast networks (ABC, CBS, NBC) in their nightly news broadcasts, under the presumption that the initial coverage is crucial for "framing" a new phenomenon in a way that narrows the options and centrally influences later understandings (Linsky 1986). This time period also corresponds, as Brody demonstrates in Chapter 10 of this volume, to the rally in public opinion behind President Bush, and to the bulk of Dorman and Livingston's (Chapter 3) "establishing phase" of the crisis. I have chosen ABC, CBS, and NBC, despite the erosion of their audience and the proliferation of other televised news, because they continue to reach a larger news audience than other news outlets, and because they still designate as well as reflect newsworthiness.

I will argue that the newsmaking process in the United States embeds bias into the news because of (not in spite of) its use of prima facie neutral procedures. The Persian Gulf Crisis began, at least from the perspective of the Bush administration, as an unfortunate accident with the unforeseen invasion of Kuwait, but the news media's routine practices tended to constrain its disruptive meanings and to transform an out-of-control accident into a controllable crisis.[7] In particular, the news media's reliance upon institutional newsbeats and a "hierarchy of credibility" among them limited access to the debate during the crucial early weeks over the commitment of troops and the possibility of using military force.

The System of Newsbeats

Like most organizations, the news media attempt to manage their workloads by routine, standard operations. Yet if news consists of the new and the fresh, how, to recall Tuchman's (1973) famous phrase, can journalists "routinize the unexpected"? In American journalism, the answer has been: send reporters to places where news is likely to happen. So the journalistic world is broken down into newsbeats, the territorial or topical domains individuals are assigned to cover routinely (see Fishman 1980). There, reporters can latch onto a continuing story that serves as an ongoing focus for their work and a multi-episode serial for the audience. A newsbeat thereby embodies an organizational commitment to stories from that site or on that subject.

In all news, but particularly on television where the news is viewed as a complete package to be divided up into its component parts, a complementarity of newsbeats minimizes redundancy and allows for some range of different newsmakers, perspectives, and understandings of ongoing events. In seeking material that will gain them a prominent place in the broadcast or newspaper, reporters seek out the script which the newsbeat most often evokes—how a bill becomes a law for a legislative reporter, the march of scientific progress for a medical journalist, etc.— and which best distinguishes their newsbeat from those of their competitors for the newshole. This script is also handy for indicating the most newsworthy moment—when it moves from one phase to the next

(Fishman 1980)—and the bigger picture, suggesting the meaning of a given episode in the overall script and where the script will go next (Schudson 1986).

Even after finding a newsworthy event (the *what* and the *when*), reporters must decide *who* to cover. To enhance the credibility and importance of their account, they turn to "authoritative sources," those presumed to be in positions to know information or to move the continuing story along. Some political actors—those able to claim the status of an authoritative source at a newsbeat—are favored over others. Yet given their aspirations to professional autonomy, journalists contest any evidence that they are extensions of the powers-that-be. Conflict is a necessary component of newsworthiness, if only to provide the tension that will carry the account along toward its ultimate denouement. At the same time, the continued dominance of impartiality in legitimizing journalistic authority in the United States means that reporters themselves cannot be seen to be the sources of ideological criticism or the instigators of conflict. In the words of Don Hewitt, executive producer of CBS's *60 Minutes*, "The dilemma is how to be critical without being partisan."

There are two key solutions to Hewitt's journalistic quandary: gravitate toward the extant conflict among authoritative sources; and avoid any judgment over the goals being sought and instead assess the effectiveness of the agreed-upon sources' pursuit of their own goals, either by focusing on matters of strategies and tactics or by contrasting earlier promises with later performance. The potential for journalists to open up public debate is therefore contingent and variable. When potentially divergent authoritative sources are silent or, perhaps, silenced (Bennett 1989, 1990), or when there is little performance against which to compare the promises (e.g., at the beginning of a presidential term; see Grossman and Kumar 1980), journalists are constrained. Likewise, as certain continuing stories become dominant, certain newsbeats may gain prominence over others in moving the stories along, further restricting access to the news.

Coverage changes when it is channeled through different newsbeats.[8] The choice of where to station reporters to cover a crisis is thus crucial. In a foreign policy story, four institutional beats come most into play: the White House, State Department, Pentagon, and Capitol Hill.

THE WHITE HOUSE

The president is the central newsmaker in American politics today, partly because of theories of governance through individual leadership and partly because American journalists write stories with individual protagonists. Instead of concentrating on the presidency as an institution, White House reporters focus on the president as a person making decisions and issuing orders. Since presidents' personal involvement is crucial to a story, reporters' contact with the president can be highly regulated and stage-managed.

Yet White House stories need not always be favorable to the president. Reporters tend to see presidential actions as motivated more toward *political strategy* of maintaining leadership and power rather than toward policy, and they can always use file footage or go elsewhere in Washington to garner critical quotes (see Cook 1992). As with campaigns, White House correspondents focus on the game of who's ahead and who's behind and the strategies designed to win the next round. But what the game is about, and its range and focus all depend crucially on who the opponents are. In foreign policy, these antagonists could be outside or inside the United States; if domestic actors are relatively silent, the opponents abroad—genuine or imagined—may loom larger, enabling the president to act the symbolic role of the embodiment of the nation in strategizing against external threats.

STATE DEPARTMENT

The State Department beat, by contrast, is oriented more toward *policy formulation*. In part, this reflects the centrality of performative language in the making of foreign policy. Given that any words attributed on the record to an official automatically become taken as policy, desk officers are skittish about loose language and they negotiate careful statements to be read at the daily televised noon briefing. State Department reporters thus must become well-versed in what Hess (1984, 68) termed "nuance journalism."

Nonetheless, this briefing is crucial not only for reporters, who can get an official statement of American policy toward the global events of the day; it also forces a deadline for the regional desks in hammering out that official policy. Partly because it is as definitive as one can get in the world of government, partly because it is on the record, and partly because it parallels the reporters' task of analyzing a confusing outside world, the daily briefing provides the crucial ingredients of State Department correspondents' reports. Instead of the strategic concerns among the White House reporters, what news-watchers receive is the closest that the American media have to *explication de texte*.

THE PENTAGON

Formal processes of newsmaking are less visible at the Pentagon. The newsbeat there is intimate; estimates of the number of "regulars" are between ten and twenty (Heise 1979; Sims 1983), and reporters and press officers with adjacent large, unpartitioned spaces interact informally. On-the-record briefings are a far less frequent ritual than the daily counterparts at the White House or State. The difficulty for Pentagon reporters, particularly for television, is not getting information as much as finding persons willing to comment on the record. Consequently, they must seek other sources, often elsewhere in Washington (see Martin 1991).

Thus, the Pentagon beat is a topical beat. While reporters are geographically based there, they often take on the title of "military affairs correspondent" or "defense correspondent," just as reporters located at the Supreme Court become topical reporters on the law. This *substantive emphasis* enables reporters to interact more smoothly with their sources at the Pentagon, by shared understandings and languages, and fits their relationship to their audience, nicely enunciated by Robert Trautman of Reuters: "To report to the average guy who is paying taxes how his money is being spent; and what he should be worrying about and what he should not be worrying about" (in Sims 1983, 23). The continuing story then stresses preparedness, and pushes Pentagon reporters to be guns-and-ammo substantive experts concerned with means rather than ends.

CAPITOL HILL

In comparison with the highly regulated interactions with officials at executive beats, reporting on Capitol Hill is much more freewheeling. After all, there are 535 competing sources who are authoritative to one degree or another; reporters may wander the halls at will; and most arenas of congressional decision-making are open, further increasing reporters' choices of what to cover and who to cite. But much if not most of the members' media activities are directed at local publicity, leaving a minority (albeit a sizable minority) committed to pursuing the national spotlight. This range is further reduced by reporters' focus on strategically situated members who may move the legislative process along or who can symbolize two sides of a contested issue before Congress.

Capitol Hill reporters are, like their White House counterparts, political correspondents, focusing on strategies and the game.[9] But the focus of the game is different, less on leading and ordering than on debating and legislating. Without a legislative vehicle or a pending legislative decision, Congress surfaces in the news as an element in someone else's story, most often reacting to executive initiatives. But under the right conditions, Capitol Hill reporting can set the agenda, identify and clarify two sides to an issue, and even open up the debate to the public.

HINTERLANDS

Networks have worked of late to "de-Washingtonize" their coverage. They maintain bureaus scattered across cities in the United States, but these bureaus have been increasingly cut back or abolished. Difficulties of scheduling and coordination, differences in time zones, and the presumption that little local news is of interest to a national audience mean that relatively little breaking news can be generated outside of New York and Washington. But the networks seek a national audience and must maintain at least the image of a coast-to-coast broadcast. Since the varied diet of news consumers is presumed to include closing "kicker" pieces that are more thoughtful or lightweight, and—conveniently for the news media—not necessarily tied to the breaking stories of the day, television routinely produces "evergreens"—unscheduled, less perishable news stories that can come from a variety of locales.

In contrast to the Washington and New York stories which emphasize officialdom and expertise, hinterlands stories frequently feature average Americans, either in accounts of their reaction to large-scale national and international events that affect their lives, or in feature stories whose interest far outweighs their importance. In contrast to the institutional and topical newsbeats in Washington and New York, then, hinterlands stories do provide an entrée for nonexperts and nonofficials to be heard in the news.

In short, the newsbeat system offers one way to divide up the world for news organizations to process their daily product. But although it offers a range of possible news, it favors certain institutions and certain actors above others and thereby shapes the public meaning of ongoing events. I now turn to an examination of the impact of the newsbeat system in shaping the coverage following Iraq's invasion of Kuwait.

The Nightly News and the Newsbeats: The Persian Gulf Crisis in August and September 1990

From the Vanderbilt *Television News Index and Abstracts,* an assistant and I coded all nightly news stories that made use of film for the three broadcasts, according to their newsbeat: whether *institutional* ("with the president" whether in Kennebunkport or at the White House; State Department; Pentagon; Capitol Hill; United Nations), *topical* (business, environment), or *geographical* (the hinterlands, i.e., the U.S. outside of Washington or New York, or a foreign capital), with residual categories for interviews and commentaries from the studio and for general-assignment reporters. After noting the lengths of the stories, we coded each time that a source was quoted on film, as shown by a bracketed description in the *Index;* these sound bites represent the televised equivalent of a quote and offer individuals the chance to state their cases without additional mediation on the reporter's part.[10]

Tables 1a and 1b present the week-to-week results of this coding for August and September 1990. Note the gradual rise and decline in news coverage, as measured in seconds of film stories, on the crisis, peaking in the week of August 20–26 and gradually diminishing thereafter. Since Funkhouser's (1973) classic article, we have long known that the short attention-span of the news media produces an "attention cycle," even for crisis news. The Persian Gulf Crisis was no exception. We should also note that Congress was out of session for almost all of August and did not reconvene until mid-September, so the locale that Washington journalists most often use to gauge opposition to presidential initiatives (see Hess 1981) was essentially unavailable.

Though the Persian Gulf Crisis was international from the start, it was reported largely by reporters from Washington newsbeats or from the studio. One might question whether the studio is a domestic location or not, but we shall see that the sources quoted or interviewed there were overwhelmingly American. Thus, in this time period in general, and in seven of the nine weeks examined, the air time of film stories devoted to domestic newsbeats outnumbered that from foreign locales, sometimes by as much as two to one. Importantly, the dominance of domestic over foreign reports held for the saturation period of August 13–26, and re-emerged toward the end of this time period when reporters had gained access to Baghdad and Saudi Arabia, both of which had been off limits in early August.

The three key domestic newsbeats were the White House, the State Department, and the Pentagon. In August and September, 28 percent of all the air time on the crisis was reported by journalists from one of the three points of the "Golden Triangle." This percentage fluctuated less across the weeks studied than the percentages allotted to foreign newsbeats, which were more responsive to ongoing events. In general, all other domestic newsbeats lagged far behind, but business reporters and, to a lesser extent, Capitol Hill correspondents got a sizable chunk of the

TABLE 1a. Coverage of the Persian Gulf Crisis News by Domestic Newsbeats, August 2–September 30, 1990

	8/2–5	8/6–12	8/13–19	8/20–26	8/27–9/2	9/3–9	9/10–16	9/17–23	9/24–30	TOTAL
White House	19:30	42:40	33:00	33:00	35:00	16:40	24:40	13:20	8:10	226:00
	(15%)	(13%)	(9%)	(9%)	(11%)	(8%)	(12%)	(11%)	(7%)	(10%)
State	2:00	16:20	28:10	31:00	39:10	12:40	5:20	6:50	7:10	148:40
	(2%)	(5%)	(8%)	(9%)	(12%)	(6%)	(3%)	(5%)	(6%)	(7%)
Pentagon	19:30	44:20	43:00	38:50	29:10	9:50	18:40	22:30	9:30	235:20
	(15%)	(13%)	(12%)	(11%)	(9%)	(4%)	(9%)	(18%)	(8%)	(11%)
Capitol Hill	7:40	9:50	4:20	—	2:30	6:10	9:40	4:20	5:10	49:40
	(6%)	(3%)	(1%)		(1%)	(3%)	(5%)	(3%)	(4%)	(2%)
Business	12:10	22:50	10:00	8:50	8:10	2:00	1:50	6:20	12:10	84:20
	(9%)	(7%)	(3%)	(2%)	(3%)	(1%)	(1%)	(5%)	(10%)	(4%)
Studio	21:50	39:20	38:30	38:20	43:50	20:40	6:30	13:50	21:10	244:00
	(17%)	(12%)	(11%)	(11%)	(14%)	(9%)	(3%)	(11%)	(17%)	(12%)
General assignment D.C/N.Y	—	12:00	14:00	15:00	8:50	6:40	7:10	4:10	2:40	70:30
		(4%)	(4%)	(4%)	(3%)	(3%)	(4%)	(3%)	(2%)	(3%)
Hinterlands	4:10	22:10	16:50	29:00	12:40	5:30	20:10	10:20	2:10	123:00
	(3%)	(7%)	(5%)	(8%)	(4%)	(2%)	(10%)	(8%)	(2%)	(6%)
TOTAL DOMESTIC	86:50	209:30	187:50	194:00	178:20	80:10	94:00	81:40	68:10	1181:30
	(68%)	(62%)	(54%)	(54%)	(56%)	(36%)	(47%)	(65%)	(56%)	(55%)

Source: Vanderbilt *Television News Index and Abstracts*.

Note: These figures represent the total minutes and seconds devoted to film stories on the Persian Gulf Crisis reported from the respective newsbeat, and the percentage of the total of all film stories (domestic and foreign) on the crisis.

TABLE 1b. Coverage of the Persian Gulf Crisis News by Foreign Newsbeats, August 2–September 30, 1990

	8/2–5	8/6–12	8/13–19	8/20–26	8/27–9/2	9/3–9	9/10–16	9/17–23	9/24–30	TOTAL
U.N.	—	—	—	3:50	—	—	—	—	9:00	12:50
				(1%)					(7%)	(1%)
London	8:40	4:10	9:50	4:20	4:20	4:00	2:30	2:40	—	41:30
	(7%)	(1%)	(3%)	(1%)	(1%)	(2%)	(1%)	(2%)		(2%)
Israel	11:40	11:50	13:50	7:00	4:00	—	2:00	—	2:20	52:40
	(9%)	(3%)	(4%)	(2%)	(1%)		(1%)		(2%)	(2%)
Cairo	9:20	45:50	17:00	14:30	—	4:50	—	—	—	91:30
	(7%)	(14%)	(5%)	(4%)		(2%)				(4%)
Moscow	2:00	4:10	—	2:30	4:20	12:20	4:50	—	—	28:10
	(2%)	(1%)		(1%)	(1%)	(6%)	(2%)			(1%)
Persian Gulf/	10:00	12:10	59:30	56:20	48:40	41:10	32:50	25:20	14:40	300:40
Saudia Arabia	(8%)	(4%)	(17%)	(16%)	(15%)	(19%)	(16%)	(20%)	(12%)	(14%)
Jordan	—	47:00	44:40	56:20	30:50	23:50	22:10	—	6:20	231:10
		(14%)	(13%)	(16%)	(10%)	(11%)	(11%)		(5%)	(11%)

Tokyo	—	2:10 (1%)	2:20 (1%)	2:40 (1%)	—	1:50 (1%)	1:50 (1%)	—	5:40 (5%)	16:30 (1%)
Ankara	—	2:40 (1%)	—	1:40 (0%)	—	—	—	—	—	5:20 (0%)
Baghdad	—	—	13:40 (4%)	9:10 (3%)	45:40 (14%)	35:30 (16%)	31:30 (16%)	16:50 (13%)	14:50 (12%)	167:10 (8%)
Damascus	—	—	2:00 (1%)	—	—	—	—	—	—	3:40 (0%)
Teheran	—	—	—	4:20 (1%)	—	—	—	—	—	4:20 (0%)
Paris	—	—	—	2:20 (1%)	—	—	—	—	—	2:20 (0%)
Berlin	—	—	—	1:50 (1%)	—	—	—	—	—	8:30 (0%)
Helsinki	—	—	—	—	—	18:00 (6%)	—	—	—	18:00 (1%)
TOTAL FOREIGN	41:40 (32%)	130:00 (38%)	162:50 (46%)	166:50 (46%)	137:50 (44%)	141:30 (64%)	106:00 (53%)	44:50 (35%)	52:50 (43%)	984:20 (45%)

Gulf Crisis news in the first week. After Congress returned from recess, Capitol Hill correspondents contributed a larger percentage of the air time in mid-September, as did reporters from the hinterlands.

In total air time, the Pentagon beat was at least the co-equal of the White House here. But if one examines only those film stories that led the broadcast, the dominant role of the White House newsbeat becomes clear. Of the 141 broadcasts when the Gulf Crisis led the news in August and September, 31 (22 percent) began with the White House reporter, far greater than the 10 percent of air time allocated to the White House beat. By comparison, the percentage (12) of lead stories by Pentagon reporters is about the same as the percentage (11) of the air time originating at the Pentagon. Indeed, by comparing tables 1 and 2, we receive an interesting lesson in who is allowed to initiate stories, with the White House and Baghdad reports being far more prominent among the lead stories than in the total air time; reports from the Gulf itself or from Saudi Arabia, from the studio, and from the hinterlands are far less likely

TABLE 2.   Locales of Persian Gulf Crisis Lead Stories on the Nightly News, August–September, 1990

	ABC	CBS	NBC	TOTAL	(%)
White House	9	7	15	31	(22)
Baghdad	9	11	7	27	(19)
Pentagon	4	5	8	17	(12)
Amman	6	6	4	16	(11)
State Department	8	2	3	13	(9)
Gulf/Saudi Arabia	0	6	1	7	(5)
Studio	4	1	2	7	(5)
Cairo	2	1	3	6	(4)
Business	2	1	1	4	(3)
Capitol Hill	1	0	2	3	(2)
General Assgnmt. D.C./N.Y.	0	2	1	3	(2)
United Nations	1	1	1	3	(2)
Helsinki	1	0	1	2	(1)
Moscow	1	0	1	2	(1)
London	0	1	0	1	(1)
Damascus	0	0	1	1	(1)
Iraq-Turkey Border	0	0	1	1	(1)
TOTAL	48	44	52	144	

Source: Vanderbilt University *Television News Index and Abstracts.*

TABLE 3. Domestic Newsbeats Compared: Total Airtime, Lead Stories, and Earliest Lead Stories from Foreign Sources, August–September, 1990

	Percent of Total Airtime from Domestic Newsbeats	Percent of Lead Stories from Domestic Newbeats	Percent of Earliest Stories when Lead Story was from Foreign Newsbeats[1]
White House	19%	40%	31%
State Department	13	17	23
Pentagon	20	22	17
Capitol Hill	4	4	5
Business	7	5	2
Studio	21	9	17
General assgmt. D.C./N.Y.	6	4	3
Hinterlands	10	—	2
TOTAL	100%	101%	100%

Note: Totals may not add to 100% due to rounding error.

[1] N = 64, excluding two broadcasts with no domestic coverage when the lead was a Persian Gulf story reported from abroad.

to have led the news than the air time would have suggested. Viewers of the network news, who tend to learn more from lead stories than others (Robinson and Levy 1986), would thus be forgiven if they began to envision the dispute as one strictly between Baghdad and the White House.

White House reporters were also advantaged by being turned to most often when the lead story on the Gulf Crisis came from a foreign locale, as we see in table 3. In this task, however, White House reporters received competition from State Department correspondents, who were substantially more likely to be elicited for response to a foreign lead than would have been predicted by their overall percentage of the air time, presumably because spokespersons enunciated official U.S. positions in State Department briefings. But, however one measures the prominence of particular newsbeats, there is one key conclusion: the executive branch was a crucial place for newsmaking and the legislative branch was not. And although the air time allotted to other domestic beats—especially hinterlands and business—was greater than that given to Capitol Hill, table 3 makes clear that the executive branch held a privileged place in initiating domestic stories and in responding to foreign developments.

Domestic Newsbeats and Sources in the Persian Gulf Crisis News, August and September 1990

These results need not imply that potential critics of the executive branch were shut out of the news. In particular, White House reporters rely on congressional sources as well, given the political slant often placed on presidential news, the attractiveness of the White-House-versus-Capitol-Hill script, and, following the decisions in 1979 by the House and in 1986 by the Senate to televise their floor proceedings, the easy availability of ready-taped comments from members on a variety of topics. In order to gauge the impact of the hierarchy of newsworthiness among newsbeats, then, one must examine which sources were most often used at each locale. Table 4 reports the number of sound bites that individual sources contributed at each newsbeat. Some intriguing patterns emerge.

1. Domestic newsbeats rarely included foreign sources. Even ambassadors based in Washington received only sporadic access to the news. In short, when international news is reported stateside, it relies heavily on domestic political actors.

2. At the White House newsbeat, the president was the key actor, providing almost half of the overall sound bites, far more than the 15 percent total for his Cabinet members or his national security staff. But members of Congress, especially Democrats, were allowed to speak in reports filed from the White House, providing 18 percent of the sound bites. Congress was not shut out from the news simply because of the minuscule air time allocated to Capitol Hill correspondents. The power of the script of presidential-congressional conflict was strong enough to include the president's ostensible opponents. Whether these opponents opposed very much, of course, is another matter.[11] The news media must have noticed the initially strong consensus behind the presidential actions and the absence of criticism of the administration's past policy in the only congressional debates on the Gulf Crisis before the August recess (this despite the fact that it was Congress, not the president, who had been urging a tougher line on Iraq). Thus, journalists may well have concluded that the political discord, usually gauged between the Republican president and the Democratic Congress, was not to be found over the principle of responding militarily to Iraqi aggression. At the beginning of the sessions after Congress returned from its August recess, there were occasional one-minute speeches that raised doubts about "blood for oil" and the size of the military build-up.[12] Though these were automatically fed to network bureaus, no legislative vehicles provided a

focus for debate. Such critical comments, both easily available and uttered by officials, may have been deemed less than newsworthy either because there was no continuing story without a bill or because of reporters' concern to use only quotes that symbolized the overall mood of Congress. In either case, the incipient congressional opposition to the buildup began to emerge only as the amount of air time devoted to the crisis declined; the window of opportunity had shut.

3. State Department correspondents relied heavily upon the official department spokesperson for their soundbites (56 percent of the total), despite their dubious television pizzazz, with considerably less attention to political figures inside or outside of the State Department. Some of the dominance of Richard Boucher and Margaret Tutwiler among the on-the-record sources may well be attributed to Secretary of State Baker's avoidance of publicity in these two months, but the domination of official statements—and the presumable journalistic understanding of the State Department beat as reflecting policy more than politics—is striking.

4. Pentagon reporters' sound bites were divided largely four ways: among key politicians (the president, defense secretary, and Pentagon spokesperson); among military officers, especially Generals Colin Powell and Norman Schwarzkopf; among soldiers; and among defense and foreign policy experts, many of whom were former military officials. The greater salience of the last named group as compared to the other Washington institutional beats indicates again how the Pentagon is the most substantively focused of the "Golden Triangle."

5. The studio was used primarily for conversations with defense and foreign policy experts and with fellow journalists. Officials were seldom included. The studio locale was rarely used to start a broadcast. Instead, anchors frequently used the time after the lead stories to make sense of the developments from other newsbeats. In such a manner, journalists tried to maintain a balance between their contradictory urges to be impartial disseminators on the one hand and interpretive investigators on the other.[13] Having allowed the officials in the lead stories to set forth their views, journalists and experts then busied themselves with making sense of the official agenda.

6. Finally, protestors, peace activists, conscientious objectors, and Arab-Americans—the group I have termed "oppositional"—had virtually no access to the news except through general-assignment reporters either in Washington and New York or in the hinterlands. In effect, at this early stage in the framing and normalization of an accidental crisis, reporters did not use sources that they knew beforehand to be

TABLE 4.   Domestic Newsbeats and Sources in Persian Gulf Crisis News, August–September, 1990

	Newsbeat							
	White House	State	Pentagon	Capitol Hill	Business	Studio	Hinterlands	Gen. Assgnmt.
Officials								
Bush	99	9	11	5	4	6	—	2
Baker	3	7	1	2	—	4	—	—
Cheney	1	1	14	—	—	—	—	1
Other cabinet members	1	1	—	1	3	1	—	—
Sununu	2	—	—	—	—	—	—	1
Scowcroft	9	1	4	—	—	—	—	1
Pickering	7	3	—	—	—	—	—	—
Econ. advisor	—	—	—	1	2	—	—	—
Other govt./exec.	3	4	—	1	2	—	1	1
Powell	—	—	10	—	—	—	—	—
Schwarzkopf	—	—	6	—	—	—	—	—
Other mil. officer	—	—	16	—	—	1	2	—
Member of Congress (Dem.)	27	4	12	24	6	7	8	2
Member of Congress (Rep.)	11	—	5	18	1	2	3	—
Local/state official	—	—	—	—	2	2	2	—
Fitzwater	5	2	5	—	—	—	—	—
State Dept. spokesperson	4	40	6	—	—	1	1	—
Pentagon spokesperson	—	—	12	—	—	—	—	—

Experts and business people

Economist	2	1	3	4	29	3	6	—
Pollster	2	—	—	—	—	—	—	—
Oil/gas exec./expert	—	—	—	3	25	—	10	5
Airline/auto expert	—	—	—	1	4	—	2	2
Defense/foreign policy expert	4	9	32	—	4	41	1	6
Consumer advocate	—	—	—	—	5	—	5	—
Other business	—	—	1	3	9	1	9	1
Other journalist	—	—	—	1	—	31	2	—

Oppositional

Arab-American	—	—	—	—	—	1	4	—
Peace activist	—	—	—	—	—	—	3	4
Protestors/CO	—	—	—	—	—	—	4	2

Nonexperts/nonofficials

Soldier	4	—	26	—	—	6	16	18
Soldier relative	—	—	2	—	—	1	23	10
Hostage/escapee	—	11	—	—	—	8	3	14
Hostage relative	3	18	—	—	—	4	12	7
Veteran	2	—	—	—	—	—	6	2
Person-in-street	—	—	1	10	20	—	70	8

(*continued*)

TABLE 4. (*Continued*)

				Newsbeat				
	White House	State	Pentagon	Capitol Hill	Business	Studio	Hinterlands	Gen. Assgnmt.
Foreign sources								
Western head of state/ foreign sec.	8	4	3	—	—	4	—	1
Arab head of state/foreign sec.	1	—	2	—	—	5	—	—
Iraqi ambassador	7	14	2	—	—	2	1	1
Kuwaiti ambassador	2	1	2	1	—	—	—	—
Saudi ambassador	3	—	1	2	—	2	—	—
Other ambassador	1	3	—	—	—	4	—	—
Other foreign official	1	2	2	—	1	2	—	2
Foreign expert	—	—	—	—	1	3	—	—
Foreign soldier	—	—	2	—	—	1	—	—
Foreign person-in-street	—	—	—	—	—	1	—	2
TOTAL	212	135	181	77	119	142	194	93

oppositional unless they were covered in reports that were segregated from the official voices heard at the institutional newsbeats.

Moreover, even these reports were limited, either by focusing on a peripherally related topic to the military buildup—discrimination against Arab-Americans was a particularly popular topic[14]—or by offering contrasting viewpoints to the oppositional voices, as when the lone story on conscientious objectors in this period (NBC on September 15, 1990) used sound bites both from COs and military recruiters.

There is one strong exception, however, to this overall pattern of neglect, and an instructive one. As we have seen, soldiers and their relatives were frequently asked to comment on the mobilization. Thus, television was ready when an education professor at the University of Wisconsin-Milwaukee named Alex Molnar published an open letter to Bush as an op-ed piece in the *New York Times* on August 23, entitled "If My Marine Son is Killed. . . ." This hard-hitting op-ed article connected the almost televisual scenes of Molnar's good-bye to his son with a panoply of different criticisms of the military buildup: the contrast between the privilege of President Bush, Vice President Quayle, and Secretary of State Baker versus the sacrifices of the soldiers; "a Government that no longer has a non-military foreign policy;" the sudden switch from a pro-Iraq tilt before the invasion; and the risk of young lives for "cheap gas."

Falling into the newsworthy category of "Marine parent" from the heartland, Molnar thus had access that others did not. Indeed, with his articulateness, he was able to parlay his op-ed piece into sound bites on each of the three broadcast networks. But each network used Molnar differently. NBC, on the evening of August 23, showed a closer by Fred Briggs in Milwaukee, featuring excerpts from the open letter. CBS, by contrast, fit Molnar in as one of a series of critics of the mobilization in the only story in this period that focused exclusively on dissent. Jerry Bowen's story from Los Angeles, on August 30, was sixth in the opening flow—following reports from Amman, the State Department, the White House, the Pentagon, and Saudi Arabia—and referred to the beginnings of dissent. But CBS, instead of focusing on Molnar's story, made him part of a series of usual suspects from the distant past (Ramsey Clark, Ron Kovic, and George McGovern) that resoundingly echoed the Vietnam script. For its part, ABC showed an Ann Compton story from Kennebunkport on August 23 which raised questions about Bush's continuing his Maine vacation and used Molnar to criticize Bush's "unseemly" behavior when young people might die in the Gulf. In short, even though Molnar was able to gain access to all three network news programs, he could not control the context in which his quotes would appear; the coverage thus diverged among the three networks from NBC's, closest to the original op-ed piece, to CBS's, with its stereotyped frame of dissent, and ABC's, with its preoccupation with Bush's style and self-presentation above the substance of the mobilization itself.

In other words, opposition to the military option was not absent, but to find any amplification in television news, such opposition had to be strategically placed to fall into a category that reporters already considered to be newsworthy for other reasons. That, in turn, meant that critics were less successful at controlling the context in which they appeared and could easily lose control over their larger message.

7. Nonelites were most prominent in reports from the hinterlands, which were kept both distinct from and well after the stories on the decision-makers in Washington. The populist impulse that Hallin and Mancini (1984) note in American television news was blunted by the focus on persons-in-the-street, consumers at the gas pumps, and relatives of soldiers or hostages; as Levine (1977) has pointed out, as the news descends through its presumed hierarchies, the more television portrays news happening to people rather than people instigating news. Implicitly, too, the separation of stories between officialdom in Washington and the populace in the hinterlands—and the tendency I have already noted of the latter to react to the former far more frequently than the other way around—had the effect of symbolically distancing citizens from the potential for debate over the military buildup.

Conclusion

The seemingly simple choices of the news media of where to allocate their personnel and which reporter to feature most heavily in the developing story had impressive consequences on the trajectory of the story. And by emphasizing particular newsbeats, the news selects particular newsmakers and particular perspectives on the invasion, its meaning, and its aftermath. As those actors and perspectives become certified as newsworthy, a self-fulfilling prophecy ensues; yesterday's news becomes the basis for the next day's story lines and allocation of newsbeats, and on we go.

The news about the Persian Gulf Crisis in its initial two months was reported more heavily from domestic newsbeats than from foreign newsbeats. Newsbeats in Washington, and the executive branch in particular, were dominant. The administration was usually able, through television news, to initiate stories and to respond to foreign developments, and as long as the White House, State Department, and Pentagon were publicly in accord with one another, the news from these three newsbeats might only give different facets—politics, policy, and implementation—of a single approach.

In the first two months of the Gulf Crisis, the White House was favored for the lead story with strong emphasis upon the person of George Bush, front and center; the State Department was an important location for reaction to lead stories from abroad and stressed official policy statements; and the Pentagon newsbeat, second for second, was actually the best-represented, with particular attention to matters of method and expertise. These three newsbeats together were responsible for 52 percent of the overall air time from domestic newsbeats and a staggering 79 percent of the domestically derived lead stories on the crisis. Given the possibilities for coordinating the "line of the day" through the White House Office of Communication (Maltese 1992), the administration was able to dominate early coverage.

The news did not, to be sure, completely shut out potential critics. But those that fell into categories that were oppositional were largely neglected, and only those critics who met other standards of newsworthiness, by being a key member of Congress or a soldier's parent, were admitted to the debates on the news, and only in a position of responding to administration initiatives. Although opposition was not then absent, even at this earliest stage in the continuing story, the Gulf Crisis presented limited opportunity for the media to foster full and open debate about American involvement, given their tendency to process an unforeseen accident through institutional newsbeats and thereby domesticate it. The media's routine practices thus helped to transfer the crisis from the arena of political debate to the realm of "managerial democracy" (Bennett 1989).

Yet, to return to the contrast posed by the French and American news broadcasts, none of this is inevitable. While American journalists no doubt would see the division of the news into institutional newsbeats that overrepresent the executive branch as natural, comparative studies of the news tell us that there are alternative ways to organize the world that journalists could apprehend in a routine day-to-day fashion. If it is the case that the news media have become a national political institution (Cook 1991), their rules and procedures, as with all institutions, are the result of historical developments and standing decisions that can be modified to produce the sort of political processes that we would prefer.

Perhaps none of this should be terribly surprising to students of the American news media and foreign policy, particularly in "crises." Many accounts have noted the impact of the "journalism of deference" (e.g.,

Dorman and Farhang 1987), how presidents dominate crisis reporting to their advantage (e.g., Nacos 1990), or how the range of disagreement in the news hinges upon the "indexed" range of dissensus within Washington opinion in general and Congress in particular (e.g., Hallin 1986; Bennett 1990).

However, I should reinforce the point that the media did not single-handedly accomplish the removal of the Persian Gulf Crisis from the arena of full debate. The Washington news media rely upon Congress to provide readings on presidential performance, to raise questions about executive initiatives, and, in general, to provide the other side in the legendary "two sides of the story" (see Hess 1981). Mass-mediated opposition to the military buildup in the first weeks of the crisis was undoubtedly hindered by the congressional recess from August 4 to September 10, 1990. But that is only part of the story, because the numbers here suggest that members of Congress, in spite of the paucity of stories reported by Capitol Hill correspondents in the first two months of the crisis, were far from absent from the coverage at other newsbeats, particularly the White House. The congressional response was encapsulated by the ostensible leader of the opposition, Thomas Foley, Speaker of the House, who noted on August 28, 1990, that the president had "strong across-the-board support from members of Congress, both the Senate and House, Democrats and Republicans alike," and voiced concern only "about burden-sharing."[15] Without either leaders or a critical mass of members who would raise questions that could symbolize larger discontent and concern in Washington or in the country at large, the isolated one-minute speeches that backbenchers began to give against the military mobilization when Congress returned from its recess were unlikely to gain prominence in the news.

Nor was the congressional response to the Iraqi invasion of Kuwait unusual. Barbara Hinckley, in a forthcoming book, has studied the history of congressional responses to presidential foreign policy initiatives since World War II. She has found that Congress's engagement with the president is not only spotty but ritualistic. As long as presidents accept the symbolic importance of consultation with Capitol Hill, Hinckley concludes, Congress tends not to contest presidential decisions, least of all in "crisis" situations.

In the first two months after Iraq invaded Kuwait, the public may well have been informed about what the president's plans, opinions, and assessments were, how the State Department reacted to overseas developments, and how the military mobilization was being carried out. But the public rarely had an opportunity in these crucial first weeks either to witness or enter into much of a debate about the pros and cons of the military option. That failure was not purely the media's doing. Instead, it was the result of two sorts of risk-averseness: Congress's reluctance to challenge a president during an international event that was labeled a crisis, and the news media's chronic dependence upon officialdom to provide the main focus of their work and the sources of their criticism.

Notes

Earlier versions of this paper were presented at workshops of the Social Science Research Council in Seattle and Washington, D.C., and at the annual meeting of the International Communication Association in Miami, May 21–25, 1992. In addition to my colleagues at these meetings, my thanks go to Lewis Friedland for useful comments. A Division II Research Grant from Williams College funded the capable research assistance of Eric Zimmerman, who coded the broadcasts from the Vanderbilt *Television News Index and Abstracts*.

1. TF1 broadcast anchored by Patrick Poivre d'Arvor, January 10, 1991. TF1's nightly news habitually receives the highest ratings of any of the four national news broadcasts in France.

2. Between McWethy and Zelnick, to be sure, Jennings consulted the on-tap expert of the evening, William Quandt of the Brookings Institution. After another commercial, Jennings returned to quiz Laurie further—revealing that the latter had received nothing but pessimism about such a settlement—and only then turned to David Ensor at the United Nations, followed by the resident experts (Anthony Cordesman, Judith Kipper, and Quandt).

3. For a similar conclusion comparing Italian and American television news broadcasts, see Hallin and Mancini (1984).

4. O'Heffernan, Chapter 11 in this volume, shows how elites are attentive to foreign policy news, meaning that this process need not be mediated by the mass public.

5. Admittedly, the program—on lesbian mothers—was not on an item that the news media have considered to be important in the past, and August is usually a slow news time in general.

6. For documentation on this point, see Roshco's (1992) excerpts from 1990 State Department press briefings prior to the invasion.

7. Routinization per se need not lead to reassuring news. As Eliasoph (1988) has noted from her participant-observation at Pacifica Radio, news could routinely depend on critical sources, but journalists rarely accept such presumptions of *where* news happens and *who* is an authoritative source.

8. For the best comparison of newsbeats at different agencies, see Hess (1984). This section also draws upon, for the White House, Crouse (1973), Grossman and Kumar (1980), Kernell (1986) and Hertsgaard (1988); for the

State Department, Cohen (1963) and Chittick (1970); for the Pentagon, Heise (1979) and Sims (1983); for Congress, Hess (1985) and Cook (1989). The importance of what I call "hinterlands" stories in television network news is well delineated by Epstein (1973) and Gans (1979).

9. Indeed, since 1988, when I studied the congressional reporters (Cook 1989), cutbacks in news operations—especially on the three broadcast networks—have meant that lone reporters in each case cover Capitol Hill as part of their job as "Washington political correspondents." Increasingly, Congress is covered as part of other Washington-wide stories (Hess 1993).

10. I should note that the Vanderbilt *Index* is far more problematic to use in coding favorable or critical statements, which are often only listed as, for example, "Senator X comments on invasion." Consequently, this analysis does not consider the balance of favorable to critical sound bites but instead focuses on which sources were admitted to the news under what conditions.

11. Most of the House debate, such as it was, consisted of Foreign Affairs Committee chair Dante Fascell staving off parliamentary objections from Republicans who disliked the change in the daily schedule and/or wished to add amendments. The fuller debate in the Senate included only one momentary doubter, Arlen Specter, who noted "substantial similarities between the Tonkin Gulf resolution and this resolution," but then quickly added "my hope that we will not have to undertake the forceful measures called for in this resolution." See *Congressional Record* (daily edition), August 2, 1990, pp. H6311–H6321 and pp. S11895–S11907. Specter's comments are found on p. S11902.

12. A recent study of one-minute speeches (Browning 1992) shows that the vast majority of them are concerned with national policy rather than with parochial concerns.

13. The terminology comes from Weaver and Wilhoit's (1986) analysis of a 1981 national survey of American journalists. About 62 percent of their sample endorsed an "interpretive/investigative" role but 50 percent favored an "information dissemination" role, with over half of each group endorsing the other role at the same time (see fig. 5.1).

14. Charles Thomas filed a story from Detroit on Arab-American reaction on August 12 (ABC); Connie Chung reported on anti–Arab-American violence on September 2 (CBS); Tom Foreman contributed a closer on Hollywood bigotry against Arabs on September 5 (ABC); and finally, Bill Lagatutta reported from California on anti–Arab-American discrimination on September 23 (NBC), although the story did point out that Bush would meet the next day with Arab-Americans to condemn discrimination, an action that all three networks dutifully covered in turn.

15. Quoted in *Congressional Quarterly Almanac, 1990,* pp. 729–30.

References

Bennett, W. L. 1989. "Marginalizing the Majority: Conditioning Public Opinion to Accept Managerial Democracy." In Michael Margolis and Gary A. Mauser, eds., *Manipulating Public Opinion: Essays on Public Opinion as a Dependent Variable,* pp. 321–362. Pacific Grove, Calif.: Brooks-Cole.

————. 1990. "Toward a Theory of Press-State Relations in the United States." *Journal of Communication* 40, 2: 103–25.

Browning, R. X. 1992. "Speaking Up and Speaking Out: One-Minute Speeches in the House of Representatives." Paper presented at the Off the Video Record conference, Public Affairs Video Archives, Purdue University, West Lafayette, Indiana, November.

Chittick, W. O. 1970. *State Department, Press, and Pressure Groups: A Role Analysis.* New York: Wiley-Interscience.

Cohen, B. C. 1963. *The Press and Foreign Policy.* Princeton: Princeton University Press.

Cook, T. E. 1989. *Making Laws and Making News: Media Strategies in the U.S. House of Representatives.* Washington, D.C.: Brookings Institution.

————. 1991. "Are the American News Media Governmental? Testing the 'Fourth Branch' hypothesis." Paper prepared for delivery at the annual meeting of the International Communication Association, Chicago, May.

————. 1992. "Covering the News and Staging the News: Media Events and Broadcast Network News in the First Six Months of the Bush Presidency." Paper presented at the Off the Video Record conference, Public Affairs Video Archives, Purdue University, West Lafayette, Indiana, November.

Crouse, T. 1973. *The Boys on the Bus.* New York: Ballantine.

Dorman, W. A., and M. Farhang. 1988. *The U.S. Press and Iran. Foreign Policy and the Journalism of Deference.* Berkeley: University of California Press.

Eliasoph, N. 1988. "Routines and the Making of Oppositional News." *Critical Studies in Mass Communication* 5: 313–34.

Epstein, E. J. 1973. *News From Nowhere: Television and the News.* New York: Vintage.

Fishman, M. 1980. *Manufacturing the News.* Austin: University of Texas Press.

Funkhouser, G. R. 1973. "The Issues of the Sixties: An Exploratory Study in the Dynamics of Public Opinion. *Public Opinion Quarterly* 37: 62–75.

Gans, H. J. 1979. *Deciding What's News.* New York: Pantheon.

Grossman, M. B., and M. J. Kumar. 1980. *Portraying the President: The White House and the News Media.* Baltimore: Johns Hopkins University Press.

Hallin, D. C. 1986. *The "Uncensored War": The Media and Vietnam.* New York: Oxford University Press.

Hallin, D. C., and P. Mancini. 1984. "Speaking of the President: Political Structure and Representational Form in U.S. and Italian Television News." *Theory and Society* 13: 829–50.

Heise, J. A. 1979. *Minimum Disclosure: How The Pentagon Manipulates the News.* New York: W. W. Norton.

Hertsgaard, M. 1988. *On Bended Knee: The Press and the Reagan Presidency.* New York: Farrar, Straus and Giroux.

Hess, S. 1981. *The Washington Reporters.* Washington, D.C.: Brookings Institution.

————. 1983. "The Golden Triangle: The Press at the White House, State and Defense." *Brookings Review* (Summer): 14–19.

————. 1984. *The Government/Press Connection: Press Officers and Their Offices.* Washington, D.C.: Brookings Institution.

————. 1985. *The Ultimate Insiders: U.S. Senators in the National Media.* Washington, D.C.: Brookings Institution.

————. 1993. "The Decline and Fall of Congressional News." Paper prepared for delivery at the conference on Congress, the Media and Public Opinion, American Enterprise Institute, Washington, D.C., May.

Hinckley, B. Forthcoming. *Less Than Meets the Eye: Congress, the President, and Foreign Policy.* Chicago: University of Chicago Press.

Kernell, S. 1986. *Going Public: New Strategies of Presidential Leadership.* Washington, D.C.: Congressional Quarterly Press.

Levine, G. F. 1977. "Learned Helplessness and the Evening News." *Journal of Communication* 27, 4 (Autumn): 100–105.

Linsky, M. 1986. *Impact: How the Press Affects Federal Policy Making.* New York: W. W. Norton.

Maltese, J. A. 1992. *Spin Control: The White House Office of Communications and the Management of Presidential News.* Chapel Hill: University of North Carolina Press.

Martin, D. C. 1991. "Covering the Pentagon for Television: A Reporter's Perspective." In Loren B. Thompson, ed., *Defense Beat: The Dilemmas of Defense Coverage,* pp. 83–93. New York: Lexington Books.

Nacos, B. L. 1990. *The Press, Presidents, and Crises.* New York: Columbia University Press.

Robinson, J. P., and M. R. Levy. 1986. *The Main Source: Learning from Television News.* Beverly Hills: Sage.

Roshco, B. 1992. "When Policy Fails: How the Buck was Passed When Kuwait Was Invaded." Discussion paper D-15, Joan Shorenstein Barone Center on the Press, Politics, and Public Policy, Harvard University.

Schudson, M. 1986. "Deadlines, Datelines and History." In Robert Karl Manoff and Michael Schudson, eds., *Reading the News.* New York: Pantheon.

Sims, R. 1983. *The Pentagon Reporters.* Washington, D.C.: National Defense University Press.

Smith, J. C. 1992. *George Bush's War.* New York: Henry Holt.

Tuchman, G. 1973. "Making News by Doing Work: Routinizing the Unexpected." *American Journal of Sociology* 79: 110–31.

Weaver, D. H., and G. C. Wilhoit. 1986. *The American Journalist: A Portrait of U.S. News People and Their Work.* Bloomington: Indiana University Press.

six

Jarol B. Manheim

Strategic Public Diplomacy

*Managing Kuwait's Image
During the Gulf Conflict*

The United States is par excellence a country where public opinion plays an important role, inspiring, orienting, controlling the policy of the nation. Nothing can be achieved or endure without it, and its veto is final. It is characterized by the fact that it is both more spontaneous than anywhere else in the world and also more easily directed by efficient propaganda technique than in any other country.

André Siegfried, *America at Mid-Century*

We disseminated information in a void as a basis for Americans to form opinions.

Frank Mankiewicz, Vice Chairman,
Hill and Knowlton Public Affairs Worldwide

Teachers get awards. We get blamed for teaching.

Lauri J. Fitz-Pegado, Senior Vice President,
Hill and Knowlton Public Affairs Worldwide

Though the centrality of communication to the conduct of diplomacy has long been evident, both scholars and practitioners have devoted more systematic attention to this relationship in recent years than previously. This renewed emphasis can be characterized as addressing four distinctive aspects of diplomatic activity: government-to-government, diplomat-to-diplomat, people-to-people, and government-to-people contacts. The first of these refers to the traditional form of diplomacy, the exchange of formal messages between sovereign states. The new emphasis here is typified by Raymond Cohen (1987), who explores the nuances of form in diplomatic exchanges with particular attention to the rituals and cues that accompany and give added meaning to the various communiqués. The second, commonly termed "personal diplomacy," refers to the individual-level interactions among those involved in diplomatic contacts. The value ascribed to personal diplomacy is often cited at an institutional level as a rationale for summitry (e.g., for the seemingly routinized meetings of American and Soviet/Russian leaders or of the leaders of the principal Western economies), and has been addressed as a subject of scholarly inquiry by Harold Saunders (1988), who ascribes particular importance to the interpersonal relationships among diplomats themselves. The third, often referred to as "public diplomacy," is characterized by cultural exchanges such as the Fulbright Program, media development initiatives, and the like, all designed to explain and defend government policies and portray a nation to foreign audiences. The last, another form of public diplomacy which was identified by W. Philips Davison (1974) and Richard Merritt (1980), includes efforts by the government of one nation to influence public or elite opinion in a second nation for the purpose of turning the foreign policy of the target nation to advantage. It is this latter aspect of diplomatic activity that provides the context for the present analysis.

In its earliest incarnation, the twentieth-century study of what was then commonly referred to as "propaganda" was extensive indeed. The research of Carl Hovland, Harold Lasswell, Wilbur Schramm, Morris Janowitz, Irving Janis, and others, received substantial government support, especially following the outbreak of the Second World War, and gave impetus to the development of social psychology and to early interest in political communication. (For examples of this work, see Hovland, Lumsdaine and Sheffield 1949; and Institute of Communications Research 1955.) In the United States, propaganda was at once an accepted instrument of government—as exemplified by George Creel and the Committee on Public Information—and an object of fear to be investigated by the House Committee on Un-American Activities, depending, in large measure, on the direction of informational flow (Lee 1952). The study of propaganda during this period took two principal tracks, one, as noted, directed at the psychological mechanics of influence, and the second at the specific techniques by which propagandists ostensibly plied their trade. The first of these tracks led scholars to a more general and largely empirical examination of attitudes and such attitude-related processes as change or inoculation against change. The second, which led to an interest in political public relations, advertising, and marketing, tends to be expressed in more anecdotal and generally more normative terms. A review of scholarship on propaganda from this period lies beyond the scope of this essay, but it is important to note that both approaches have had enduring influence in such disciplines as communication, political science, and psychology.

More recently, the term "public diplomacy" has come into vogue to characterize activities that would once have been described as propaganda. The term was reportedly coined in 1965 by Edmund Gullion of the Fletcher School of Law and Diplomacy at Tufts University (Malone 1988, 12). Tuch (1990) defines public diplomacy as "a government's process of communicating with foreign publics in an attempt to bring about understanding for its nation's ideas and ideals, its institutions and culture, as well as its national goals and current policies." Thus, the Voice of America (and the international broadcast services of other countries), created in 1942 to counteract the presumed effects abroad of Nazi wartime broadcasts, now engages in public diplomacy, as do the libraries maintained overseas by the United States Information Agency, the participants in the Fulbright exchange program, and other persons and agencies. In no small measure, this change in label represents a lesson learned from the propagandists themselves, that what one calls an object helps to determine how it is perceived by others. But in part, it also represents a sort of gentrification of the art of influence reflective of the greater legitimacy that attends to such functions in a world more accustomed to bombardment by media messages.

On two occasions, Congress has held hearings to examine the organization, conduct, and effectiveness of U.S. efforts at public diplomacy (U.S. House of Representatives 1977, 1987). The general conclusion has been that such activities could productively be expanded and improved. In the present context, however, the most revealing governmental inquiry might be that conducted in the late 1970s by the U.S. General Accounting Office (GAO). In a 1979 report (U.S. GAO, 1979), the GAO summarized the public diplomacy activities of seven countries—France, Great Britain, Japan, West Germany, China, and the Soviet Union, as well as the United States—and assessed their implications for U.S. foreign policy. After noting that public diplomacy had become a major instrument of foreign policy for the United States and other nations and describing the U.S. effort as smaller than those of both allies and adversaries, the GAO offered six avenues for improvement: greater cooperation with public diplomacy efforts of U.S. allies to increase efficiency, improved financial management, expanded emphasis on the teaching of English (e.g., through VOA broadcasts), limited legalization of the domestic distribution of USIA-produced materials (actually, for a brief period at the time of the report this agency was called the International Communication Agency, a name soon discarded because of the similarity of its acronym with that of the CIA), adequate compensation of overseas public diplomacy representatives, and a more systematic assessment of Soviet public diplomacy in the U.S. Leaving aside the "bean counter" mentality that seems to characterize these recommendations, they do reflect as well the general governmental approach to public diplomacy during this period. That approach was grounded in a belief that relatively straightforward efforts to disseminate information that accorded with U.S. national interests to the largest possible audience in the greatest number of countries, while keeping a bit of a wary eye on those targeting their efforts in the other direction, would best serve the interests of the United States. Scholarship within this framework (e.g., Green 1988; Malone 1988; Smith 1980; Tuch 1990) has tended to focus on issues in the management, general content and direction, and integration with larger foreign-policy interests and initiatives, of public diplomacy efforts, though Signitzer and Coombs (1991) take a more conceptual approach, arguing for a more explicit convergence of public-relations practice with theories of cultural communication.

The most contemporary approach to this set of phenomena, and the one that will frame the balance of this essay, is perhaps best described as an emphasis on "*strategic* public diplomacy." Strategic public diplomacy is the international manifestation of a relatively new style of information management that Manheim (1991a), drawing on use of the term by some practitioners, has termed "strategic political communication." In this view, political communication encompasses the creation, distribution, control, use, processing, and effects of information as a political resource, whether by governments, organizations, or individuals. *Strategic* political communication incorporates the use of sophisticated knowledge of such attributes of human behavior as attitude and preference structures, cultural tendencies, and media-use patterns to shape and target messages so as to maximize their desired impact while minimizing undesired collateral effects. Strategic public diplomacy, then, is public diplomacy practiced less as an art than as an applied transnational science of human behavior. It is, within the limits of available knowledge, the practice of propaganda in the earliest sense of the term, but enlightened by half a century of empirical research into human motivation and behavior.

As early as 1966, scholars and practitioners had begun to recognize the potential for developing a more sophisticated approach to the conduct of public diplomacy. In that year, the Bernays Foundation (named for Edward L. Bernays, commonly regarded as the father of modern public-relations practice) sponsored a series of lectures on the topic at Tufts University. Later published in an anthology (Hoffman 1968), these essays covered the applicability of such bodies of knowledge as public opinion research, national cultures, group dynamics, psychological operations, and semantics and linguistics to the problem at hand. Participants included Lloyd Free, Margaret Mead, Lewis Coser, and Daniel Lerner, to name but a few. Subsequently, Fisher (1972) outlined in a rather more orderly fashion the social scientific knowledge base on which increasingly sophisticated efforts at public diplomacy might be grounded. He argued that expanding communications technologies and greater public participation in foreign affairs policy-making were challenging the traditional means of conducting international relations in ways that must be taken into account. Davis (1977), in a case study of Nigerian politics surrounding the period of that country's civil war, pointed to the significance of public relations and other consultants in representing the political interests of governments and various subnational organizations to external audiences, notably in the United States and other Western industrial countries. These efforts, he found, were of value not only in framing images held by the audiences of the various foreign clients, but in translating those images into relatively advantageous policy outcomes. And a few years later, Merritt (1980) suggested that governments had indeed developed a greater appreciation for the role of information campaigns as instruments of their respective foreign policies, and for the more or less subtle techniques available to them to implement such efforts. The effectiveness of these campaigns, and some of their limitations, were subsequently documented by Manheim and Albritton (1984, 1986, 1987; Albritton and Manheim 1983, 1985; Manheim, 1987) in a series of studies which identified and tested a model of image change in which the goals of image enhancement vary depending upon the characteristics of the initial media portrayal of the image object in question, and which specified conditions under which the model succeeds or fails to predict or account for image changes. Amaize and Faber (1983) studied patterns of international advertising undertaken by national governments and their agencies.

More recently, Manheim has explored the structure of foreign-interest representation in the United States (1991b) and the nature of the decision-making of both U.S. and foreign governmental actors, and of U.S. political consultants who work in behalf of foreign interests, focusing on both the strategic (1988, 1990a) and the tactical (1990b, 1990c) aspects of public diplomacy. Anderson (1989) has offered a case study of the Reagan administration's marshaling of the tools of strategic public diplomacy to influence U.S. media and public perceptions of Nicaragua and the Sandinistas, while Choate (1990) has presented an extensive examination of the representation of Japanese governmental and corporate interests in the domestic political arena of the United States. In particular, Choate has demonstrated the intertwining of political and commercial interests, in effect, the partnership of government and business, in the design and conduct of public diplomacy, at least by some countries. Finally, Fisher (1987, 134–35), not surprisingly, given his earlier contribution, has called for a more pro-active role for the

USIA in U.S. foreign-policy making, first by fostering more systematically the psychological infrastructure that would sustain a more sophisticated U.S. effort, and second by bringing its expertise in communication and in psychology to bear in the formative stages of the policy process rather than in implementation alone. There is some evidence that Fisher's call was being heeded, if not by the State Department, at least by the Department of Defense (Kriesel 1985).

From these studies and related literature, when considered in the aggregate, we know that:

- There exists a knowledge base in such disciplines as communication, journalism, political science, and psychology sufficient to guide relatively sophisticated efforts at strategic communication, which efforts can be employed to further the interests of governments in the international system.
- Such strategic approaches to public diplomacy, grounded in social scientific knowledge regarding attitude structures and change, media-use habits, newsroom decision-making, and the like, have been demonstrated to be effective under certain circumstances, and ineffective under other, more or less clearly delineated ones.
- In particular, differential strategies, derived from such notions as cognitive balance theory (e.g., Festinger 1957) or psychological inoculation (e.g., McGuire 1964; Pfau and Kenski 1990), have been identified and evaluated under differing conditions defined by characteristics of extant news portrayals of the image-object in question, and relevant case studies illustrating several such conditions have been developed.
- An increasing number of governments are coming to appreciate the potential utility of taking a more strategic view of their external communications. This assertion is supported by both aggregate statistics on such activity and by a small number of case studies of decision-making in such countries as Nigeria, the Philippines, Pakistan, and South Korea.
- Specifically, many governments around the world (roughly 160 according to the most recent Department of Justice foreign-agent registration records), in addition to their own trained staffs of public diplomatists, engage the services of U.S. lobbyists, public-relations consultants, and others, to assist them in communicating with the U.S. media and public. Some, but not

all, of these efforts could be characterized as having "strategic communication" components.

• For a variety of reasons, ranging from the "obtrusiveness" of issues to the economics of newsroom decision-making, strategic communication campaigns can be more effective when directed at issues or actors in foreign affairs than when employed in domestic politics.

• The industry which serves these governments in the United States has grown rapidly over the past quarter-century. The number of registered firms has doubled during this period, and the number of individuals employed in their service has more than tripled.

• Typically, governments with special needs or problems or with generally negative images in the United States are the most likely to engage in strategic communication, but strategies are available for, and employed by, those with positive images as well.

The Gulf Conflict: A Battle of Images

In this context, it is little wonder that public diplomacy and other strategic communication efforts were central to the development of the Gulf conflict from its very inception. Virtually every major player participated in these efforts.

For Saddam Hussein, the principal objective was to shape the debate in the United States—through the selection of language frames ("guests" rather than "hostages"), visual frames (the "baby formula" factory, complete with a sign in English), and overt censorship—to limit the range of politically acceptable responses available to the Bush administration. For the administration, on the other hand, the principal objective was to shape the debate to maximize its freedom of action and to build support for a military response. This was achieved through image management (e.g., Saddam Hussein as "Hitler"), but also through news management, as with the media pools and the Home Town News Program, both calculated to minimize the importance of potentially critical national reporters. And for the Pentagon, the principal objective was to preserve its political legitimacy (i.e., to avoid the "Vietnam syndrome") and to protect itself against the additional budget-cutting pressure that would surely follow a less-than-exemplary showing. The army, in particular, pursued its objectives in part through a strategy of inoculating media and public opinion in advance against the shock of such possible events as the use of chemical warfare (Manheim, 1993).

Among the most interesting of the strategic communication efforts during the period, however, were those undertaken by and in behalf of the Kuwaitis, who had the least ambiguous objective of all: They wanted their country back. To achieve that, they turned to Hill and Knowlton Public Affairs Worldwide.

Of the hundreds of firms providing U.S.-directed public affairs services to international clients, perhaps the most prominent and most comprehensive is Hill and Knowlton Public Affairs Worldwide. Founded by John W. Hill in Cleveland, Ohio, in 1927 (Donald Knowlton was brought in as a partner a few years later), Hill and Knowlton today employs some 1,900 people in sixty-five offices in twenty-four countries worldwide, and serves more than a thousand clients, including more than half of the *Fortune* 100. It maintains a networking relationship with forty-eight additional U.S. firms and twenty overseas, the net effect of which is to extend its reach nationwide and abroad. The company's total revenues in 1989 reached $164 million, nearly four times their 1981 level.

By any measure, Hill and Knowlton is a major player in international public relations and public affairs. It was one of only three firms in 1987 (out of more than 800) to provide services to clients representing more than twenty countries. Unofficial, but more recent, figures show that, between November 10, 1990, and May 10, 1991, Hill and Knowlton received some $14 million in fees and expenses from thirty-one foreign clients (Anonymous 1991b). Selling both expertise and a network of contacts, Hill and Knowlton was a natural object of Kuwaiti attention. A visit by company executives Robert Gray and Frank Mankiewicz to the Kuwaiti ambassador on the very heels of the invasion assured that they received it (Mutson 1992, 28).

Images of Kuwait

It was, in the event, not direct representatives of the exiled government of the emir who called at the firm's Washington Harbour offices a day or two after the invasion, but rather representatives of the newly formed Citizens for a Free Kuwait. Though virtually all of the total fees of $10.8 million (including expenses) that Hill and Knowlton collected over the brief life of its contract originated with the emir or his government, the existence of the intermediary organization made it possible for the company to disclaim any responsibility for defending the government, and to emphasize instead the commitment of its clients to democracy in Kuwait.

Citizens for a Free Kuwait included a variety of Kuwaitis in the United States, among them businessmen, political exiles, students, and some who simply happened to be in the U.S. on vacation at the time of the invasion. All had awakened on August 2 to find themselves homeless. Among the leaders of the group, and those with whom Hill and Knowlton eventually dealt, were former Kuwaiti minister of education Hassan al Ibrahim, Fawzi al Sultan of the World Bank, and Ali al Tarah, cultural attaché at the Kuwaiti Embassy in Washington. The group soon formed additional branches in London and elsewhere.

Hill and Knowlton's principal on the account was Lauri Fitz-Pegado, senior vice president and managing director of the International Public Affairs Division, a Latin America specialist who holds degrees from Vassar and the Johns Hopkins School of Advanced International Studies. Fitz-Pegado, who joined Hill and Knowlton after five years as a foreign service officer, has represented interests in some twenty countries since joining the firm in 1982. Her base of operations was a river-view office dominated by a political map of the world, a collection of State Department area handbooks, and a Rolodex worthy of any Washington power broker.

In interviews with the author, Fitz-Pegado and Frank Mankiewicz, vice chairman and managing director for Public Affairs, described the Hill and Knowlton effort as a twenty-four-hour-a-day, seven-day-a-week undertaking, one that Fitz-Pegado characterized as "the project of a lifetime." Though it is generally the case that public-relations firms see international clients as providing them with unique challenges, Fitz-Pegado saw this particular client as more challenging still. "We were," she said, "dealing with people who were traumatized. You had to be a bit of a psychologist to get the job done." She found it an emotionally draining experience. Part of the problem was that the clients did not understand the rationale for much of the company's effort. For example, one theme Hill and Knowlton emphasized early in its effort to build a pro-Kuwait constituency in the U.S. was the relative freedom of Kuwaiti women. Unlike those in Saudi Arabia, for instance, Kuwaiti women were permitted to drive, and, the company's materials noted, even served as university rectors. Fitz-Pegado tells, however, of one Kuwaiti spokesman-to-be who could not grasp the purpose of what he saw as a trivialization of the issues. How can you ask me to spend my time talking about women driving, he wondered aloud, when last week my daughter was raped by the Iraqis? More generally, it was difficult for people who had just escaped from danger and were worried about their families to focus on themes and messages. On more than one occasion during media-training sessions, the clients broke into tears.

Hill and Knowlton reportedly engaged in little direct lobbying, but that is not to say that the firm did not employ to the fullest its Washington connections. According to sources at Amnesty International, which later publicly disassociated itself from a claim to which Amnesty had given currency, it was Hill and Knowlton that gave to the group the story of Iraqi soldiers pulling newborns from their incubators so that these machines could be removed to Iraq. More significantly, the story also made an appearance on Capitol Hill, where a young woman identified only as Nayirah told a hearing of the Congressional Human Rights Caucus, chaired by Representative Tom Lantos, that she had witnessed this event firsthand. After John R. MacArthur, publisher of *Harper's Magazine*, revealed in a *New York Times* op-ed piece the fact that Nayirah was, in fact, the daughter of the Kuwaiti ambassador to the U.S., it was also disclosed that Hill and Knowlton had helped to prepare her testimony, which she had rehearsed before video cameras in the firm's Washington headquarters. This rehearsal took place, as it happened, just down the hall from the offices of the caucus itself, which had for some time been the rent-free tenant of Hill and Knowlton. (The caucus also received a $50,000 contribution during this period from Citizens for a Free Kuwait [Krauss 1992].) Similar, though less publicized, testimony was presented before the United Nations Security Council by a woman identified only as a Kuwaiti refugee, but who later turned out to be Fatima Fahed, wife of the Kuwaiti minister of planning and a prominent Kuwaiti television personality (Strong 1992).

According to Kuwaiti doctors and other prospective witnesses interviewed by Middle East Watch, a human-rights group, the incident never occurred, a position that was rejected by the U.S. Embassy in Kuwait (Cushman 1992, A11; Priest 1992a, A17). A subsequent private investigation by Kroll Associates, a U.S. firm paid by the Kuwaiti government, found that Nayirah's testimony was based on a single, brief incident, but that perhaps half a dozen Kuwaiti infants were, in fact, removed from incubators during the occupation (Priest 1992b, A14). True or not, this story clearly affected George Bush, as evidenced by the frequency with which he cited it, including in an important turn-of-the-year interview with David Frost.

Most of the firm's efforts were focused on media training (their clients, who normally dressed in Western-style business suits, were instructed, for example, to change into Arab dress when appearing on television), drafting speeches and scheduling speaking tours, monitoring and analyzing legislative initiatives, distributing video and other materials, and tracking public opinion. Hill and Knowlton maintained a television crew in Saudi Arabia to produce its own video, and also provided a channel through which video produced by the Kuwaiti resistance was distributed to outside news services and networks. The firm arranged for events in Kuwait to be highlighted during the Thanksgiving Day National Football League telecast (Anonymous 1991b).

Of the fees received by Hill and Knowlton, Mankiewicz indicated that approximately $2.6 million were distributed to subcontractors, principally the Wirthlin Group, a polling firm based in Alexandria, Virginia, and founded by Richard Wirthlin, a long-time White House insider who had served as Ronald Reagan's pollster. The firm conducted daily tracking polls on Kuwait's image and related variables, much on the model of tracking polls conducted for candidates in political campaigns.

According to Dee Allsop, the Wirthlin Group's vice president for communications and marketing research and the company's principal representative on the account, polling began with a nationwide benchmark survey on August 20. This was followed with daily tracking surveys from early September through late October, then with biweekly surveys until mid-December, when polling ceased as it became clear that the objective of the overall campaign—moving the U.S. to act decisively in Kuwait—was about to be achieved. The tracking polls each contained some thirty items, and were administered by telephone to two hundred respondents. Principal categories of measurement included the mood of the country, levels of support for the president and for U.S. policy in the Gulf, a series of world-leader and country thermometers, and a bank of specific questions on attitudes toward the Gulf conflict. Wirthlin provided a three- to four-page written report on each survey, and sometimes briefed representatives of Citizens for a Free Kuwait directly. (Partial results of these surveys are reported in Wilcox, Ferrara and Allsop, 1991.)

In addition to tracking polls, the Wirthlin Group conducted approximately eight focus groups for Hill and Knowlton and the Kuwaitis, including one group of between thirty and forty subjects who watched a series of videos (e.g., interviews and news coverage from CNN and *Nightline*) while their reactions to both spokespersons and messages were monitored electronically. Wirthlin also piggy-backed Kuwait-related questions on its quarterly Congressional Omnibus survey of Capitol Hill staffers in October, and followed up with a special survey of top staffers in December. Finally, again in December, the firm conducted the first of what was intended to become a series of studies of school-children's attitudes toward Kuwait. The objective here was to attract media interest, but by then there was more Kuwait-related action in other news venues, and, in any event, the contract was terminated shortly afterward.

Analysis

A key question in the present essay is the extent to which Hill and Knowlton's efforts in behalf of Kuwait accord with, or differ from, the more general knowledge base developed in earlier research. It is not possible to answer that question definitively, but we are able to note several points of convergence.

First, the literature tells us that strategic communicators will employ systematically the theory and tools of social science to manage client images in much the manner these same techniques are used in domestic political campaigns. Fitz-Pegado disclaims any such knowledge base for herself other than that of an area specialist, saying that she focuses instead on the particular circumstances and perspectives of each client. In addition to Middle East area specialists, however, the team of twenty professionals she assembled to serve the Kuwaitis included economists, media-relations specialists, foreign-policy experts, foreign-aid experts, health-policy specialists, and, of course, pollsters. And in addition to the daily tracking surveys, message development was based on a series of focus-group sessions conducted in various locations around the country. Speakers were selected and placed based on the results of these group sessions, with Kuwaiti women and the wives of American hostages sent to some locations, men and "business types" elsewhere. Frank Mankiewicz characterized the media effort as operating at the "wholesale rather than the retail" level, but messages were targeted differentially to, for example, the black press and the labor press. Clearly, this was more than a "seat-of-the-pants" operation.

Second, the literature tells us that public affairs consultants will focus on themes they believe will resonate among the target audience. Here, the initial theme was that Kuwait was the most open and democratic society in the Persian Gulf region. In addition to the emphasis noted above on women's rights, in this early phase of the campaign Hill and Knowlton pointed to the high percentage of its gross national product that Kuwait had been providing as foreign assistance to Third World countries, and focused on the client's commitment to democratic values and institutions, a theme which has been shown elsewhere to have specific persuasive value.

The tracking surveys showed no trend in the level of support for the Kuwaiti government (recall that the government was not, ostensibly, the client) through the period; it remained steady at just under 60 percent. But in mid-September, the focus groups yielded some important information. They showed that the public reacted, not to the themes of democracy and human rights in Kuwait, but to Saddam Hussein. The focus-group data made clear that the critical factor was response to Saddam as the enemy, while Kuwait was merely a symbol of his atrocities. To Allsop and others working on the contract, who set out initially with some fifty prospective messages from which they sought to cull those that reinforced what people were already feeling, this suggested a two-track strategy. The primary theme was to be designed to reinforce anti-Saddam sentiment. The initial themes portraying Kuwait as pro-Western, a U.S. ally, and a progressive country, were to be accorded secondary, supporting status. Research then turned to finding the best media for this message combination.

Though the Kuwaitis did not seem especially to like the advice they were receiving, they did accept it, and emphasis on the victimization theme was increased. In this regard, Hill and Knowlton helped their client to avoid one potential pitfall of such a theme by specifically and repeatedly advising them to eschew talking in public about what the United States government should do in response to the crisis. This advice was generally followed, though the Kuwaiti ambassador to the U.S. did make some public statements that were more direct.

Third, the literature tells us that image consultants will vary their strategy depending on the extant characteristics of the client's image. With respect to specific cues associated with Kuwait and the Gulf, we have already seen evidence of this phenomenon. In addition, some research suggests that visibility-raising informational campaigns are likely to prove most viable where there is low public ego-identification or involvement with a given image object but where general public sentiment is favorable. In the present instance, Frank Mankiewicz characterized the initial condition as being low in involvement when he described the Hill and Knowlton effort as disseminating "information in a void as a basis for Americans to form opinions," and the Wirthlin polling data showed a substantial level of popular support for the Kuwaiti government. There is no direct evidence from our interviews that the staff of Hill and Knowlton were operating from an explicit awareness of the social scientific knowledge base in this area when serving the Kuwaiti account. To the contrary, they describe their actions as grounded in their many years of experience. But if not theory-*driven*, it does appear that, at the least, they were behaving in a manner consistent with theory-*grounded* predictions, and a significant increase in December in popular support for U.S. military action may constitute evidence of their effectiveness.

Fourth, the literature on persuasion suggests that attitudes can best be created or influenced where the new or discrepant message displays thematic consistency. In the present instance, we know that several interests were represented in the communication environment, and that diverse messages were being distributed. Any one of them might be rendered more effective if reinforced by another, apparently independent source.

With that in mind, it is worth noting that, one week before Iraq's invasion of Kuwait, Hill and Knowlton had merged with the consulting firm of Wexler, Reynolds, Fuller, Harrison and Schule. As part of the arrangement, Craig Fuller assumed leadership of the Hill and Knowlton Washington operation. He began his new duties the very week that Iraq invaded Kuwait, a fact that Gray and Mankiewicz may have communicated to the Kuwaiti ambassador during their initial visit. Craig Fuller's principal claim to fame was his long service as chief of staff to the then vice president of the United States, George Bush. After Fuller left the government, when Bush chose John Sununu to head his presidential staff, he maintained his ties to the White House to the extent that he was tapped to organize the 1992 Republican National Convention that renominated his former boss. More to the point, throughout the period in question he frequently visited the White House to discuss political strategy. This provided a unique opportunity for a coordinated communication effort, one which Fuller later told a *60 Minutes* audience he did try to facilitate. As he put it on another occasion, "Getting [the Kuwaitis'] message across was completely in line with the goals of the Bush administration. By helping the Kuwaiti citizens, it was clear we would be helping the Bush administration" (Mufson 1992, 29).

Finally, in addition to the points summarized above, the literature also tells us that the effectiveness of a strategic communication campaign will be reduced, or its effects perhaps reversed, if the effort itself becomes the object of public controversy. In this case, the nature and extent of the communication campaign—and the controversy associated with the Nayirah testimony and other of its aspects—did not become widely known until after the objectives of the campaign had been achieved, so any penalties would necessarily be imposed in some secondary arena. It is impossible to do more than speculate on what those penalties might be, but it is tempting to argue that growing doubt about President Bush's motives in the Gulf was at least nurtured by increased public, media, and elite awareness and resentment of the communication effort, and that the subsequent and very marked decline in the fortunes of Hill and Knowlton's Washington office—which included declining revenues, downsizing of staff, and the very public departure of important clients and staff (Anonymous 1992; Lee 1992)—were hastened by the blow to the firm's credibility that was dealt to it in the aftermath of the Gulf conflict.

Hill and Knowlton's association with Citizens for a Free Kuwait ended in January 1991, before the eventual U.S.-led counterstrike and liberation. As Hill and Knowlton sees it, the company's effort to educate both its client and the American people succeeded. The Kuwaitis' perceptions of Americans changed, their political sophistication increased, and over time they were able to do more on their own, and support for eventual U.S. military action was generated. As some Kuwaitis saw it at the time, however, they were paying a great deal of money and getting little in return (Matlack 1991, 1159). Whichever view one takes, it is clear that the public-relations effort continued long after the contract with Hill and Knowlton was terminated, coming more and more under the direct control of the Kuwaiti government as its authority was progressively reasserted. By May 1991, Kuwait had contracts with four U.S. public-relations firms, and by June the government had in place an elaborate effort to show Americans the extent of the country's devastation, a plan which included travel to Kuwait by commerce secretary Robert Mosbacher, federal and state officials, congressmen, and business executives, variously paid for by the Kuwaiti government, its embassy in Washington, and even, at the Kuwaitis' request, such U.S. companies as Fluor Corporation, which had extensive interests in the region (Anonymous, 1991a, 1991c; Auerbach, 1991).

References

Albritton, R. B., and J. B. Manheim. 1983. "News of Rhodesia: The Impact of a Public Relations Campaign." *Journalism Quarterly* 60: 622–28.
———. 1985. "Public Relations Efforts for the Third World: Images in the News." *Journal of Communication* 35: 43–59.
Amaize, O., and R. J. Faber. 1983. "Advertising by National Governments in Leading United States, Indian and British Newspapers." *Gazette* 32: 87–101.
Anderson, R. 1989. "The Reagan Administration and Nicaragua: The Use of Public Diplomacy to Influence Media Coverage and Public Opinion." Paper

presented at the Annual Meeting of the Speech Communication Association, San Francisco.

Anonymous. 1991a. "Nine Firms Working for Kuwait; Big $ to Rendon, Neill, CGS&H." *O'Dwyer's FARA Report* 1 (March): 1–2. New York: J. R. O'Dwyer.

———. 1991b. "Hill and Knowlton's Six-Month FARA Fees Hit $14.2 Million." *O'Dwyer's FARA Report* 1 (July): 1–2. New York: J. R. O'Dwyer.

———. 1991c. "Kuwait Awards PR to Keene, Shirley." *O'Dwyer's FARA Report* 1 (July): 1. New York: J. R. O'Dwyer.

———. 1992. "H&K's FARA Fees Plunge as Work for Kuwaiti Citizens Group Ends." *O'Dwyer's Washington Report* 2 (February): 1, 4–5.

Auerbach, S. 1991. "Kuwaitis Paid for Mosbacher Trip." *Washington Post,* June 5, p. A13.

Choate, P. 1990. *Agents of Influence.* New York: Alfred A. Knopf.

Cohen, R. 1987. *Theatre of Power: The Art of Diplomatic Signalling.* London: Longman.

Cushman, J. H., Jr. 1992. "U.S. Offers Proof of Iraqi Atrocity." *New York Times,* February 6, p. A11.

Davis, M. 1977. *Interpreters for Nigeria: The Third World and International Public Relations.* Urbana: University of Illinois Press.

Davison, W. P. 1974. "News Media and International Negotiation." *Public Opinion Quarterly* 38: 174–93.

Festinger, L. 1957. *A Theory of Cognitive Dissonance.* Evanston: Row, Peterson.

Fisher, G. H. 1972. *Public Diplomacy and the Behavioral Sciences.* Bloomington: Indiana University Press.

———. 1987. *American Communication in a Global Society.* Revised edition. Norwood, N.J.: Ablex.

Green, F. 1988. *American Propaganda Abroad: From Benjamin Franklin to Ronald Reagan.* New York: Hippocrene Books.

Hill and Knowlton. 1990. "Facts and History." Corporate brochure.

———. N.d. "International Public Affairs: The Power of Communication." Corporate materials.

Hoffman, A. S., ed. 1968. *International Communication and the New Diplomacy.* Bloomington: Indiana University Press.

Hovland, C. I., A. A. Lumsdaine, and F. D. Sheffield. 1949. *Experiments on Mass Communication.* Vol. 3. New York: John Wiley and Sons.

Institute of Communications Research. 1955. *Four Working Papers on Propaganda Theory.* Urbana: University of Illinois.

Krauss, C. 1992. "Congressman Says Girl Was Credible." *New York Times,* January 12, p. A11.

Kriesel, M. E. 1985. "Psychological Operations: A Strategic View." In *Essays on Strategy: Selections from the 1984 Joint Chiefs of Staff Essay Competition.* Washington: National Defense University Press.

Lee, A. M. 1952. *How to Understand Propaganda.* New York: Rinehart and Company.

Lee, G. 1992. "PR Firm Loses Bid to Curb Ex-Employees." *Washington Post,* September 25, p. F1–2.

Malone, G. D. 1988. *Political Advocacy and Cultural Communication: Organizing the Nation's Public Diplomacy.* Lanham, Md.: University Press of America.

MANAGING KUWAIT'S IMAGE   147

Manheim, J. B. 1987. "A Model of Agenda Dynamics." In Margaret L. McLaughlin, ed., *Communication Yearbook 10*. Beverly Hills: Sage, pp. 499–516.

———. 1988. "Political Culture and Political Communication: Implications for U.S.-Korean Relations." Paper presented at the Annual Meeting of the American Political Science Association, Washington, D.C.

———. 1990a. "Rites of Passage: The 1988 Seoul Olympics as Public Diplomacy." *Western Political Quarterly*: 279–95.

———. 1990b. "Coming to America: Head-of-State Visits as Public Diplomacy." Paper presented at the Annual Meeting of the International Communication Association, Dublin, Ireland.

———. 1990c. "'Democracy' as International Public Relations." Paper presented at the Annual Meeting of the American Political Science Association, San Francisco.

———. 1991a. *All of the People, All the Time: Strategic Communication and American Politics*. Armonk: M. E. Sharpe.

———. 1991b. "Image Making as an Instrument of Power: The Representation of Foreign Interests in the United States." Paper presented at the Annual Meeting of the International Communication Association, Chicago.

———. 1993. "The War of Images: Strategic Communication in the Gulf Conflict." In Stanley Renshon, ed., *Political Psychology of the Gulf War*. Pittsburgh: University of Pittsburgh Press, pp. 155–71.

Manheim, J. B., and R. B. Albritton. 1984. "Changing National Images: International Public Relations and Media Agenda Setting." *American Political Science Review* 78: 641–54.

———. 1986. "Public Relations in the Public Eye: Two Case Studies of the Failure of Public Information Campaigns." *Political Communication and Persuasion* 3: 265–91.

———. 1987. "Insurgent Violence Versus Image Management: The Struggle for National Images in Southern Africa." *British Journal of Political Science* 17: 201–18.

Matlack, C. 1991. "Dead in the Water?" *National Journal*, May 18, pp. 1156–160.

McGuire, W. J. 1964. "Inducing Resistance to Persuasion: Some Contemporary Approaches." In L. Berkowitz, ed., *Advances in Experimental Social Psychology*. Vol. 1, pp. 191–229. New York: Academic Press.

Merritt, R. L. 1980. "Transforming International Communications Strategies." *Political Communication and Persuasion* 1: 5–42.

Mufson, S. 1992. "The Privatization of Craig Fuller." *Washington Post Magazine*, August 2, pp. 14–19, 26–31.

Pfau and Kenski. 1990. *Attack Politics: Strategy and Defense*. New York: Praeger.

Priest, D. 1992a. "Kuwait Baby-Killing Report Disputed." *Washington Post*, February 7, p. A17.

———. 1992b. "Report Faults Iraqis in Babies' Death." *Washington Post*, June 30, p. A14.

Saunders, H. 1988. "'Us and Them'—Building Mature International Relationships: The Role of Official and Supplemental Diplomacy." Presentation before the University Seminar in Political Psychology, The George Washington University, Washington, D.C., April 11.

Signitzer, B., and T. Coombs. 1991. "Public Relations and Public Diplomacy: Conceptual Convergences." *Public Relations Review* 17: 137–47.

Smith, A. 1980. *The Geopolitics of Information: How Western Culture Dominates the World.* New York: Oxford University Press.

Strong, M. 1992. "Portions of the Gulf War Were Brought to You by the Folks at Hill and Knowlton." *TV Guide,* February 22, pp. 11–13.

Tuch, H. N. 1990. *Communicating with the World: U.S. Public Diplomacy Overseas.* New York: St. Martin's Press.

United States General Accounting Office. 1979. *The Public Diplomacy of Other Countries: Implications for the United States.* Washington, D.C.: Government Printing Office.

United States House of Representatives. 1977. *Public Diplomacy and the Future.* Hearings before the Subcommittee on International Operations of the Committee on International Relations. Washington, D.C.: Government Printing Office.

———. 1987. *Oversight of Public Diplomacy.* Hearings before the Subcommittee on International Operations of the Committee on Foreign Affairs. Washington, D.C.: Government Printing Office.

Wilcox, C., J. Ferrara, and D. Allsop. 1991. "Before the Rally: The Dynamics of Attitudes Toward the Gulf Crisis Before the War." Paper presented at the Annual Meeting of the American Political Science Association, Washington, D.C.

Persons Interviewed

Allsop, Dee T., Vice President for Communications/Marketing Research, The Wirthlin Group.

Fitz-Pegado, Lauri J., Senior Vice President and Managing Director, International Public Affairs Division, Hill and Knowlton Public Affairs Worldwide.

Mankiewicz, Frank, Vice Chairman and Managing Director, Public Affairs, Hill and Knowlton Public Affairs Worldwide.

seven

Daniel C. Hallin and
Todd Gitlin

The Gulf War as Popular Culture and Television Drama

It is a commonplace of opinion research that the public does not much care about foreign policy. There is, however, one very dramatic exception: war. No political event inspires more public interest or emotion than war. This is why, if war is "the health of the state," it is also the health of the news media, at least in terms of audience size. During the Gulf War twenty of the twenty-five largest newspapers had circulation gains.[1] On television, to give a few examples, CNN had an 11.7 prime-time rating January 15–21, higher than the network ratings and better than ten times normal;[2] for the morning news shows, meanwhile, ratings were up about 15 percent a few weeks into the war, and these normally entertainment-oriented shows stayed with heavy coverage of the war into the February sweeps period.[3] And when local stations in Buffalo, New York, interrupted daytime programming for repeated live coverage of homecomings of Gulf troops, we were told, it was the first time they hadn't gotten calls complaining about soap operas being canceled.

War, moreover, is more than a news story. It is genuinely a part of popular culture in a way that politics rarely is, at least in the contemporary United States. This is manifested in participatory political activities—flying the flag, wearing yellow ribbons, giving blood, attending rallies, and forming support groups of various kinds. It can also be seen, more prosaically, in the proliferation of products through which people participate symbolically in the war: T-shirts, bumper stickers, games and toys, and a host of more exotic consumer items, from crayons to condoms.[4] Media which are not normally concerned with politics make an exception for war, from "Entertainment Tonight" to *People* magazine. And once the war is over, the media put out "Commemorative" or "Collector's" editions and videos.[5]

War is one of the few political activities in which ordinary people participate directly. The modern state drew the masses into political life in two distinct ways. It conceded them the right to vote, of course. It also mobilized them for war. The "Rights of Man and Citizen" is one side of the legacy of the French Revolution; the *levée en masse*, the citizen army and the total mobilization of society to support it, is the other side (Dyer 1985; Kerber 1990). Ordinary people care about war, even a distant one like the Gulf War, because their families and communities are disrupted and the lives of their sons and daughters are at stake. At the same time, common people take center stage in political life: they can die, but they can also become heroes. Even those at home are called upon to sacrifice and are offered the opportunity to become heroes, as the home front is integrated into the war effort. As modern political life has lost the kind of mass mobilization that once characterized electoral politics, the experience of participation in war, actual or vicarious, is now essentially unique.

People care about war because they have a clear stake in it—the lives of their neighbors or loved ones. But something else, less "rational" is also involved: imagination is as important as interest. War is an enormously appealing symbolic terrain, a source of images and stories that can be extremely seductive to its audience—and certainly also to those who are in the business of selling images and stories. The fact that war involves ordinary people in a contest of epic proportions and ultimate consequence interacts with the populism of journalism, especially television journalism, with its hunger precisely for stories that concern the lives and feelings of ordinary people and yet have implications for the entire community. To those who make the decision to engage in it, war is above all a political policy. But the mass public, and the media that address that public, relate to it primarily in very different terms, as an arena of individual and national self-expression.

We need to say a little at the outset about what it means to approach the subject of television and the war as a phenomenon of popular culture. In the pages that follow, we will be looking at television coverage of the war in some detail, down to the level of analyzing individual phrases of narration and the lighting of video shots. To someone interested in the effect of the media on public opinion, all this may at first glance seem trivial, since none of it is likely to be a very powerful predictor of public-opinion variables toward the war. If we want to account statistically for support or opposition, a simple count of favorable or unfavorable stories, or perhaps of the number of sound bites for and against the war, is likely to be adequate, and anything more subtle is not going to add significantly to the variance explained.

From the point of view of cultural analysis, on the other hand, we have explained little until we know what the war means to those who support or oppose it, and how its meanings are interpreted and circulated by the media. This is not simply a matter of empathy, or anything so "soft-headed." The assumption behind this perspective is that people's responses to the world, whether it is the response of a citizen rallying to the war effort, donning a yellow ribbon and telling a pollster he or she supports the war, or of a journalist selecting one shot or another, are structured by a framework of meanings which define war as noble or ignoble, opposition as an exercise of political judgment or a breach of community loyalty, and so on. In pushing our analysis of television content beyond the kinds of variables most useful for predicting public opinion as measured by surveys, we are trying not to broaden but to deepen our understanding of the opinion-formation process: that is, we are not trying to add additional predictors, but to connect responses of support or opposition to the enduring frameworks of meaning in which they are anchored.

In its early days the study of public opinion and political communication was often concerned with "nonrational" elements in political life (e.g., Adorno et al. 1950; Lane 1959; Lasswell 1960). The trend in recent years has been toward rational-choice theory and information-processing approaches. These have been extremely productive in many ways. But it seems to us that in the case of war it becomes particularly clear that they leave a good deal unexplained. In a sense, we are arguing for a return to the kind of concern with "nonrational" elements of political meaning that characterized an earlier generation of scholarship. Our approach is different from that of the earlier generation mainly in that we approach political meaning more from the point of view of culture than individual psychology.

Our analysis here will be mostly interpretive rather than causal. This is not, however, because we believe that causal and interpretive understandings of the social world are mutually exclusive, or that cultural analysis excludes causal explanation. And from time to time we will try to clarify the complex network of reciprocal causation that clearly is involved in the relations among the news media, the public, the government, and other actors. In particular, we will try to show that in an event like the Gulf War, in which public opinion moves strongly in one direction, there is a powerful "backflow" of influence onto those we normally think of as the shapers of public opinion.

For the most part, however, causal analysis would require data of a sort that a single case study cannot provide. If American television were organized differently, and thus had reported the war differently, would public opinion have developed in a different way? Perhaps, but we will never know for sure, and only comparative data might give us some approximation to an answer. We will end by speculating about the effect of Gulf coverage, not on public opinion during the war itself, but on something that seems to us ultimately more significant: the society's understanding of the meaning of war.

This study covers network evening news and CNN coverage of the Gulf during the period of the actual fighting, roughly from the January 15, 1991, deadline until a few days after the fighting stopped. It also covers local news in two markets for which extensive material was available to us: Buffalo and Chicago. We did a quantitative content analysis of part of this material, seventy-five broadcasts from the period from January 14 to March 2, selected from among the three network evening news shows, miscellaneous CNN time periods (mostly from 6 to 7 or 10 to 11 P.M. Eastern time), and the 6:00 P.M. broadcasts of the three Buffalo stations. The sample was constructed by selecting two broadcasts randomly from each date, though in some cases missing material forced us to substitute an adjacent date or drop a particular date. We also did a number of interviews, particularly with personnel from the Buffalo stations. Buffalo is of course only one among many local markets. But from what we have seen of coverage in other local markets and from comments of other scholars on our analysis of the Buffalo coverage, we believe it is reasonably representative of local news across the country.

War, as we have argued, can be seen as both a political policy and an expressive activity. Television coverage of the Gulf War, especially at the network level, included both elements. The second, however, heavily outweighed the first: in our sample, about 20 percent of the stories could be described as political reporting, by a fairly generous definition. In the discussion that follows we will set aside television's coverage of the war as a political story, and look specifically at war as popular culture. We will organize the discussion around two major themes in television's portrayal of the Gulf War, war as an agon—a contest and a job—and war as ritual, creating and celebrating community solidarity.

Agon

War is the ultimate expression of "purposive-rational" action: that form of human activity that involves the rational mobilization of means to achieve a given end. It was one of the first human activities to be submitted to reason in this sense: one of the first professions to develop its knowledge and practice in a systematic way, and a key testing ground of new technology and also of social organization—of techniques for organizing large numbers of human beings to accomplish collective ends (McNeill 1982). There are other great social enterprises that approach war as an expression of purposive-rational action—the landing of a man on the moon, for example—but none seem to have quite the drama of war.

Perhaps this is related to the abstractness of war's end. Wars are fought for concrete political reasons. But these are often forgotten quickly enough, and the goal of war becomes simply to win, to defeat the other great social enterprise to which one is opposed. This is related to the fact that the means of war is killing, and whatever its political purpose may have been, the means in a sense turns into the end for those directly involved: war becomes a struggle for the ultimate end, to preserve one's life. In the abstractness or purity of its aim, namely, to win, war is like sport, another activity which has enormous potential to capture the human imagination. But war is grander in scale, and has the added mystery of being real. War is the most dramatic expression of the human ability to exercise power, to bend the world to our will.

For television, the Gulf War was above all a story of American prowess: a story of the firmness of American leaders, the potency of American technology, and the bravery, determination, and skill of American soldiers. It was the story of a job well done. Several key elements of television's presentation of the war are related to this theme.

First, television presented the war as a personalized contest between Saddam Hussein, on the one side, and George Bush and the Americans generally, on the other. Two quotations from NBC news give some sense of the importance of the personal figure of Hussein to the narrative structure of the war story. The day of the U.N. deadline, the NBC broadcast began with images of Iraqi crowds and then an American soldier expressing his determination; anchor Tom Brokaw then said, "Good evening. Two men, one in Washington and one in Baghdad, backed by two mighty military machines, are now in a short countdown to a showdown. . . ." The day the war ended, Brokaw began the broadcast, "His men and military machines crushed, Saddam Hussein finally surrenders. . . ."

Second, television focused heavily on the skill and character, the "toughness and stamina" (NBC), of the American soldiers. "Our top story tonight: They don't call them Top Guns for nothing," began the anchor at WBBM, the CBS station in Chicago. "From the pilots of B-52s carpet bombing Iraqi desert troops [video: closeup of B-52s flying in formation] to the red-hot fighter pilots scoring a big victory tonight, America is winning the aerial battle." Not every story was so melodramatic. But virtually all reporting on the troops emphasized their skill and sense of purpose. Here it is important to keep in mind the situation of the soldier at war. Many American soldiers, like Americans at home, had doubts about the war as a political policy. But when the war actually began, it is not surprising that they put aside these doubts to focus on doing their job as well as they could; to a large extent, of course, their lives depended on doing just this. To the extent that television adopted the point of view of the soldiers, therefore, it too tended to dismiss both political doubts and moral qualms. A number of stories explicitly con-trasted the soldiers, "just doing their jobs," with the protesters at home.

To the rank-and-file soldier, war is a job. To the military planner, it is a science. Like the soldier, the military planner puts aside most thoughts of torn flesh and of political ends to focus on the rational application of force to defeat the enemy. The technical perspective of the military plan-ner was a third prominent element of television coverage. It entered the reporting in several ways. First, there was heavy coverage of military briefings. (One striking difference between coverage of the Vietnam and Gulf wars, is that the military briefing in Saigon only made the evening news three times between 1965 and 1975 [Lawrence W. Lichty, per-sonal communication].) During the Gulf War, with access to the front limited both by military restrictions and by the technological nature of the war, journalists had few other sources of information, and the brief-ings became the center of war coverage.) Second, each network retained as consultants military specialists who could provide analysis of strategy and tactics. Finally, the journalists themselves often took up the techni-cal point of view. "Good evening," Tom Brokaw began, introducing the NBC evening news for February 12, "From the air, sea and with artillery they pounded Iraqi troops and armor concentrations in Southern Kuwait for three hours. It was the real thing, yet it was also a useful test of the complexities of mounting an all-out attack with so many forces from many different nations." In this respect, war coverage is not unlike election coverage, with its emphasis on strategic "game-plans" (Hallin 1992).

Finally, in this technological war, the machines were no less central as "characters" of the television drama than the soldiers. They were in fact often spoken of as if they were human actors: "Hailed as one of the first heroes in the Gulf War, [the Patriot missile] uses quick thinking to out-smart the enemy" (CNN, January 22). And an analysis of the visual im-ages in our sample showed that images of technology dominated the visual representation of the conflict, taking up to 17 percent of total television time, considerably more than any other major category. Images of soldiers (including officers but not top military officials), took up about 11 percent of TV time. The technologies employed in the Gulf War were in fact impressive, even if they were not so infallible as they were presented at the time. And it is probably not surprising that they left the journalists "wide-eyed," as CNN anchor David French put it. French proclaimed himself "wide-eyed" after being "honored" with a ride in an F-15E, a most successful photo opportunity for the air force (CNN, January 18). And of course these technologies were also extraordinary visual material for television.

The Gulf War looked quite different from an ordinary news event. In part, this was because of the unusual sense of power conveyed by the images—the armor surging forward, the F-15E thrusting into the air with afterburners glowing, the sixteen-inch guns of the battleship *Wisconsin* belching fire. But there was something else distinctive about many of these images: they were beautiful. Turn off the sound, look at the visual texture of most evening news, and you will notice that it changes sharply between the news and the commercials. The commercials have a kind of beauty, a romantic or awesome quality, that the news normally doesn't. During the Gulf War, however, the separation between the news and the commercials was much less clear. Probably the most striking similarity was in the lighting. One of the things that gives the images in commercials their romantic quality is strong backlighting, often with a light source shining from behind the scene into the eye of the viewer. Many of the scenes in Gulf War coverage were lit in this way. One of the most common images was that of the fighter-bomber taking off or landing at sunrise or sunset; 38 percent of film reports from Saudia Arabia had at least one such image.

It has been a common assumption since the Vietnam War that television changes the experience of war because it shows literally the horror of combat. This is not borne out by research on Vietnam coverage, which was far less bloody than is often assumed (Hallin 1986). Television has always been reluctant to risk offending viewers or advertisers by showing graphic footage of war. In any case, the Gulf War shows us something very different: that television has the capacity to aestheticize war. It did this by dramatizing the war, with the narrative of a confrontation between good and evil personified and many devices that gave war coverage far more the character of a show than an ordinary news broadcast—logos, and music, for instance, combined in dramatic openings like those quoted above. And it did it by emphasizing images that conveyed awe and beauty. In this way, TV journalists linked their occupational taste for visual narrative with the society's deep longing and appreciation for affirmative ritual.

Community

We have seen how the networks began their coverage of the Gulf War, with the story line of a confrontation between Saddam Hussein and George Bush and their "mighty military machines." Now we turn to local television. The day after the war began, for example, following reports on how people cope with the tensions of war and on an antiwar protest, anchor Irv Chapman of ABC-affiliate WKBW in Buffalo observed:

> There is no question that the Persian Gulf War is tearing at the very fiber of our nation. The feeling of suddenly being on the brink of war without quite being certain how or why we got to this point. The divisions of opinion about the Gulf crisis can be seen not only in our big cities, but in the smaller communities as well.

The story, reported from a small town near Buffalo, with a graphic saying, "Your Town U.S.A.," showed people in a diner "debating the only real issue of the day."

The last story on the broadcast that day focused on the display of flags and ribbons. "Red, white, and blue are not the only colors patriotic Americans are showing these days," Chapman said introducing that story. And the reporter continued, "Americans may question this country's involvement in the Middle East, but if flag sales are any indication, one thing there is no question of is this country's level of patriotism." The story began and ended with audio of Lee Greenwood's, "God Bless the U.S.A." Then the anchor signed off by indicating to the audience that the news staff, too, "all have our colors on"—all were wearing yellow ribbons.

Television news, especially at the local level, is centrally concerned with community. As Phyllis Kaniss has pointed out (1991), this is in part an economic imperative for local news, which needs to create a symbolic sense of common interest which will unify the fragmented metropolitan news audience. Perhaps, too, it reflects a general cultural yearning in a society characterized most of the time by individualism and fragmentation. It is very common for the news media, above all local TV news, to focus on events or activities that "bring people together"—the effort to aid victims of a natural disaster, for example, or poignant tragedy that becomes a focus of collective empathy. For local TV news, the Gulf War was above all the story of a threat to the solidarity of the community, and eventually, a celebration of community spirit. This theme was present in network news as well, but was far more prominent at the local level.

On the eve of the war, at a time when the public was about equally divided on whether to fight, the primary focus in local coverage was on that division, and there was considerably more coverage of dissent and domestic debate on local than on national broadcasts, the national news having gone on to the "military matchup."

Within a few days, however, the focus shifted from debate to consensus: one might say that the war was shifted from the secular to the sacred realm. The rallying of the community behind the troops and the flag became the primary story for local news, and the journalists celebrated that rallying as a manifestation of community spirit: "I've said it before," said the anchor of WKBW as he signed off (January 17), "we are the city of good neighbors."

In Buffalo, the anchors of two of the three network affiliates donned yellow ribbons. WGRZ also wrapped the anchor desk in a huge yellow ribbon, put an American flag on the set behind the anchors, and from January 18 ended each show with a posed shot of people—usually children—waving American flags, and a graphic saying, "Colors of Freedom." It also adopted a logo for the opening of the broadcast with a still of a soldier and the words: "When Your Country Calls: America at War." Many stations promoted support-the-troop efforts they had a hand in organizing, usually called Operation Something (since war had become the nation's model for collective action), e.g., Operation Yellow Ribbon, which WGRZ helped organize to assist families of servicemen. When you came to donate you could "meet Channel 2 personnel." The news was full of stories about what "you can do" to help the war effort, and about "home-town heroes" organizing support for the troops.

The Journalist and the Public

In order to understand what is going on here we need to raise the question of the journalist's relation to the public. It is clear that this relation is at least as important to understanding television and the Gulf War as is the relation with elite actors more traditionally explored by research on media and foreign policy. Journalists were clearly responding to strong sentiments at the grass-roots level, and had relationships at this level just as complex and significant as the relationships with elite sources which scholars have examined so extensively.

It is also clear that it is not adequate to say that television "reflected" public opinion, if this is meant as something passive or neutral. Television certainly did not simply report that Americans were for the most part rallying to support the troops, the President, and Operation Desert Storm. It celebrated and identified with this rallying; this was a "sphere of consensus" event in which the conventions of "objectivity" were for the most part set aside.

In part, the effect of public opinion on Gulf War reporting was felt negatively. Journalists, especially at the national level, commonly refer to hostile reactions from viewers when they stepped outside the consensus in support of Desert Storm. But the bandwagon effect during the Gulf War was really more positive than negative: it was a tendency to get "swept away" or "carried away"—phrases that occurred again and again in our interviews—by the tides of public opinion, rather than simply fear of going against them. "Everything was so pro-American," said Stacey Roder, executive producer at WGRZ, Buffalo. "You couldn't *buy* a yellow ribbon in this town. . . . This community came together like I've never seen it before. . . . It's very easy to get caught up in that." To an extent, this can be seen as a promotional stance. Just as retailers liked to be involved in Desert Storm hoopla because "it's strengthening their ties to the community,"[6] so the local stations found the war an excellent promotional opportunity, and were involved in activities like Operation Yellow Ribbon or an initiative by the Promotions Department at WKBW Buffalo to take cameras to local malls, offering residents an opportunity to tape messages to the troops.

Television's involvement in the "rally effect," however, cannot be understood as something purely instrumental. It is also clear that television journalists often developed close relationships with the people directly involved in the war who were their main characters, and that these relationships were compelling and rewarding for them. Local television often served as a conduit for private communication between soldiers and their families. In Buffalo, for example, around Christmas, the air force flew crews from all three local stations to the Gulf area to report on a local reserve unit, the 914th Tactical Air Group. WGRZ personnel carried things to soldiers in the Gulf from their families, produced a video Christmas card, with footage of a base Christmas party, stories of support activities, and highlights of Bills football games to show to the troops, then filmed video Christmas cards from the troops to show to families back home.

Local television also served as an important means by which family members could express themselves publicly during the war. If war allows ordinary citizens to be heroes in a way that is not normally possible, this is true largely through the media. We heard many stories, for example, of families, sometimes even families of soldiers killed in action, contacting local stations on their own initiative to offer to speak or to offer video cassettes. When local TV people talk about calls and letters from viewers, they often stress positive rather than negative calls: people calling to offer video material, to promote a support activity, to respond to initiatives like Operation Yellow Ribbon or to ask how they can help.

The closeness of the journalists' relationship with the families, especially, meant that local coverage was largely centered around their perspective. The families served in the coverage as a synecdoche for the community. Buffalo news personnel whom we interviewed emphasized the importance of being sensitive to the feelings of the families, and cited their concerns in discussing the news agenda. Rich Kellman, for example, an anchor at WGRZ, asked by us whether journalists had an obligation when covering a war to maintain the customary professional distance from the story, said:

> You're always facing the problem of when you become complicit. In war it's compounded because you're dealing with emotions, fears people have. You have to evaluate government statements critically. On the other hand, you have to give comfort to people. . . . People depend on us as neighbors. [They] don't see the distance. You have an obligation not to be cavalier with their feelings.

And Fred DeSousa of WKBW said, "The most basic question of the war, as far as I was concerned, was whether my son or my dad or whoever is going to come home alive. . . . Not the politics. Families don't care about the politics."[7]

Finally, the relationship local journalists had with the families made the war in many ways a positive experience for them. A number of journalists told us about letters they had gotten months after the war, or hugs upon seeing people once again, thanking them for their kindness in helping with these kinds of activities. "This was one of the few occasions," WGRZ producer Stacey Roder told us, when journalism felt like much more than a job, "when you felt you made a difference in people's lives. . . . You did something that made people feel better."

War as Ritual

"People in the community search for meaning," said WGRZ anchor Rich Kellman. "Local TV serves as a local psychotherapist or priest or rabbi.

Help people give meaning to events: that's how I saw my role as anchor. What you're doing is active listening, you take what people are saying and interpret it, amplify it." The analogy with religion is quite apt. The war became a ritual of what Durkheim called civil religion, affirming the unity of the community. The journalists' function in covering this sort of story is essentially a priestly one: they are not expected to stand back from consensus, to be objective, but to celebrate. Like all rituals, the war required participation; everyone was expected to be involved, and the journalists both emphasized "what you can do" and made it clear that they too were "involved." Like all rituals, the war was treated as an affair of the "heart" more than of the "head": the emphasis was on people's feelings. Finally, like other rituals, symbols were crucial to the experience.

Perhaps the most revealing evidence that religious analogy is applicable to Gulf War reporting is the fact that the symbols of patriotism most directly connected to the war were typically treated in the news as interchangeable with symbols of religion in the traditional sense. So one journalist introduced a report on the National Day of Prayer proclaimed by the president by saying, "Chicagoans raised their voices in a patriotic tribute to our troops in the Gulf (WBBM, February 3)." And in a story on WKBW, Buffalo (January 17), on local residents using "surface-to-air prayer," the reporter said: "American patriotism is at an all-time high. Many people are turning to God." As she said "American patriotism," the visual was a tight shot of a crucifix. The camera then pulled back, as she said "many people are turning to God," to show a flag on the wall next to the crucifix. Images of people praying took up about 5 percent of television time on the Buffalo stations.

Kellman, after comparing the journalist to a priest or rabbi, added that news could be seen as myth. And indeed, what literary theorist Philip Wheelwright (1965, 159) once wrote about the mythopoeic consciousness applies strongly to Gulf War coverage:

> there is a strong tendency of the different experiential elements to blend and fuse in a non-logical way. And not only that, but the self-hood of the worshipper tends to blend with them; that is to say, he becomes a full participant, not a mere observer.

Conclusion

The nation's rallying to the Gulf War and the media's amplification of it transcended by far the language and motives of politics in the strict

sense. Political justifications for the war were expressed, mostly center-
ing around the persona of Saddam Hussein and the analogy between
Hussein and Hitler. But once the war was on, these were largely mar-
ginal to public discourse. For the most part, in fact, all the participants in
that discourse, soldiers, families, military briefers, ordinary citizens, and,
not least, journalists, were expending considerable effort to separate
their feeling about the war from the mundane and contentious realm of
politics. This may be in part because the end of the Cold War has left the
country without a clear ideological framework for justifying war. But the
truth is that, at the level of popular culture, war has always been understood largely in nonpolitical terms (Fussell 1989; Taylor 1991). The soldiers were trying to focus on staying alive and beyond this, on doing
their job, accomplishing their mission, demonstrating their prowess and
that of their country. The families were focused on supporting their
loved ones, and honoring those who died. And the community at large
was focused on being good neighbors to those families and to the soldiers. The journalists mediated all of this, participated, indeed, in the
process, and thereby supplied themselves with an ever-replenished
stock of stories through which the conventions of journalism meshed
with the viewers' ritual needs. Many critics, and journalists themselves,
have blamed military censorship for their rosy coverage of the war. But
we believe this emphasis is misplaced. Journalists had other reasons for
enthusiastic participation in the ritual of the war. The war had a narrative logic full of suspense, crescendoes, and collective emotion. It was
the stuff of high drama—valuable not only for high ratings but for high
excitement in the community and the newsroom alike. It made for
bonds of solidarity between the populace and its troops. And in popular
culture, this is the point of war. The primary role of the media in wartime
in the Anglo-American world has long been to maintain the ties of sentiment between the soldiers in the field and the home front. Accordingly,
journalists engage, as Buffalo anchor Rich Kellman put it, in active listening, taking popular sentiment, combining it with ideas and imagery
produced at an elite level (in the White House or Pentagon briefings)
running it through their own ideology or collective memory (adding, for
example, images of World War II or sixties' protest), and returning it to
the public in the form of myth, the myth of war as expression of prowess
and community.

The most important effect of the media's myth-making is probably
the long-term, not the short-term, effect—its effect on our general cultural understanding of war. After World War II an extremely positive,
romantic image of war came to dominate American culture. It was mod-

ified significantly by Vietnam, as one can easily see by comparing war films from the Vietnam period with those of from World War II and the Korean War. And this made a difference—though obviously not a decisive one—when the Gulf War came around: in the pre-Vietnam period one did not see the relatively respectful coverage of dissent or the focus on public doubts and fears that marked early Gulf War coverage.

Now Americans have experienced, through television, a war that fits very closely that old, romantic image—clean, successful, largely painless, exciting, and suffused with the good feelings of potency and solidarity alike. It is possible that the Gulf War will turn back the cultural clock, and restore the image of war the nation held before Vietnam. However, this is far from a foregone conclusion. Collective memory is not fixed by the initial representation of a historical event but developed through repeated retellings. It may be that the shortness of the Gulf War and its very painlessness to the U.S. will mean that it does not become a culturally defining event in the way other wars have. That it was followed so quickly by a deep recession and the fact of Saddam Hussein's survival already seem to have dampened its impact. But if the image of war that comes to be etched in the nation's collective consciousness is what we saw on television during the Gulf War, it will presumably be easier to generate enthusiasm and harder to mobilize opposition the next time around, whatever the political context.

Notes

Daniel Hallin's work on this chapter was supported by a fellowship at the Freedom Forum Media Studies Center. The authors would like to thank Daniel Levy for research assistance, and John Kirton, Lawrence Lichty, and Lew Friedland for crucial assistance in obtaining video material. Thanks also to fellows at the Freedom Forum Media Studies Center for valuable comments on the project.

1. Mark Fitzgerald, "War Boosts Readership," *Editor & Publisher,* May 11, 1991, pp. 7–8.

2. "War Boosts CNN Ratings," *Broadcasting,* January 28, 1991, pp. 23–24.

3. "Morning Shows: Network's Wake-Up Call to Arms," *Broadcasting,* February 11, 1991, pp. 52–53.

4. Scott Shuger, "Operation Desert Store," *Los Angeles Times Magazine,* September 29, 1991, pp. 18–21, 24; James Malanowski, "What So Proudly We Sold," *Spy,* November, 1991, p. 29; Adriene War and Alison Fahey, "Retailers Rallying 'Round the Flag," *Advertising Age,* February 11, 1991, p. 4; "War-Related Products Face 'Profiteering' Tag," *Marketing News,* March 18, 1991, p. 1. As the

last title suggests, there was always ambivalence among marketers about whether it was wise to use the war. But many found it attractive enough to do so.

5. Joel Elson, "War Is Won on the Video Front, Too," *Supermarket News,* June 10, 1991, p. 20.

6. War and Fahey, "Retailers Rallying."

7. Interview, April 30, 1992.

References

Adorno, T., E. Frenkel-Brunswik, D. Levinson, and N. Sanford. 1950. *The Authoritarian Personality.* New York: Harper.

Dyer, G. 1985. New York: Crown.

Fussell, P. 1989. *Wartime: Understanding and Behavior in the Second World War.* New York: Oxford University Press.

Hallin, D.C. 1986. *The "Uncensored War": The Media and Vietnam.* New York: Oxford University Press.

————.1992. "Sound Bite News: Television Coverage of Elections, 1968–1988." *Journal of Communication* 42:5–24.

Kaniss, P. 1991. *Making Local News.* Chicago: University of Chicago Press.

Kerber, L. K. 1990. "May All Our Citizens Be Soldiers and All Our Soldiers Citizens: The Ambiguities of Female Citizenship in the New Nation." In *Women, Militarism and War,* ed. Jean Bethke Elshtain and Sheila Tobias. Savage, Md.: Rowman and Littlefield.

Lane, R. E. 1959. *Political Life: Why People Get Involved in Politics.* New York: The Free Press.

Lasswell, H. H. 1960. *Psychopathology and Politics.* New York: Viking.

McNeill, W. H. 1982. *The Pursuit of Power: Technology, Armed Force, and Society Since A.D. 1000.* Chicago: University of Chicago Press.

Taylor, J. 1991. *War Photography: Realism in the Press.* London: Routledge.

Wheelwright, P. 1965. "The Semantic Approach to Myth." In *Myth: A Symposium,* ed. Thomas A. Sebeok. Bloomington: University of Indiana Press.

How Public Opinion Is Shaped by the News

eight

Shanto Iyengar and
Adam Simon

News Coverage of the
Gulf Crisis and Public
Opinion

*A Study of Agenda-Setting, Priming,
and Framing*

When Saddam Hussein decided to invade Kuwait, he set in motion an uninterrupted torrent of news coverage. For the next six months, television viewers were fixated on the Iraqi occupation of Kuwait, the American military buildup, the launching of Operation Desert Storm, and the eventual liberation of Kuwait. The situation in the Gulf represented the single "big story" in the daily flow of public affairs information. Of all prime-time network news broadcasts between August 1990, and March 1991, more than one-third, by elapsed time, were devoted to the conflict (see below for a description of the content analysis).

Not only was the Gulf the subject of extensive news coverage, there is ample evidence that Americans were in fact recipients of this coverage. In January 1991, for example, 70 percent of the public reported that they followed news about the Gulf "very closely." Television news viewing in general surged during this period, and nearly 80 percent of the public reported "staying up late" to watch news of the conflict (Gallup Organization 1991a). Another symptom of this surge in viewer interest was the transformation of CNN into a major source of information with ratings points in the double digits.

The events leading up to the Gulf War provide a powerful "natural experiment" for examining the effects of news on the crystallization and development of public opinion. This chapter examines, in the context of the Gulf War, three classes of media effects. The first ("agenda-setting") is generally defined as the ability of the news media to define the significant issues of the day. We document this effect by tracking the proportion of the public nominating the Gulf Crisis as the nation's most important problem. The second effect ("priming") concerns the relationship between patterns of news coverage and the criteria with which the public evaluates politicians. We demonstrate that the public weighted its opinions concerning foreign policy more heavily when evaluating President Bush in the aftermath of the Iraqi invasion of Kuwait. Finally, we address "framing," the connection between qualitative features of news about the Gulf (in particular, the media's preoccupation with military affairs and the invariably episodic or event-oriented character of news reports) and public opinion. Here the results suggest that the pattern of episodic framing induced individuals to express greater support for a military as opposed to diplomatic resolution of the crisis.

Agenda-setting, priming, and framing are only three of the ways in which news coverage shaped the public's response to the Gulf Crisis. The threat of an imminent full-scale war between the United States and Iraq represented an occasion for rallying behind the administration (Brody, Chapter 10 in this volume). Additionally, the one-sided "official" message inherent in most news reports was bound to persuade most Americans of the wisdom of President Bush's actions (Zaller, Chapter 9 in this volume). However, these effects on public opinion (particularly the rally and persuasive effects) have been documented by other researchers, and will not be discussed here.

AGENDA-SETTING

Issues enter and leave the center stage of American politics with considerable speed. In October 1989 the problem of illegal drug usage was foremost in Americans' minds. Seventy percent of the public referred to drugs as a major national problem. This extraordinary level of public concern prompted the administration to announce a major initiative to deal with the problem. In February 1991, however, drug usage was cited as a national problem by a mere 5 percent of the public. The most plausible explanation of such dramatic shifts in political priorities is that the amount of news coverage accorded various political issues will dictate the degree of importance the public attaches to these issues. This argument is referred to as media "agenda-setting."

Early agenda-setting studies (conducted in the 1960s) were plagued by a number of conceptual and methodological difficulties, including, most notably, confusion between cause and effect. Did the convergence of newspaper readers' political concerns and newspaper content, for example, mean that the news had set the audience agenda, or did it mean that editors and journalists had tailored their coverage to appeal to the political concerns of their readers? In response to such ambiguities, communications researchers began to track the rise and fall of public concern for particular issues and events in relation to changes in the pattern of news coverage. With few exceptions, these time-series studies uncovered evidence of significant media agenda-setting effects (see Rogers and Dearing 1988, or McCombs 1992, for a review of these studies).

The time-series analyses further refined the agenda-setting paradigm by incorporating measures of the actual severity of issues (i.e., "real-world cues"), in addition to the level of media coverage, as potential determinants of the public agenda. As the level of unemployment increased, for instance, more people mentioned unemployment as a major national problem independently of how much news coverage the media provided (Behr and Iyengar 1985; MacKuen 1981). In addition to the state of economic conditions, the level of presidential rhetoric was also found to influence the public's issue agenda. When the president addressed the nation on a particular problem and the address was televised nationwide, he was able to boost public concern independently of the amount of other news coverage accorded that problem (Behr and Iyengar 1985). Finally, in a further elaboration of the interrelationships between events, network news, and public opinion, Behr and Iyengar (1985) demonstrated that agenda-setting was generally unidirectional; news coverage affected the level of public concern, but public concern did not, in turn, affect the focus of television news.

The most recent evidence on agenda-setting provides the strongest support to date for the proposition that agenda-setting is not reciprocal. Using laboratory experiments to manipulate the content of television newscasts, Iyengar and Kinder found that relatively short exposures to news coverage of particular issues were sufficient to induce significant shifts in viewers' beliefs about the relative importance of various issues (see Iyengar and Kinder 1987).

Agenda-setting effects have been captured for all forms of mass-media coverage, in both experimental and survey-based studies, and with open-ended indicators in which respondents identify the "most important problems facing the country" as well as with closed-ended items in which they rate the importance of particular issues. These effects have been observed for both local and national problems. In all these areas, research has shown that individuals habitually refer to issues or events "in the news" when diagnosing current social and political ills. In this study, we examine the effect of Gulf-related media coverage on the salience of national problems. We expect that increases in media coverage will be accompanied by increases in the percentage of the respondents who nominate the situation in the Persian Gulf as the nation's most important problem.

PRIMING

While the term "agenda-setting" reflects the impact of news coverage on the importance accorded issues, the term "priming effect" refers to the ability of news programs to affect the criteria by which political leaders are judged (for a detailed discussion of priming, see Iyengar and Kinder 1986). Priming is really an extension of agenda-setting, and addresses the impact of news coverage on the weight assigned to specific issues in making political judgments. In general, the more prominent an issue in the national information stream, the greater its weight in political judgments (Iyengar and Kinder 1986).

Priming by television news has been established in several experiments, for evaluations of presidents and members of Congress and across a wide range of political judgments including evaluations of political performance and assessments of political leaders' personal traits. In general, news coverage of political issues induces stronger priming effects in the area of performance assessments and weaker priming effects in the area of personality assessments.

The evidence demonstrating the existence of priming is not drawn exclusively from laboratory experiments. A recent study based on national survey data found that the public's support for U.S. intervention in Central America became twice as influential as a determinant of President Reagan's popularity in the period immediately following the disclosure that funds from the sale of arms to Iran had been used to finance the Contras (Krosnick and Kinder 1990). In this context we expect increased media coverage of the Gulf to increase the weight respondents accord the foreign policy domain relative to the economic policy domain when they evaluate the president.

FRAMING

Research on framing has studied the effects of alternative news "frames" on the public's attributions of responsibility for issues and events. The concept of framing has both psychological and sociological pedigrees. Psychologists typically define framing as changes in judgment engendered by alterations to the definition of judgment or choice problems. The psychological evidence derives mainly from the work of Kahneman (1982) and Kahneman and Tversky (1984). The sociological perspective on framing derives from work by Bateson (1972) and Goffman (1974), and tends to focus on the use of "story lines," symbols, and stereotypes in media presentations. This literature typically defines news frames in terms of ideological or value perspectives (for illustrations, see Gamson 1989; Gamson and Modigliani 1986; Gitlin 1980). Attributions of responsibility for political issues are of interest for a variety of reasons, not the least of which is that the concept of responsibility embodies an especially powerful psychological cue. Social psychologists have demonstrated that attitudes and actions within a wide variety of areas are altered by the manner in which individuals attribute responsibility (see Iyengar 1991, for a review of this research).

Attributions of responsibility are generally divided into causal and treatment dimensions. Causal responsibility focuses on the origin of the issue or problem, while treatment responsibility focuses on who or what has the power either to alleviate or to forestall alleviation of the issue (for illustrative discussions of responsibility, see Brickman et al. 1982; Fincham and Jaspars 1980). To illustrate with the issue of poverty, causal responsibility concerns the processes by which people become poor while treatment responsibility would seek to establish what could be done to alleviate (or perpetuate) poverty.

Typically, the networks frame issues in either "episodic" or "thematic" terms. The episodic frame depicts public issues in terms of concrete instances or specific events—a homeless person, an unemployed worker, a victim of racial discrimination, the bombing of an airliner, an attempted murder, and so on. Visually, episodic reports make for "good pictures." The thematic news frame, by contrast, places public issues in some general or abstract context. Reports on reductions in government welfare expenditures, changes in the nature of employment opportunities, the social or political grievances of groups undertaking terrorist activity, changes in federal affirmative-action policy, or the backlog in the criminal justice process are examples of thematic coverage. The thematic news frame typically takes the form of a "takeout" or "backgrounder" report directed at general outcomes or conditions and frequently features "talking heads."

Given the nature of television news—a twenty-one minute "headline service" operating under powerful commercial dictates—it is to be expected that the networks rely extensively on episodic framing to report on public issues. Episodic framing is visually appealing and consists of "on-the-scene," live coverage. Thematic coverage, which requires interpretive analyses, would simply crowd out other news items. In fact, television news coverage of political issues is heavily episodic. Two-thirds of all stories on poverty broadcast between 1980 and 1986 concerned a particular poor person (see Iyengar 1991, for details). Similarly, of the nearly two thousand stories on terrorism, 74 percent consisted of "live" reports of some specific terrorist act, group, victim, or event while 26 percent consisted of reports that discussed terrorism as a general political problem.

Our examination of framing effects is divided into two parts. First, we assess the degree to which network news coverage of the Gulf Crisis was episodic. Second, we examine the effects of exposure to television news during the crisis on respondent's policy preferences. Respondents were provided with a choice between a military or diplomatic response to the crisis. For reasons outlined later, we expect that increased exposure to television news will be associated with increases in support for the military response.

Method

DATA

Our analysis draws on three sources of data. First, we use polls taken by the Gallup Organization between April 1990, and March 1991 (see Gallup 1991b, for details). All these polls used a probability sampling procedure and were based on more than 1,500 respondents.

Our second source of data is a content analysis of network news coverage of the Persian Gulf. One network (ABC) was selected at random. A graduate-student coder then randomly sampled two broadcasts per week, (one for the first three days of coverage) from each Monday through Friday between August 2, 1990, and May 4, 1991. Using the Vanderbilt *Television News Index and Abstracts*, the coder performed a text-based analysis of 79 broadcast news reports. This sample represents 40 percent of the total number of news programs broadcast during this period.

Finally, we used the National Election Study surveys from 1988, 1990, and 1991. Each survey used probability sampling and personal interviews with respondents. In addition to the indicators we use, respondents were asked about political parties, institutions, public officials, and topical issues. The 1988 survey was administered between November 12, 1988, and January 10, 1989 ($N = 2,040$). The 1990 survey was administered between November 7, 1990, and January 26, 1991 ($N = 2,000$). Virtually all respondents in this survey (97 percent) were interviewed before the outbreak of the air war on January 16, 1991. The 1991 survey reinterviewed a subset of respondents from the 1990 survey ($N = 1,385$) in June and July of 1991 to form the NES "Panel Study on the Consequences of War."

MEASURES AND PROCEDURES

The only measure taken from the Gallup surveys was the most-important-problem question: "What do you think is the most important problem facing this country?" The aggregate proportion of respondents mentioning the economy, the budget deficit, the drug/crime problem, and the Persian Gulf was recorded for each poll. These percentages were then compiled to create a time series for these four problems.

Several different measures were extracted from the text-based coding of the Abstracts of ABC's "World News Tonight" stories relating to the Gulf and recorded, beginning with the amount of time taken up by each. The average amount of Gulf-related coverage per month was then calculated by summing the total number of minutes from that month's sampled broadcasts and dividing by the number of reports sampled. The proportion of news coverage allocated to the Gulf was determined by dividing the coverage of the Gulf by all coverage.

The central theme and the source of each Gulf-related story also were recorded. We classified the themes into four subject-matter categories corresponding to news coverage of diplomacy, military activity, and the ramifications of the conflict for Iraqi and American society. The number of minutes of news coverage allocated to official sources (basically, members of the Bush administration or the Department of Defense) were divided by the total amount of news to produce a measure of "official journalism." Finally, the *Abstracts* were examined to determine whether news reports were *primarily episodic* or *primarily thematic*. While episodic coverage focuses on specific events, thematic coverage is broader in scope and refers to the policy debate, historical background, or possible political consequences connected with Gulf-related actions. The amount of episodic coverage was then compared to the amount of thematic coverage.

A subset of 40 of the 79 sampled broadcasts was independently coded by a second graduate student. The level of intercoder agreement was greater than 90 percent. Similar levels of intercoder reliability (using the same episodic vs. thematic classification scheme) have been reported in previous research on television coverage of political issues (Iyengar, 1991).

In testing the priming and framing hypotheses, we relied on a number of survey items taken from the NES surveys. In the case of priming, we used a series of questions on presidential performance. These were worded as follows. (NES variable numbers for 1988, 1990, and 1991 are included in parentheses.) "Do you approve or disapprove of the way George Bush [or Ronald Reagan] is handling our relations with foreign countries?" (v256, v206, v2119). And, "Do you approve or disapprove of the way George Bush [or Ronald Reagan, for 1988] is handling the economy? (v227, v204, v2123). These questions were coded (1) *approve strongly*, (2) *approve not strongly*, (3) *disapprove not strongly*, and (4) *disapprove strongly*. The dependent variable in the priming analysis was the "feeling thermometer" question, which asked respondents to rate George Bush on a zero to 100-degree scale, with higher ratings indicating more positive feelings (v154, v237, v2205).

The variable of interest in the framing analysis is a measure of policy preference taken from the 1990 study. It consisted of the following two questions. First (v738), "Which of the following do you think we should do now in the Persian Gulf: pull out U.S. forces entirely; try harder to find a diplomatic solution; tighten the economic embargo; or take tougher military action?" Respondents who mentioned the tougher military response were scored as 1 and respondents who did not mention this response as 0. Second (v737), "Do you think we did the right thing in sending U.S. military forces to the Persian Gulf, or should we have stayed out?" The responses to this question included (3) *right thing*, (1) *stayed out*, (2) other. The two questions were significantly correlated ($r = .30$) and were summed to form an index of policy preference that ranged from 0 (preference for a diplomatic response) to 4 (preference for a military response).

We incorporated two measures of television exposure from the 1990 survey into the framing analysis. The first tapped respondents' self-reported frequency of news watching, "How many days in the past week did you watch the news on television?" (v127), for which the number of days was coded (0 to 7). The second was an index of general political information. Following Converse (1962) and Price and Zaller (1991), we assumed that old information begets new information and that individuals most likely to receive and retain news coverage of the Gulf are those already relatively informed about public affairs. Respondents answered a battery of seven political-identification questions, including Dan Quayle, George Mitchell, William Rehnquist, Mikhail Gorbachev, Margaret Thatcher, Nelson Mandela, and Tom Foley (v835 to v841). One point was awarded for each correct answer to produce a 0 to 7 scale of general political information.

Respondent's partisanship, race, gender, and education were included in both the priming and framing analyses as control variables. Partisanship (v274, v643) ranged from *strong Democrat* (0) to *strong Republican* (6). Race (v412, v1428) was coded as white (0) and all else (1). Gender (v413, v1427) was scored 0 for female and 1 for male. Education (v422, v1208) was coded on seven levels from *less than eight grades* (1) to *college* (7). Finally, one additional control variable was included in the framing analysis. This was the respondent's attitude toward defense spending (v924) which ranged from (1) *greatly decrease defense spending* to (7) *greatly increase defense spending.*

ANALYSIS

Before discussing the specific statistical tests used in the analysis, we summarize the previous discussion and formally state the three media-effects hypotheses under consideration.

H1 (agenda-setting): Increases in the level of media coverage accorded to events in the Persian Gulf will be associated with increases in the proportion of respondents naming the Gulf Crisis as the nation's most important problem.

H2 (priming): The weight respondents accord foreign policy performance when evaluating the president will significantly increase during and after the Gulf Crisis.

H3 (framing): Respondents reporting higher rates of exposure to television news will express greater support for a military over a diplomatic response to the crisis.

As a test of agenda-setting, we plotted the average amount of Gulf-related coverage per month against the percentage of Gallup respondents who nominated the Gulf, the economy, the budget deficit, or drugs/crime as the nation's most important problem. Because of the limited number of data points, we relied on a simple correlation in order to test the statistical significance of the relationship between Gulf coverage and the proportion of respondents who named the Gulf as the nation's most important problem. We used multiple regression techniques to test the priming and framing hypotheses. The regression specifications were as follows. For priming, the feeling thermometer rating was regressed against foreign policy performance, economic performance, party identification, education, and race. For framing, the index of policy preference was regressed against the information index, self-reported television news exposure, party identification, education, gender, and race. The specification also included a pair of interactive terms between gender, race, and the index of information. These interactive terms capture the differential effects (if any) of information on policy preference among men and women and whites and minorities.

Results

AGENDA-SETTING

How did the Iraqi invasion of Kuwait affect the political agendas of Americans? In July, immediately prior to the invasion, Americans were preoccupied with domestic problems. Drug usage and crime, the state of the economy, and the federal budget deficit were the issues most likely to be nominated as the most important problems facing the nation. This trio of issues was mentioned by more than 50 percent of survey respondents. In figure 1, we trace the trend in responses to the Gallup Poll's "most important problem" question between July 1990 and March 1991 in relation to the amount of television news-coverage of the Gulf.

Beginning in August, the Gulf absorbed virtually all network news time. The sheer amount of news peaked (at over two hours of news coverage in August) immediately following the Iraqi invasion. Between September and December, news from the Gulf averaged approximately sixty minutes per month. The onset of the air war in January and Operation Desert Storm in February raised the level of coverage to about ninety minutes per month. Thus, there was an initial period of saturation coverage followed by a steady state of heavy news which culminated in two months of virtual saturation coverage.

Turning to the issue-salience data, the conflict in the Gulf achieved parity with the economy and deficit as an agenda item as early as October. By November, references to the Gulf had surpassed mentions of the economy to become the preeminent national problem in the eyes of Americans. At its peak (in February), the Gulf came in for a greater share of public attention than the economy, deficit, and drugs combined. Just as rapidly, the Gulf disappeared from the public agenda. Following the cessation of hostilities, responses to the most-important-problem question reverted to their preconflict state, with one notable change; while the economy shared center stage with drugs and the deficit prior to the conflict, at the end of the war the economy had come to overshadow all other domestic issues. Overall, the amount of media coverage accorded to the Gulf situation and the proportion of respondents nominating it as the nation's most important problem were highly correlated ($r = .85$).

Most discussions of agenda-setting are unidirectional in nature—

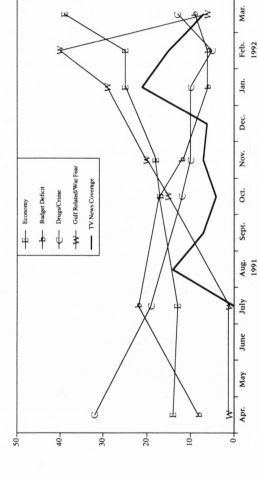

Fig. 1. Trends in Issue Salience and Gulf-Related News Coverage (Y Axis: Percent Nominating or Average Minutes per Month, X Axis: Month)

increases in news coverage are thought to bring about increases in the salience of particular issues or events. The evidence in figure 1, however, not only highlights the dramatic surge in the salience of the Gulf conflict, but also indicates the bidirectional nature of the agenda-setting process. That is, the emergence of the Gulf as the most important national problem was accompanied by a sudden (and pronounced) decline in the prominence of drugs and the budget deficit. In effect, intensive news coverage generated by a "crisis issue" not only elevates the prominence of the target issue but also removes other issues from public attention. It is important to note, however, that this "hydraulic" pattern did not apply to the economy. While references to economic problems remained relatively stable during the early phases of the conflict (October–November), the economy actually gained in salience between November and February. By March, the economy was clearly the preeminent agenda problem—references to economic problems exceeded references to all other domestic issues. It is possible that the continual coverage of the Gulf prompted viewers to consider simultaneously the economic and military risks posed by the conflict, thus elevating their concern for economic problems. Alternatively, the public may have been responding on the basis of prevailing economic conditions; that is, as the economy worsened, more people identified it as a significant problem.

PRIMING

In the context of the Gulf crisis, the priming hypothesis predicts that over time Americans will assign a greater weight to their beliefs and opinions concerning foreign policy in general when forming impressions of George Bush in 1990. Our data stem from the 1988, 1990, and 1991 NES postelection surveys. In each year, we analyzed the effects of the public's ratings of presidential performance on the economy and foreign policy on their overall feelings toward George Bush. These results are given in table 1.

The evidence is consistent with the priming hypothesis. Foreign policy performance assessments tended to override economic assessments in their impact on thermometer ratings of George Bush during the Gulf Crisis while the reverse was true in 1988. A similar analysis (not reported here), using ratings of overall presidential performance as the dependent variable, produced identical results. These results are also suggestive of the hydraulic pattern found in the agenda-setting section above. Increases in the impact of foreign policy performance assessments on global evaluations of the president were accompanied by small

TABLE 1.   Determinants of Feelings toward George Bush

	1991		1990		1988	
	b	s.e.	b	s.e.	b	s.e.
Foreign policy performance (disapprove)	−9.24	.53	−6.00	.29	−4.40	.56
Economic performance (disapprove)	−7.08	.53	--4.96	.31	−7.95	.57
Gender (male)	.41	1.64	−1.01	.83	−1.43	.98
Party (Republican)	1.29	.27	2.09	.22	4.12	.28
Education	−.76	.32	−.49	.25	−.33	.31
Race (nonwhite)	−5.88	1.63	−1.03	1.20	1.52	1.45
Adj. R²	.47		.47		.47	
N	1,228		1,925		1,713	

Note: Entries are multiple regression coefficients and standard errors estimated with controls for education, gender, partisan identification, and race. In 1988, both performance questions referred to Ronald Reagan.

decreases in the importance of economic evaluations. Overall, the evidence suggests that the Gulf conflict altered the principal basis of President Bush's popularity from the state of the national economy to foreign policy matters. Because the public rated Bush more favorably on foreign policy, their overall impression of the president was made more positive; his mean feeling thermometer rating rose from 60 in 1988 to 64 in 1990 and 71 in 1991.

FRAMING

We examined the prime-time news broadcasts by ABC News between August 1990 and April 1991 (see figures 2–3). Not surprisingly, television news coverage of the Gulf was heavily episodic or event-oriented. The typical news story transmitted information about specific developments or "live" occurrences. Each day, viewers were provided the next "episode" in the developing confrontation between the United States (and its allies) and Iraq. Rarely were viewers provided "background" in the form of analyses of the antecedents of the conflict, historical precedents for similar territorial disputes, information about the socioeconomic and cultural makeup of Iraqi and Kuwaiti society, or other such contextual presentations. The *diplomatic* and *military* categories are self-explanatory. Stories included in the *Iraq* and *U.S.* categories (which were collapsed into a single category in figure 3) included reports on the economic consequences of the military buildup, reports of ethnic strife

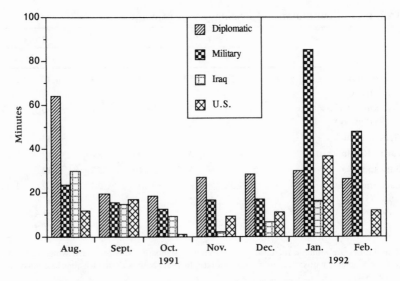

Fig. 2. Trends in Gulf-Related News Coverage by Subject Matter

(in the case of Iraq), public opinion and the elite debate, the impact of
the crisis on civilian life, etc.

Reports on ongoing diplomatic efforts accounted for most coverage
throughout the period except during the months of January and February, which were characterized by a flurry of reports on the ground war.
Within each subject-matter category (but particularly in the case of
news reports on diplomacy), episodic reports overwhelmed thematic reports by a huge margin.

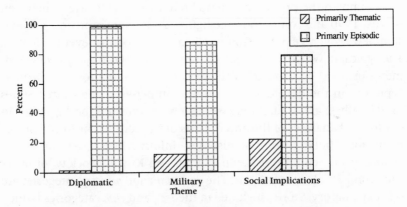

Fig. 3. Mix of Episodic and Thematic Framing in Gulf-Related Coverage

How might this pattern of predominantly episodic news coverage affect public opinion towards the Gulf conflict? Previous research has investigated the effects of the episodic and thematic news frames on viewers' attributions of responsibility for various political and social issues (including poverty, unemployment, crime, terrorism, racial inequality, and the Iran-Contra affair). Under thematic framing, viewers tended to assign responsibility for national problems to general societal factors, including cultural norms, economic conditions, and the actions or inactions of public officials. When television news coverage presents a general or analytic frame of reference for national problems, the public's reasoning about causal and treatment responsibility is societal in focus. Under episodic framing, however, viewers attributed responsibility for national problems not to societal or structural forces but to the actions of particular individuals or groups. For example, when poverty, crime, and terrorism were depicted in episodic terms, viewers attributed causal and treatment responsibility primarily to poor people, criminals, and terrorists. Confronted with a parade of news stories describing particular instances or illustrations of national issues, viewers focus on individual and group characteristics rather than historical, social, political, or other such general forces. In this respect episodic framing encourages reasoning by resemblance—people settle upon causes and treatments that "fit" the observed problem.

In the context of the Gulf Crisis, the important policy question concerned the appropriate strategy for ending the Iraqi occupation of Kuwait, e.g., a question of treatment responsibility. Given the pervasive use of episodic framing, it was anticipated that exposure to television news coverage of the Gulf would tend to strengthen a preference for punitive (i.e., military) over diplomatic or economic remedies. This hypothesis is based on the evidence cited above that episodic framing of "public order" issues such as terrorism and crime instills attributions of punitive treatment responsibility. Since the conflict in the Gulf may be considered analogous to issues of law and order (Iraq as the transgressor, Kuwait as the victim, the U.S. as the law enforcer), it was anticipated that exposure to television news would enhance viewers' preference for military over diplomatic responses to the Iraq occupation of Kuwait.

We attempted to examine this particular connection between television news coverage and public opinion by using our two measures of exposure to television news (self-reported frequency of exposure and the general political information index) and the index tapping support for military over diplomatic solutions to the conflict. We relied on two

TABLE 2.   Support for Military over Diplomatic Response

	b	s.e.	p-level
TV news exposure	.02	.01	.03
Information	.07	.03	.03
Gender X information	−.09	.04	.02
Race X information	.10	.06	.08
Gender (male)	.67	.11	<.001
Race (nonwhite)	−.76	.13	<.001
Party (Republican)	.07	.01	<.001
Defense spending (favor)	.20	.02	<.001
Education	.07	.02	<.001
Adj. R^2		.19	
N		1,763	

Note: Entries are unstandardized multiple regression coefficients, standard errors, and their corresponding significance levels.

different indicators of exposure to television news. Following Zaller (Chapter 9 in this volume), we assumed that the effects of information on support for a military response would be stronger among groups with relatively low levels of political information. Therefore, we computed two interactive terms between information and respondents' race and gender. These interactions were then included in the regression equation. Finally, we also controlled for respondents' preferences concerning military spending on the grounds that those who favor increased military spending would be more hawkish on the Gulf. The results of this analysis are provided in table 2.

Partisanship, race, gender, and education all affected respondents' policy preferences concerning resolution of the conflict. Republicans, males, those with more education, and whites tended to support the military option. Support for increased defense spending was strongly associated with a more militaristic outlook toward the conflict. Both indicators of exposure to television news exerted significant effects; the more informed respondents who watched the news more frequently were more apt to favor a military response. The effects of information were markedly stronger among women and minorities, suggesting that groups relatively inattentive to public affairs were especially affected by exposure to news of the crisis. (Women, for example, received a mean score of 1.8 on the information index in 1990 while men received a mean score of 2.5.)

Overall, then, there were statistically significant traces of the expected relationship. Exposure to episodic news programming strengthened, albeit modestly, support for a military resolution of the crisis.

Discussion

The evidence presented here indicates that television news coverage of the conflict in the Persian Gulf significantly affected Americans' political concerns and the criteria with which they evaluated George Bush. Prior to the crisis, Americans were preoccupied with economic problems and crime, and their feelings toward George Bush were colored primarily by economic considerations. Following the Iraqi invasion of Kuwait, the Gulf Crisis became the public's paramount concern, and evaluations of George Bush became more dependent upon foreign policy considerations. Finally, we find support for the hypothesis that exposure to episodic framing of the crisis increased viewers' support for a military resolution of the conflict.

As Walter Lippmann noted nearly seventy years ago, we tend to know little about "what is happening, why it happened and what ought to happen" (1992, p. 39). But in modern times we do have "pictures in our heads," courtesy of ABC, CBS, CNN, and NBC.

It is now well established that television news has a significant impact on public opinion. The Gulf War was a mediated issue par excellence, and the results shown here, that American public opinion would follow the course of television news coverage, were predictable. The influence of the media inevitably gives rise to a host of questions concerning the determinants of news coverage and the practice of public-affairs journalism.

In a simpler era, Lippmann drew a distinction between "news" and "truth," and first posed the question—fundamental to democratic functioning—of how closely the news could be said to reflect the "truth." The discrepancy between the two has surely been increased by the present governmental domination of the flow of information. As the examples of Grenada, the Gulf, and Somalia make clear, print and broadcast news coverage of world events involving the use of United States military force have tended to propagate the worldview and policy preferences of the incumbent administration. The media portrayed Grenada as a hotbed of communist insurgents hatching terrorist plots and jeopardizing American lives. Saddam Hussein was portrayed as a modern Hitler, bent on annexing Kuwait and controlling the world's supply of petroleum. In Somalia, the deployment of U.S. troops was seen in exclusively humanitarian terms.

Journalists have attributed their tendency simply to repeat the governmental "party line" to the unavailability of other sources of information; as correspondent John McWethy has described the journalist's predicament: "When you are in a situation where your primary source of information is the U.S. Government, . . . you have to make an assumption that the U.S. Government is telling the truth . . ." (quoted in Hertsgaard 1988). In our analysis of network news reports on the Gulf, more than 50 percent of all reports examined emanated directly from official spokespersons. Even allowing for the most benevolent and accessible of administrations, this de facto "stranglehold" over the news guaranteed that there would be a certain disjuncture between actual events and the media's depiction or interpretation of events. The successes of American technology, such as the interception of Iraqi Scud missiles and the destruction of military installations by "smart" bombs, and the "malevolence" of the Iraqis, as demonstrated by the deliberate igniting of oil wells, were the staples of news coverage. Contrary themes such as the devastation of a third-world nation, the enormous scale of civilian casualties, or the deliberate burial alive of Iraqi conscripts in their trenches, were ignored. The practice of "official" journalism thus assured that the public's and the president's understanding of this international crisis would be congruent.

Notes

We are indebted to Sharmaine Vidanage for her invaluable research assistance, and to two anonymous reviewers for comments on a draft of this chapter. Preparation of the chapter was supported in part by a National Science Foundation Graduate Fellowship to Adam Simon.

References

Bateson, G. 1972. *Steps Toward an Ecology of the Mind: Collected Essays in Anthropology, Psychiatry, and Epistemology.* San Francisco: Chandler.

Behr, R. L., and S. Iyengar. 1985. "Television News, Real-World Cues, and Changes in the Public Agenda." *Public Opinion Quarterly* 49:38–57.

Brickman, P., J. Karuza, Jr., D. Coates, E. Cohn, and L. Kidder. 1982. "Models of Helping and Coping." *American Psychologist* 37:368–84.

Converse, P. E. 1962. "Information Flows and the Stability of Partisan Attitudes." *Public Opinion Quarterely* 26:578–99.

Fincham, F. D., and J. M. Jaspers. 1980. "Attribution of Responsibility: From Man the Scientist to Man as Lawyer." In L. Berkowitz, ed., *Advances in Experimental Social Psychology.* Vol. 16. New York: Academic Press.

Gallup Organization. 1991a. "Buildup to War." *January Monthly Report*, pp. 2–13.

Gallup Organization. 1991b. "The Persian Gulf War." *February Monthly Report*, pp. 2–6.

Gamson, W. A. 1989. "News as Framing." *American Behavioral Scientist* 33:157–61.

Gamson, W. A., and A. Modigliani. 1986. "Media Discourse and Public Opinion on Nuclear Power." Manuscript. Boston College, Social Economy Program, Boston.

Gitlin, T. 1980. *The Whole World Is Watching.* Berkeley: University of California Press.

Goffman, E. 1974. *Frame Analysis: An Essay on the Organization of Experience.* Cambridge: Harvard University Press.

Hertsgaard, M. 1988. *On Bended Knee.* New York: Farrar, Straus, and Giroux.

Iyengar, S. 1986. "More than Meets the Eye: Television News, Priming, and Citizens' Evaluations of the President." In G. Comstock, ed., *Public Communication and Behavior.* Vol. 1. New York: Academic Press.

———. 1991. *Is Anyone Responsible?: How Television Frames Political Issues.* Chicago: University of Chicago Press.

Iyengar, S., and D.R. Kinder. 1987. *News That Matters.* Chicago: University of Chicago Press.

Kahneman, D. 1982. "The Psychology of Preferences." *Science* 246:136–42.

Kahneman, D., and A. Tversky. 1984. "Choices, Values, and Frames." *American Psychologist* 39:341–50.

Krosnick, J. A., and D. R. Kinder. 1990. "Altering the Foundations of Popular Support for the President through Priming." *American Political Science Review* 84:497–512.

MacKuen, M. 1981. "Social Communication and the Mass Policy Agenda." In M. MacKuen and S. L. Coombs, eds., *More than News: Media Power in Public Affairs.* Beverly Hills: Sage Publications.

McCombs, M. 1992. Special issue on agenda-setting, *Journalism Quarterly*, 69:4.

Price, V., and J. Zaller. 1991. "Who Gets the News?" Paper presented at the Annual Meeting of the American Political Science Association.

Rogers, E. M., and J. W. Dearing. 1988. "Agenda-Setting Research: Where Has It Been and Where Is It Going?" In J. A. Anderson, ed., *Communication Yearbook*, Vol. 11. Beverly Hills: Sage Publications.

nine

John Zaller

Elite Leadership of Mass Opinion

New Evidence from the Gulf War

Evidence from a half a century of polling in the United States supports the proposition that the more citizens know about politics and public affairs, the more firmly they are wedded to elite and media perspectives on foreign policy issues. When elites are united in support of a foreign policy, politically aware Americans support that policy more strongly than any other part of the public. When elites divide along partisan or ideological lines, politically attentive citizens are more likely than the inattentive to align their opinions with that segment of the elite which shares their party or ideology. And when elite opinion changes, political awareness is a major determinant of which members of the public follow the elite lead.[1]

The present chapter reviews the historical evidence for these assertions and presents fresh supporting evidence from the case of the Persian Gulf War.

Theoretical Background

THE PUBLIC'S DEPENDENCE ON ELITE-SUPPLIED INFORMATION

Walter Lippmann has perhaps best summarized the plight of the average citizen attempting to understand distant events:

> Each of us lives and works on a small part of the earth's surface, moves in a small circle, and of these acquaintances knows only a few intimately. Of any public event that has wide effects we see at best only a phase and an aspect. . . . Inevitably our opinions cover a bigger space, a longer reach of time, a greater number of things, than we can directly observe. They have, therefore, to be pieced together out of what others have reported and what we can imagine. (1992, p. 59)

The main sources of the public's information about distant events are, of course, the mass media and the political elites whose views are reported in them. One of the central questions in communication research, and the one with which this chapter is centrally concerned, arises from this dependence: To what extent is the public able to react critically and independently to the information it receives from the national political media, and to what extent does it simply accept what it encounters in the media?

The available evidence is not very encouraging. For one thing, most citizens are very poorly informed about public affairs in general and foreign affairs in particular. In 1983, for example, the United States government was actively supporting anticommunist guerrillas in their attacks on the Marxist government of Nicaragua. Although this was a topic of considerable partisan controversy, only 13 percent of the public knew which side the U.S. was supporting. By 1986, amid continuing and often acrimonious debate between Congress and the White House, the number able to say which side the U.S. was supporting in Nicaragua rose—but only to 38 percent. A general public with so vague an understanding of foreign policy issues cannot be counted upon to exhibit much critical scrutiny of the news and information it gets on these subjects.[2]

There is, moreover, much evidence showing that, even in situations in which people possess the information necessary to engage in informed deliberation, they will not take the trouble to do so. Rather, they tend to rely on such simple rules of thumb, as whether the advocate of a given policy is a Democrat or Republican, liberal or conservative, or whatever. It is worth reviewing the evidence on this point in some detail.

A persistent finding of the psychological literature on persuasive communication—and the foreign policy news citizens receive in the media certainly falls into the category of persuasive communication—has been that cues about the "source" of a message greatly affect how individuals judge the message. Reviewing this evidence in an influential paper, McGuire (1969, 198) wrote that the "message receiver"

> can be regarded as a lazy organism who tries to master the message contents only when it is absolutely necessary to make a decision. When the purported source is clearly positively or negatively valenced, he uses this information as a cue to accept or reject the message's conclusions without really absorbing the arguments used.

The "lazy organisms" that relied on source cues to decide whether to accept messages were probably unaware that they were avoiding any real thought about the subjects on which they received communications. As McGuire's review essay further reported, "The given message is judged as fairer, more factual, more thoroughly documented, its conclusion following more validly from its premises, and even more grammatical, when it is ascribed to a high- as opposed to a low-credibility source."[3]

The relevance of all this for how the public might be expected to deal with foreign policy news is quite clear: Few members of the general public should be expected to engage in independent thought and analysis on foreign policy issues. The most that can be expected is that they choose among competing elite and media messages—*at least in cases in which competing messages are present*—on the basis of source credibility.

If even the best-informed members of the public cannot engage in independent analysis but can only evaluate competing news messages on the basis of ideology or partisanship, and if much of the rest of the public pays too little attention to know what elites are discussing, what ought we to infer about elite and media influence on mass opinion in the domain of foreign affairs?

One inference is that elite and media influence is likely to be limited to those citizens who are sufficiently attentive to politics to be aware of what elites are saying. A second is that influence is likely to be greatest in cases in which elites achieve sufficient internal agreement to avoid undercutting each other's arguments. Putting these two ideas together, one can reach a third inference: Elite influence is likely to be greatest in times of national emergency, since that is the time when citizen attentiveness to politics peaks, and when elites are most likely to forge a unified position.

This argument has an obvious irony. It is that the citizens who are most heavily exposed to the media are invariably the most politically aware segment of the public. One might suppose that such people are most resistant to persuasion rather than, as I have argued, most susceptible. There is some validity to this supposition. The most aware citizens are, as we shall see, quite good at making ideologically informed choices between the messages of competing elites, when elites actually compete with one another. But in many cases, including some very important ones, elites do not compete, and then the most politically aware citizens are most susceptible to influence because they are most heavily exposed to an elite consensus that they have no partisan basis for resisting.

MEASURING POLITICAL AWARENESS

In order to test these suppositions, it is necessary to measure people's level of political awareness, where awareness is taken as an indicator of exposure to the mass media. Much evidence indicates that the most effective measure of awareness is a person's background level of factual information about politics. People who score high on information tests (e.g., which side the U.S. government is backing in Nicaragua) are people for whom politics is relatively important and who therefore pay attention to political news. People who know little about politics—not even, for example, the name of the vice president, as about 15 percent of the public does not—are people who either pay no attention to politics or retain little of what they do encounter.

Self-reported levels of media use, self-reported attention to an issue, and formal education can be used as substitutes for information in cases in which an information measure is unavailable. These alternative measures capture the same types of exposure effects as political information, except less well (Price and Zaller 1993). This chapter will report results from each of these types of measures, depending on what is available in a given dataset. As a way of making clear that each is intended to measure the same concept, I will refer to all of them as measures of political awareness.

Evidence of Exposure Effects in Past Studies

If political awareness is associated with greater exposure to elite discourse, and with greater ability to select critically among the "sources" of this discourse, we ought to find the following.

- In cases when elites of all political colorations agree on a policy, higher levels of political information are associated with greater support for that policy. Following Gamson and Modigliani (1966), I refer to this as the "mainstream effect." It occurs because, given support for the policy among sources of all political colorations, highly informed persons have no basis for resisting the arguments to which they are, as aware persons, heavily exposed.
- In cases when elites disagree along partisan or ideological lines, more informed people become more likely to espouse the position that is associated in elite discourse with their ideology or partisanship. Thus, greater information leads conservatives to-

ward greater support for the position of conservative elites and
leads liberals toward greater support for the liberal position. I refer to this as the "polarization effect."

THE MAINSTREAM EFFECT

There are numerous well-documented cases of the mainstream effect.
Hadley Cantril (1944), describing poll results obtained during World
War II, found that better-informed persons were more likely to support
vigorous prosecution of the war against Germany, lenient terms for the
defeated Axis powers, and a world organization to prevent the occurrence of future wars. Cantril interpreted these findings as evidence that
more informed persons had a better understanding of the nation's true
interests, but the indoctrinating effects of exposure to mainstream elite
discourse seems a more likely explanation.

Postwar studies, most notably Almond's *The American People and Foreign Policy,* found that political awareness, as indexed by education, was
associated with support for an internationalist foreign policy, including
an active role for the U.S. in the United Nations, high levels of international trade, and the Marshall Plan. These policies were, or course, pil-
lars of the country's cold-war foreign policy consensus on containment
of communism, so exposure to elite discourse again appears to promote
support for mainstream policies.

John Mueller's *War, Presidents, and Public Opinion* likewise found that
better-educated people were disproportionately likely to support U.S.
involvement in the Korean and Vietnam wars, especially in the early
stages in which these wars were overwhelmingly supported by congressional and other elites. Mueller also shows that the better-educated followed dovish as well as hawkish turns in presidential leadership, which
establishes that the better-educated were not simply more hawkish but
more closely wedded to elite opinion.

THE POLARIZATION EFFECT

But although mainstream liberals and conservatives largely supported
the Vietnam War in its initial stage, liberal elites began publicly turning
against it in 1966. By 1970, liberal ideology was solidly identified with
opposition to the war.

Given this, we should expect public opinion on the Vietnam War to
exhibit both the mainstream effect and the polarization effect. The
mainstream effect should appear early in the war, when most elites supported it, and the polarization effect should appear late in the war. As
figure 1 shows, data from the 1964 and 1970 election studies of the Cen-

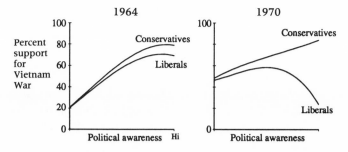

Source: 1964 and 1970 CPS surveys.

Note: Ideology is measured as the difference in ratings of liberals and conservatives on separate 100-point feeling thermometers. Awareness is measured by tests of political knowledge; scores on awareness run from the 2d percentile at the extreme of low awareness to the 98th percentile at the high end. Estimated patterns of war support are based on coefficients and modeling procedures described in Zaller (1991).

Fig. 1. Support for the Vietnam War in 1964 and 1970

ter for Political Studies at the University of Michigan confirm these expectations.

The magnitudes of the mainstream and polarization effects shown in figure 1 are quite substantial. In 1964, support for the Vietnam War increased from about 20 percent among the least politically aware segment of the public to about 75 percent among the most aware segment. (The apparent differences between liberals and conservatives in this figure do not achieve statistical significance in 1964, that is, they may reflect only chance fluctuation in the data.) In 1970, by contrast, political awareness is not consistently associated with support for the war; rather, it generates strong contradictory trends—greater support for the war among conservatives and less support among liberals. As a result, the difference in war-support rates between the most-aware conservatives and liberals is now very large—approximately 60 percentage points. (Technical information concerning these estimates is available in Zaller 1991).

It is worth noting that the elite-mass interactions that generate mainstream and polarization effects can arise in any case in which the media carry the requisite consensual or dissensual messages and cues. For example, within the domain of racial policy, political awareness is associated with greater support for most forms of nondiscrimination against blacks, but it is also associated with greater polarization between liberals and conservatives on such policies as affirmative action and busing to achieve school integration. This pattern, a recapitulation of the two halves of figure 1, reflects the mainstream elite consensus that exists in the first policy domain and the intense elite dissensus that exists in the second (see Zaller 1992, chap. 6).

A CLOSER LOOK AT THE EFFECTS OF LACK
OF POLITICAL AWARENESS

It might be suspected that the failure of politically less-aware liberals and conservatives to polarize in response to elite and media cues reflects an independent cast of mind rather than, as I have argued, lack of exposure to elite cues and messages. Figure 2, however, weighs against this objection.

The figure compares the public's responses to two questions about aid to the Contra rebels in Nicaragua in the 1980s when such aid was controversial. (Conservatives, led by the Reagan administration, wanted to furnish aid on the grounds that the Contras were fighting the Marxist government of Nicaragua; liberals argued that the U.S. had no business in the internal affairs of Nicaragua.) Those classified as "hawks" in figure 2 are ones who said, in a series of general questions, that they strongly value military strength, an aggressive posture toward potential adversaries, and uncompromising opposition to communism. Persons labeled as "doves" are those who rejected these positions, preferring to emphasize negotiations and accommodation with foreign adversaries.

The left side of the figure shows that politically aware hawks and

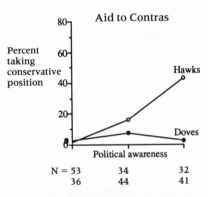
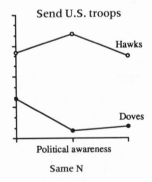

If you had a say in making up the federal budget, would you like to see: spending for aid to the Contras in Nicaragua increased, decreased, or kept about the same?

Would you strongly favor, not so strongly favor, not so strongly oppose, or strongly oppose sending U.S. troops to Central America to stop the spread of communism?

Source: 1987 NES Pilot Study.

Fig. 2. Two Questions on Central America Policy

doves differ greatly on the question of whether U.S. "aid to the Contras in Nicaragua" should be increased, decreased, or kept the same: 42 percent of the most-aware hawks, but only 3 percent of the most-aware doves, favored increased Contra aid. However, among persons in the middle and lower thirds of the awareness scale, hawks and doves scarcely differ at all—a result that raises doubts about whether the hawk-dove dimension has any utility for understanding the views of less-aware persons.

However, the right side of figure 2 shows responses to a question about whether the U.S. should send troops "to stop the spread of communism" in Central America. Here we find that respondents at every level of awareness are equally reliant on the hawk-dove dimension for structuring responses to the issue.

Why the difference in response pattern to the two items, especially among less-aware persons? The explanation lies in the background information carried in the two questions: the first, although scarcely lacking in clarity, requires citizens to know who the Contras are and what they stand for. This requirement will often go unmet among persons who are, in general, poorly informed about politics. The second question in figure 2, by mentioning communism, makes clear what is at stake, thereby enabling people inclined toward hawkish foreign policies to recognize and support them.

These results strongly suggest that at least part of the reason that poorly informed persons fail to embrace dominant elite ideologies—in this case, the failure of politically inattentive hawks to support aid to Contras—is not that they are independent-minded; it appears, rather, that they have paid too little attention to politics to know what, exactly, they are being asked about.[4]

Public Opinion in the Gulf Crisis

Numerous survey organizations asked hundreds of questions over the period of the Gulf Crisis, touching on everything from the number of casualties expected in a war to George Bush's handling of the crisis. The analysis in this chapter focuses on the handful of issues that appear to be most politically relevant: support for sending American troops to the Gulf region, and support for using military force against Iraq.

In the Gallup surveys, support for sending troops to the Gulf was measured by the following question:

Do you approve or disapprove the United States' decision to send U.S. troops to Saudi Arabia as a defense against Iraq?

When this question was initially asked in early August, 78 percent of Americans said it was right to send troops. As the news spotlight turned in September and October to the budget battle between Congress and the president, support decayed, with 66 percent saying it was right to send troops in a mid-October survey. Thereafter, attitudes were essentially steady until fighting began.

Attitudes toward use of force to evict Iraq from Kuwait varied greatly, depending on the wording of the question. The items in table 1 give a typical selection of results. Seventy percent of the public said the U.S. should take "all necessary action, including use of military force, to make sure Iraq withdraws its forces from Kuwait." Yet, in another survey at about the same time, only 45 percent said the U.S. should "engage in combat if Iraq . . . refuses to leave Kuwait." And only 32 percent wanted the U.S. to "increase the level of its troops to force Iraq to leave Kuwait."

It is natural, when confronted with such seemingly disparate results, to ask what, after all, people *really* believed. The question, however, is misleading, because most people, on most issues, do not "really think" any particular thing. With respect to a major issue like the Gulf Crisis, for example, most people monitor the news to some extent and collect information, but they rarely if ever have occasion to pull everything together into a single, coherent opinion. Hence, their thoughts remain a poorly organized mass of reactions and impressions rather than a hard-and-fast opinion. They may be angry at Saddam, put off by Kuwaiti society, worried about the cost of war, distrustful of the military—all without deciding whether or not they favor use of force against Iraq until the moment when the pollster pops the question to them. The answer they give will depend partly on the considerations that happen to be in their minds at the moment of response, and partly on how particular words in the question resonate with one another and with the context in which the question is asked.

Given all this, it is usually a mistake to take any one question as a reliable indicator of what people think (though one can still use a single question to examine time trends, or to discover what kinds of people are most likely to favor one or another side of an issue). Rather, one must analyze numerous questions in order to figure out, as best one can, where the center of opinion lies.[5]

In the case of using military force against Iraq, one might reasonably conclude from the data in table 1 that the public was divided but, on balance, cautiously willing to use force.[6] According to an impressively thorough analysis of dozens of questions asked on use of force, public

TABLE 1.   Attitude toward Use of Military Force at Time of Bush Decision on Second Troop Deployment to Saudi Arabia

Just from what you have heard, read or seen, which of these statements comes closest to how you, yourself, feel about the United States presence in the Mideast?

—The United States should begin to withdraw its troops	20%
—The United States should continue its present level of troop presence	42
—The United States should increase the level of its troops to force Iraq to leave Kuwait	32
—Don't know	7

(Gallup, November 1–4)

All in all, is the current situation in the Mideast worth going to war over, or not?

Yes	49%
No	41
Don't know	10

(Gallup, September 27–30, N = 1,000)

Do you agree or disagree that the United States should take all action necessary, including the use of military force, to make sure that Iraq withdraws its forces from Kuwait?

Agree, use force	70%
Disagree	27
Don't know	3

(ABC/*Washington Post*, November 2–4, N = 1,015)

Now that U.S. forces have been sent to Saudi Arabia and other areas of the Middle East, do you think they should engage in combat if Iraq . . . refuses to leave Kuwait?

Yes	45%
No	37
Don't know	18

(Gallup, October 18–19, N = 755)

Note: Data compiled from John Mueller, *Policy and Opinion in the Gulf War* (Chicago: University of Chicago Press, 1994).

attitudes on this issue were essentially stable over the period in which U.S. officials were deciding whether to use force (Mueller, 1994).

THE MAINSTREAM EFFECT

Because political leaders in the United States both consensually supported some aspects of the Bush administration's Persian Gulf policy and engaged in partisan debate over others, the Gulf Crisis affords opportunities to observe both the mainstream and the polarization effect. I begin with the former.

From the Iraqi invasion in August through the fall congressional elec-

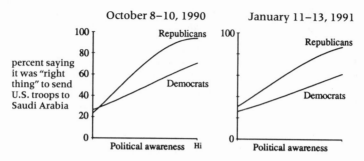

Source: CBS News-*New York Times* surveys.

Note: Estimates are based on coefficients and modeling procedures described in Appendix.

Fig. 3. Support for Policy of Sending U.S. Troops to Saudi Arabia

tion, there was no articulate opposition to the policy of sending U.S. forces to the region, and most important Democratic leaders publicly supported it.[7] Sending troops to the Gulf, thus, was a mainstream policy.

The effect of political awareness on support for this mainstream policy is shown in the left-hand panel of figure 3 (the data are from a CBS News-*New York Times* poll in late October). As can be seen, political awareness—here measured as a composite of formal education, attention to news about the Gulf Crisis, and attention to the budget negotiations in Congress[8]—is strongly associated with support for keeping U.S. troops in Saudi Arabia. Support increases from about 25 percent in the least-aware segment of the public to about 75 percent in the most-aware group. There is some partisan polarization in these data, but the dominant effect is that of a sharp, awareness-induced increase in support for Bush administration policy within all partisan groups. Five other CBS-*New York Times* polls from this period show the same pattern.[9] (See Appendix for technical details of the regression on which figure 3 is based.)

Two days after the fall congressional election, President Bush announced a decision to send several hundred thousand additional troops to the gulf. These reinforcements gave the United States, for the first time, the capacity not only to block further Iraqi aggression but to take the offensive in order to roll back Iraq's seizure of Kuwait.

Bush's troop buildup sparked harsh criticism from congressional Democrats (see Entman and Page, Chapter 4, this volume). But the criticism was as notable for what it did not contain as for what it did. In particular, no important Democratic spokesman urged Bush to withdraw American forces from the Gulf region, nor did any contend that Bush was wrong to send them there in the first place. Rather, the Democratic position was that diplomacy and economic sanctions should be given more time to work before the U.S. resorted to force.

The Democratic criticism, as we shall see, had its effect on public opinion. But, inasmuch as it refrained from challenging the basic Bush policy of sending U.S. troops to confront Iraq, it also failed to undermine public support for that policy. This can be seen in the right side of figure 3, which shows that public support for sending troops to the Gulf was essentially the same in early January as it was at the start of the crisis.[10]

In emphasizing the importance of political awareness in inducing support for the policies of mainstream elites, I do not claim that awareness is the only important determinant of public opinion. The claim, rather, is that, whatever an individual's predisposition to support a mainstream policy, greater levels of exposure to the mass media are likely to be associated with greater support for that policy.

This point is clear in figure 4, which shows the effect of awareness-induced exposure to elite and media discourse among four demographic groups: white males, white females, black males, and black females. White males have the strongest predisposition for U.S. involvement in the Gulf (and, as other evidence shows, for hawkish military policies generally), while black females have the weakest. But in each group, awareness has roughly the same tendency to induce approval for American involvement in the Gulf. Exposure to a one-sided elite discourse thus tends to override initial predispositions and to promote support for mainstream policy. (For technical details, see Appendix.)

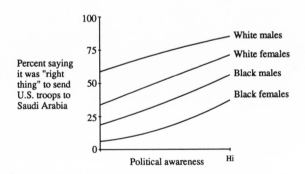

Source: CBS News-*New York Times* surveys.

Note: Estimates are based on procedures described in Appendix. Results are based on polls of January 8–10 and January 11–13.

Fig. 4. Group Differences in Support for Policy of Sending U.S. Troops to Saudi Arabia

These data, moreover, underestimate the extent to which media exposure can override personal predispositions. This can be seen from responses to another question, which was asked by the National Election Studies between November and January:

Which of the following do you think we should do now in the Persian Gulf:
- *Pull out U.S. forces entirely.*
- *Try harder to find a diplomatic solution.*
- *Tighten the economic embargo.*
- *Take tougher military action.*

For persons who dissented from the mainstream position of responding militarily to Iraq, this question provides a clear choice—"pull out U.S. forces entirely." Any of the other three responses imply support for continued U.S. military involvement. As can be seen in figure 5, the vast majority of Americans took an option other than the pullout option, thus either accepting the current level of military confrontation or urging greater military assertiveness. Even in the group most resistant to hawkish policies—African-American, Democratic women—rejection of the pullout option rises from about 55 percent at the lowest awareness level to about 85 percent at the highest level.[11]

In interpreting results from these poll questions, it is necessary to bear in mind that the data were collected at a time when the United States was on the verge of war—a war that, if it came, virtually everyone expected to be bloody. The most favorable government estimate, which was widely regarded as optimistic, was that the U.S. would suffer only

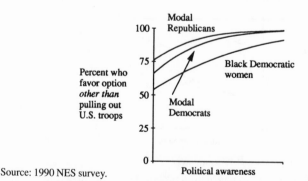

Source: 1990 NES survey.

Note: Estimates are based on coefficients and modeling procedures described in Zaller (1992, chap. 6).

Fig. 5. Support for Keeping U.S. Troops in Persian Gulf

three to five thousand casualties, including up to a thousand dead, and some observers expected American battlefield deaths to be ten thousand or more.[12]

The fact that, in this situation, a majority of the public asserted that the U.S. had been right to send troops to the Gulf, and that a larger majority declined the pullout option when offered it, is a testament to the power of elites to mobilize mass opinion through the media. As Lang and Lang (Chapter 2, this volume) show, few Americans knew anything about Iraq before the invasion of Kuwait, but after a few weeks of media exposure to the consensual view that Saddam Hussein, who was not even a communist, was too dangerous to be allowed to get away with swallowing Kuwait (see Dorman and Lvingston, Chapter 3, this volume), the country was, though not eager for war, quite prepared to accept it.

THE POLARIZATION EFFECT

We have been dealing so far with an aspect of Persian Gulf policy that commanded consensual support from mainstream elites. We turn now to three issues which provoked partisan controversy: whether Congress should pass a resolution authorizing military action against Iraq; whether the U.S. should allow more time before attacking Iraq to see if economic sanctions would work; and whether George Bush was doing a good job of handling the crisis. Each of these matters was sharply debated by partisan elites. Given this, we would expect exposure to elite discourse in the media to be associated with greater partisan polarization. That is, exposure should, for each issue, engender greater support for the conservative option among Republicans and greater support for the liberal position among Democrats.

This is what we do find in a CBS-*New York Times* poll taken a week prior to war. As shown in figure 6, awareness no longer induces greater support for the hawkish option, as it did when the elite consensus was hawkish. Rather, for all three issues, awareness induces greater partisan polarization, such that with increases in awareness, partisans gravitate more reliably toward their expected partisan positions. (See Appendix for technical details concerning figure 6.)

If there is any surprise in these results, it is that the question of whether to attack Iraq soon or allow economic sanctions more time provoked less polarization than other questions. The reason is probably that Bush never publicly advocated attacking Iraq as soon as the U.N. deadline for Iraqi withdrawal from Kuwait passed. His position was that if the U.S. showed it was prepared for war, it would be unnecessary to fight at

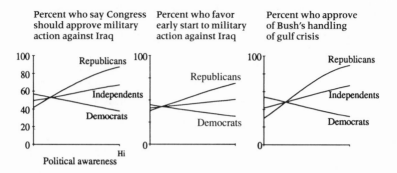

Source: CBS News-*New York Times* surveys, January 11–13.

Note: Estimates are based on coefficients and modeling procedures described in Appendix.

Fig. 6. Party Polarization on Gulf Policy

all because Iraq would back down.[13] The effect of this ambiguity was apparently to mute partisan polarization on this issue as compared to what occurred on others. The muting, however, was short-lived. Once Bush revealed his position by actually attacking Iraq, politically aware Republicans rallied overwhelmingly to support it (Zaller, forthcoming).

Altogether, then, exposure to media and elite opinion in the Gulf crisis, as indexed by political awareness, had the same effect as in past foreign policy crises: It induced support for the mainstream elite position in cases in which elite consensus existed, and it induced polarization in cases in which Democratic and Republican elites disagreed.

Conclusion

The results presented in this chapter suggest that attention to politics drives a socialization process that ties the attitudes of politically informed Americans to those of political elites. Important issues, however, remain unresolved.

ALTERNATIVE EMPIRICAL MODELS OF ELITE INFLUENCE

It is, first of all, unclear which aspect of media content most affects mass opinion. The chapters in this volume by Lang and Lang, Dorman and Livingston, Gitlin and Hallin, and Manheim devote much attention to the substantive ideas and information carried in the media, and scarcely any to partisan cues that may also have been conveyed. My chapter reverses this emphasis. Thus, for example, Dorman and Livingston attach importance to the fact that the media vilified Saddam as a new Hitler, while my analysis never mentions this aspect of press content and instead notes the bipartisan elite consensus in support of the Bush policy of military assertiveness. My assumption is that almost any negative coverage of Iraq would have been equally effective in mobilizing mass support for war, so long as partisan, ideological, and other leaders communicated to the public their belief that war was necessary.

The key question, thus, is as follows: To what extent is mass opinion affected by the substantive content of news reporting—a story's positivity or negativity, how it frames an issue, the particular arguments it makes or information it presents—and to what extent is mass opinion affected merely by the partisan cues that are embedded in media reportage?

If we look to the evidence from experimental studies of persuasion, the answer seems clear: In most politically relevant conditions, the "receiver" of persuasive messages is, as noted earlier, a "lazy organism" that will pay little attention to message content and much attention to peripheral attributes of the message, such as who the source is.[14]

Yet, because what happens in a psychological experiment might fail to capture what occurs in the real world, we would like to have real-world (or naturalistic) studies to corroborate the laboratory results. Unfortunately, we don't. There are naturalistic studies of the effect of *either* media content[15] *or* elite cues, but there is no naturalistic study, so far as I know, that rigorously analyzes the effects of one factor on mass opinion while controlling for the effects of the other.[16]

We are therefore left to base our conclusions on the evidence from laboratory studies. This evidence, though not conclusive, should give pause to those who examine media content independently of the elite cues it carries. Meanwhile, a naturalistic study of the relative importance of media content and elite cues should rank high on the agenda of future research in this area.

ALTERNATIVE NORMATIVE MODELS OF MEDIA INFLUENCE

There is also uncertainty over what role the media *ought* to play in helping to shape mass opinion. For example, the Lang and Lang chapter and the Dorman and Livingston chapter suggest that democracy will work poorly—or perhaps not work at all—unless the media provides citizens with enough contextual and other information to form balanced assessments of major issues. Implicit in this view is that, in an ideal democracy, the public should seriously evaluate each new issue, decide what it wants to have done, and authorize its leaders to take appropriate action.

The ideal, thus, is one of prospective (or forward-looking) citizen control of policy. Not unreasonably in light of the requirements of this demanding ideal, these chapters fault the press for failing to keep the public adequately informed before and during the Gulf Crisis.

An alternative ideal, more in line with the slant of my chapter, might be sketched as follows: As new issues come up, the public looks to public statements by its political leaders—partisan, ideological, religious, ethnic, and so forth—to decide what should be done, and is willing, within broad limits, to go along with what the majority of leaders advises. Then, as the consequences of elite initiatives become apparent in the form of policies that succeed or fail, the public judges its leaders accordingly. The ideal here is one of retrospective (or backward-looking) accountability of political leaders.[17] The function of the news media in this model is relatively modest: to convey the policy recommendations of leading political figures, and to indicate, after the dust has settled, whether the advice succeeded or failed. Judged in light of this ideal, media performance in the Gulf Crisis was probably adequate (though see Entman and Page, Chapter 4, this volume).

Inasmuch as these competing democratic models rest on normative concerns, data are not of much use in deciding between them, but it is still worthwhile to distinguish them.

HOW MUCH DO ELITES REALLY LEAD?

All of the writers in this volume, including me, assume a substantial amount of elite influence over mass opinion. But how clear is the evidence that elites are really leading mass opinion rather than, perhaps, following it? Not entirely clear, I believe.

Consider a case of apparent elite leadership for which we happen to have especially good opinion data: President Nixon's surprise announcement of wage and price controls in a nationally televised speech in 1971. By happenstance, a study of party activists was under way at the time of the speech. Among Republican activists interviewed before the speech, 37 percent favored controls; among those interviewed afterwards, 82 percent favored them (Barton 1974–75). Because of the quasi-experimental nature of the president's announcement and the fortuitous availability of pertinent opinion data, it seems clear that Nixon truly did lead rather than follow mass opinion in this case.

But yet, even here, there is room for doubt. A plausible argument can be made that Nixon's action on price controls, like his decision to go to China a year earlier, was, above all, an attempt to position himself for the 1972 election, and in this sense, an anticipation of what the public wanted—or would want, when prodded by the opposition party— rather than a wholly autonomous attempt to lead opinion.

The Democratic opposition to the Persian Gulf War in the late fall of 1990 appears to represent another case in which elites were both lead- ing and following at the same time. Democratic leaders supported the initial decision to send American troops to the Gulf, but were critical of the administration whenever it wanted to take offensive action against Iraq. And yet, when the moment of decision arrived in early January, enough congressional Democrats supported the Gulf War resolution to enable it to pass, and remaining Democrats made it clear that, although opposing an early start to hostilities, they would not play an obstruction- ist role if war began.

One plausible interpretation of the Democrat's equivocal opposition is that they were, by their actions in the fall, testing the depth of the pres- ident's support, but, finding it too strong to challenge, fell into line be- hind his policy. Another is that, finding the public roughly evenly divided on the question of force against Iraq at the end of their fall politi- cal offensive, Democrats felt they could follow their own best judg- ments, and that most concluded the president's position merited support. Or finally, Democrats may have felt that, however they voted, the president intended to go ahead with military action against Iraq, and that the safest course in this event was to let him have his way. If the war was successful, they could say that they only urged caution rather than really opposed it. And if unsuccessful, they could claim that they op- posed starting it prematurely.

Whatever combination of these scenarios is correct, the Democratic opposition was both leading mass opinion (since any actions it took ei- ther to support or oppose administration policies affected public opin- ion) and also following it (since all moves involved calculations of how the public would react). Thus, the relationship between elites and masses appears, in this case as, I suspect, in most others, deeply recipro- cal.

The exact combination of leading and following done by elites un- doubtedly varies from case to case and from one elite actor to another, thus requiring the analyst interested in elite-mass relations to make case-by-case judgments as well. An important thing to note about such judgments, however, is that a high degree of correspondence between elite and mass opinion, or even between changes in elite opinion and changes in mass opinion, is not, by itself, helpful for deciding the ques- tion of who is leading whom. To do this, the analyst must examine more than just public opinion data. She or he must examine the dynamics of elite decision-making—in the Congress, the executive branch, the media, and in relevant policy communities—in relation to events and to public opinion about these events. (See Chapter 12, below, for such an analysis).

Thus, the body of this chapter, in demonstrating the importance of political awareness in creating a correspondence between elite and mass opinion, is only the beginning of an investigation of the nature of elite-mass relations in the foreign policy area. A fully adequate account of elite opinion leadership is not one which sees a public that responds to elite cues in a completely mechanical fashion, though a supportive response of the public to skillfully crafted elite initiatives can usually be counted upon. Rather, it is an account in which elites—always having some ideas of their own, always looking back to see whether the public is following, and always trying to anticipate what the public will say, after the dust has settled, that it wanted all along—attempt to lead and to follow at the same time.

Appendix

This appendix provides technical information concerning the construction of the figures reported in this chapter. Since all data used in this paper are publicly available through the ICPSR at the University of Michigan, this information should enable the interested person to precisely replicate the graphs presented in the body of the chapter.[18]

Figure 1 is adapted from Zaller (1991) and figure 2 is from Zaller (1992), where technical details are reported. The remaining technical information follows.

Figures 3 and 5. The model used in all panels of these figures is a logistic function in which the independent variables are political awareness, party attachment, ideology, party X awareness, and ideology X awareness. This type of function cannot capture very much of the dynamics of public opinion, but suffices for discussion of mainstream and polarization effects.

Awareness is measured in the model as a combination of two 4-point scales, education and attention to news about the Gulf Crisis, with missing data omitted. The two awareness items are correlated at .18, which indicates low-scale reliability.[19] Party attachment combines responses to two questions into a scale that scores Republicans as -2, independent-leaning Republicans as -1, independent-leaning Democrats as $+1$, Democrats as $+2$, and all others as 0. The ideology variable counts self-described conservatives as -1, liberals as $+1$, and all others as 0.

The exact wording of the policy questions not shown in text is as follows:

> Do you think the United States did the right thing in sending troops to Saudi Arabia, or should we have stayed out?
>
> The United Nations has passed a resolution authoring the use of military force against Iraq if they do not withdraw their troops from Kuwait by January 15. If Iraq does not withdraw from Kuwait by then, do you think the United States should start military actions against Iraq, or should the United States wait longer to see if the trade embargo and other economic sanctions work?
>
> Would you want your Congressman to vote for or to vote against giving President Bush the authority to use armed force in the Persian Gulf?
>
> Do you approve or disapprove of the way George Bush is handling Iraq's invasion of Kuwait?

These items were converted to dichotomies, with 1 assigned to the response of interest and other codes set to 0. The coefficients obtained from modeling these items are in table 1. In converting the coefficients into figures, I counted as "Republicans" those who described themselves as Republicans and as conservatives; "Democrats" were Democrats and liberals. "Independents" were centrist independents. The measure of party shown in the figures thus combines the effect of party and ideology; however, party is by far the most important variable, as can be seen in table 2.

All awareness measures have been standardized. In constructing graphical estimates, I show the effects of an increase in political awareness from the 1st percentile to the 98th—that is, the effect of awareness over the middle 98 percent of the scale. Due to distributional differences, the z-scores necessary to achieve this range vary. In the October data, they are -2.53 to 1.81; in the January survey, they are -2.46 to 1.41.

Figure 4. I combined data from the January 5–7 and 11–13 to obtain a sufficient number of African-Americans for analysis. Awareness was measured in the way described earlier. The effect of awareness on the "right thing" item was statistically significant in a bivariate logistic regression within each group. The range of awareness z-scores in figures for blacks ranged from -2.84 to 1.63; for whites they ranged from -2.42 to 1.44.

TABLE 2. Regression Coefficients for Mainstream and Polarization Models

	Right to Send Troops (Oct. 8–10)	Right to Send Troops (Jan. 11–13)	Gulf Force Resolution (Jan. 11–13)	Start War Early (Jan. 11–13)	Approve Bush on Gulf (Jan. 11–13)
Intercept	0.82	0.56	0.50	-0.11	0.40
Awareness	0.62	0.46	0.16	0.10	0.23
(standardized)	(.09)	(.06)	(.06)	(.05)	(.06)
Party attachment	-0.32	-0.25	-0.30	-0.20	-0.29
(range -2 to +2)	(.05)	(.04)	(.04)	(.03)	(.03)
Ideology	-0.00	-0.04	-0.17	-0.05	-0.30
(range -1 to +1)	(.10)	(.08)	(.08)	(.08)	(.08)
Party X aware	-0.12	-0.07	-0.11	-0.08	-0.14
	(.05)	(.04)	(.04)	(.03)	(.04)
Ideology X aware	.00	0.01	-0.12	-0.08	-0.15
	(.11)	(.08)	(.08)	(.08)	(.08)

Source: CBS News-*New York Times* surveys.
Note: Model is a logistic function with negatively signed coefficients. Number of usable cases in the October data is 949; the number in January is 1,501. Standard errors are in parentheses.

Notes

I am very grateful to Darcy Geddes and Benjamin Page for comments on an early draft of this paper. The data in this paper have been drawn from various Center for Political Studies and National Election Studies surveys between 1964 and 1991, and from polls conducted by the CBS News-*New York Times* polling organization in 1990 and 1991. I am grateful to the Rockefeller Foundation, the National Science Foundation, the CBS News-*NYT* organization, and the InterUniversity Consortium for Political and Social Research at the University of Michigan for making these data publicly available.

1. For analysis of the effect of political awareness on susceptibility to attitude change during the Gulf Crisis, see Zaller, 1993.
2. Sobel, 1989. None of this is to suggest that citizens lack *any* basis for forming opinions about foreign affairs. Almost everyone has gut-level feelings concerning groups such as foreigners, protesters, and communists, and these feelings can be used as guides to opinion (Sniderman, Brody, and Tetlock 1991). General predispositions toward hawkishness, pacifism, or vigilance can also guide opinion formation (Hurwitz and Peffley 1987). And finally, established loyalties to Democratic or Republican party leaders can serve as serviceable cues to opinion formation (see, generally, Page and Shapiro 1992.) However, the ability to use partisan cues or general predispositions as a basis for reacting to events should not be confused with the capacity for informed evaluation of elite initiatives.
3. Recently, some psychological research has challenged the "lazy organism" view, but not in a way that has much relevance for assessing the capabilities of a mass political audience. See discussion in Zaller (1992, chap. 3).
4. This general line of argument parallels that taken by Converse (1964) in his classic treatment of mass belief systems.
5. For a more systematic treatment of this subject, see Zaller (1992, chaps. 2–4).
6. For similar analyses, see William Schneider, "Public Backs Gulf War as Last Option," *National Journal*, January 5, 1992, p. 5; Richard Morin, "Two Ways of Reading the Public's Lips on Gulf Policy," *Washington Post*, January 14, 1991.
7. See E. J. Dionne, Jr., "Post-Cold War Consensus Backs U.S. Intervention," *Washington Post*, August 8, 1990, p. A12; Karen Tumulty, "Bush Gets Solid Backing From Congress," *Los Angeles Times*, August 9, 1990. See also "Strategic Politicians," Chapter 12 of this volume.
8. A three-item composite measure is more reliable than any of the individual items, including the item on attention to the Gulf Crisis.
9. I report the results of the early October poll because it contained the most reliable exposure measure and hence produced somewhat stronger results than the other pools.
10. In an earlier study, I found evidence that party polarization on the "right thing" question increased in early November in response to the Democratic criti-

cism (Zaller 1992, chap. 6). This finding, which was based on NES data, does not replicate in the CBS-*NYT* data, which show that modest party polarization on the "right thing" question was present from September and did not intensify over time. The most likely explanation for this difference, I believe, is chance fluctuation; if so, the NES data, because they involve many fewer cases, are probably less reflective of actual opinion. It is possible, however, that the difference arises from a question-order artifact, since the NES question appeared in a less "politicizing" context (see Lau, Sears, and Jessor, 1990) and may for this reason have been slower than the CBS-*NYT* question to show a polarization effect.

    11. Only 16 percent of African-American Democratic women supported a pullout.

    12. The more optimistic estimate was from Les Aspin, Democratic chair of the House Military Affairs Committee. See *New York Times,* January 9, 1991, A1.

    13. Asked by reporters why he didn't threaten to use force as soon as the U.N. deadline passed, Bush replied, "Because I'm not in a threatening mode. I don't think any of us are. We are in a determined mode" (Woodward 1991, p. 331).

    14. See note 3 above and associated text.

    15. Iyengar and Kinder 1987; Fan 1988; Iyengar 1991; Page and Shapiro 1992.

    16. Studies which control for the effects of both media content and elite cues may be difficult to achieve in a naturalistic setting. As Bennett has shown, the media tend to "index" the slant of their coverage to the range of opinions that exist within the government (Bennett 1990). In consequence, periods of elite consensus on cues are likely to be periods in which the media cover only one side of the story, while periods in which partisan elites transmit opposing cues to the public are likely to be periods in which the media carry balanced coverage. With the two types of media content thus confounded, it will be hard to tell whether elite cues or media coverage has the greater impact on mass opinion.

    17. This argument parallels that of Fiorina (1981) in his study of retrospective voting in U.S. elections.

    18. I will promptly send my SPSS code via bitnet to anyone wishing to use or check it.

    19. Despite this low level of inter-item reliability, the two items produce stronger results together than either can alone. Note also that the more reliable information scale from the NES survey produces generally similar results.

References

Barton, A. H. 1974–75. "Consensus and Conflict among American Leaders." *Public Opinion Quarterly* 38:507–30.

Cantril, H. 1944. *Gauging Public Opinion.* Princeton: Princeton University Press.

Converse, P. 1964. "The nature of belief systems in mass publics." In *Ideology and Discontent,* ed. David Apter. Free Press: New York.

Fan, D. 1988. *Predictions of Public Opinion from the Mass Media.* New York: Greenwood.

Fiorina, M. 1981. *Retrospective Voting.* New Haven: Yale University Press.

Gamson, W., and A. Modigliani. 1966. "Knowledge and Foreign Policy Opinion." *Public Opinion Quarterly* 30:187–99.

Hurwitz, J., and M. Peffley. 1987. "How Are Foreign Policy Attitudes Structured? A Hierarchical Model." *American Political Science Review* 81:1099–1130.

Iyengar, S. 1991. *Is Anyone Responsible?* Chicago: University of Chicago Press.

Iyengar, S., and D. R. Kinder, 1987. *News That Matters.* Chicago: University of Chicago Press.

Lau, R., D. O. Sears, and Tom Jessor. 1990. "Fact or Artifact Revisited: Survey Instrument Effects and Pocketbook Politics." *Political Behavior* 12:217–42.

Lippmann, W. 1922. *Public Opinion.* New York: The Free Press.

McGuire, W. 1969. "The Nature of Attitudes and Attitude Change." In *Handbook of Social Psychology.* Vol. 3. Gardner Lindzey and Elliott Aronson, eds. Reading, Mass: Addison-Wesley.

Mueller, J. 1973. *War, Presidents, and Public Opinion.* New York: Wiley.

Mueller, J. 1994. *Policy and Opinion in the Gulf War.* Chicago: University of Chicago Press.

Page, B., and R. Shapiro. 1992. *The Rational Public.* Chicago: University of Chicago Press.

Price, V., and J. Zaller. 1993. "Who Gets the News: Measuring Individual Differences in Likelihood of News Reception." *Public Opinion Quarterly,* Summer.

Sniderman, P., R. Brody, and P. Tetlock. 1991. *Reasoning and Choice.* New York: Cambridge University Press.

Sobel, R. 1989. "The Polls: U.S. Intervention in El Salvador and Nicaragua." *Public Opinion Quarterly* 63:114–28.

Woodward, B. 1991. *The Commanders.* New York: Simon and Shuster.

Zaller, J. 1991. "Information, Values, and Opinion." *American Political Science Review* 85:1215–38.

———. 1992. *The Nature and Origins of Mass Opinion.* New York: Cambridge University Press.

———. 1993. "The Converse-McGuire Model of Attitude Change and the Gulf War Opinion Rally," *Political Communication* 10:369–88.

ten

Richard A. Brody

Crisis, War, and Public Opinion

The Media and Public Support for the President

The interactions of presidential policy, press content, and public opinion have been analyzed in the six presidencies from 1960 to 1984. Over the quarter-century from the Kennedy inaugural to the Reagan reelection, the American people have used evidence of policy success and failure supplied to them by the press in forming their evaluation of presidential performance. The standards of "success" and "failure," against which performance is judged, are derived from outcomes for which there is general agreement—prosperity is "good," war is "bad," and so forth—and from expectations set by the president and his administration—"if we are allowed to do this, this good thing will result." In the aggregate, the public seems to respond to policy outcomes, not to the means of achieving them; the response is pragmatic rather than ideological.

Policy proposals, as such, appear to be heavily discounted. This and the phenomenon of the rally response—which will be discussed below—are products of the dependence of the public on opinion leadership in situations of uncertainty. Proposals give rise to uncertainty because they usually generate debate, often a fairly technical debate, among political elites about the way in which public policy problems are to be solved. In any given policy area few Americans are confident that they know the best or even an effective solution to a problem. Absent a preferred solution, members of the public, if they are moved to form opinions at all, take their cue from opinion leaders in whom they otherwise have confidence. Under this account, the division in the elite will condition the impact of a given proposal on changes in public opinion. If the elite is evenly divided, the net shift in opinion is likely to be small; if the division of the elite is skewed, a definitive acceptance or rejection of the proposal is the likely outcome and this will produce a political result to which the public can respond.

Public evaluations of presidential performance have a large inertial component. This means that the public is not as fickle or "moody" as it is sometimes portrayed (see, for example, Almond 1950; Rosenau 1961). The public can and does rapidly revise its evaluation of presidential performance; these rapid shifts almost always take place in the wake of unanticipated international events—crises—which catch both the elite and the public unprepared. Ordinarily international crises add to presidential support but, given enough negative criticism by legitimate American commentators, a president can suffer a substantial loss in approval (Brody and Shapiro 1989b). Rally gains and losses are episodic; their effects pass and the precrisis inertia is reestablished.

Inertia in the system does not preclude changes in levels of support; it means that levels will change gradually. Our data indicate that by and large changes in public opinion respond to impressions of presidential success and failure formed from indications of policy outcomes reported in the news (Lodge et al. 1989). Lodge and his colleagues summarize the process as follows: First, impression formation is "on-line," that is, judgments are made as relevant information is encountered. Second, the judgments are stored in memory as summary evaluations of the attitude objects—metaphorically, an "evaluation counter" or "judgment tally." Third, it is the summary evaluation that is revised in light of new information relevant to the judgment. And fourth, "when asked to voice an opinion, people typically retrieve their [current] summary evaluation from memory" (ibid., 401). Given the fact that most people do not directly experience the world of politics, impressions of presidential success or failure are drawn from daily news. News reports prime the public to attend to areas of public policy (Iyengar and Kinder 1987) and provide the basis for the public's evaluative response (Iyengar 1991).

The public can also respond to directly experienced indications of presidential policy performance. For example, with media content controlled, Brody found a direct influence of macroeconomic indicators on support for President Reagan; this shows that the public does not rely exclusively on media. It is not clear what switches public attention from mediated to unmediated indications of policy success or failure.[1]

Previous research makes clear the dominant role played by news of results, per se, in the public's updating of its impression of presidential job performance. The dominance of results also gives rise to an anomaly: If results dominate, how do we account for the growth in positive public support in periods characterized by obvious failures of U.S. foreign policy?

International Crises and Public Opinion Rallies

In times of international crisis the public appears to depart from its reliance on policy outcomes. International crises involving the United States are often brought on by failures of United States foreign policy. Nevertheless they often occasion an increase in support for the president. Examples of foreign policy failures that led to rallies in public support for the president are found in such crises as the U-2 incident in 1960, the Bay of Pigs in 1961, the Iranian hostage crisis in 1979, the downing of flight KAL-007 in 1983, and Iraq's invasion of Kuwait in 1991. If the public behaved as it usually does in situations such as these—which offered ample evidence of policy failure—public support for the president would decline, not increase. But these "rally situations" are unusual and of interest to analysts precisely because the public responds in an unexpected fashion.

A widely accepted explanation for the rally of public opinion in international crises hypothesizes that the threat to the United States, inherent in such events, gives rise to a patriotic response on the part of the public (Mueller 1973). On this account, the patriotic response manifests itself in an increase in approval for the most visible American political institution, the presidency. The plausibility of this explanation is attested to by its persistence in the absence of direct test; no measurement of "patriotism" has even been put forward to test the hypothesis. It persists in spite of the fact that about half of the international incidents that fit Mueller's and Kernell's criteria for "rally" events are not associated with an increase in support for the president (Brody and Shapiro 1989a, 89). We shall try to offer a plausible test of the "patriotism" hypothesis in data from the Gulf rally.

An alternative explanation has been proposed by Brody and Shapiro (1989a; Brody 1991). Under this explanation, political elites frame the public's response to uncertain international events. If and when opinion leaders publicly interpret a crisis as a result of policy failure, a rally will not take place. If the elite is silent or openly supportive of the administration's position, the public will respond to the administration's generally positive one-sided view of the events—to the administration's "spin"—and rally behind the president. A rally will last as long as the president's tacit or explicit support-coalition persists.

This explanation is grounded on three assumptions: (1) The public uses available information, (2) the normal mix of information changes in international crises, and (3) the press will report criticism if it is offered by "legitimate" sources. In short a rally is brought about because elite opinion leaders change their behavior, not because the public alters its approach to evaluating the president.

From the perspective of previous research on the dynamics of public support for the president the confrontation between Iraq and the United States in the Persian Gulf presents two distinct and separate phases. The first phase begins with the August 2, 1990, Iraqi invasion of Kuwait and ends in the middle of October 1990. This period is a typical "rally" evincing a large increase in public support for the president (Mueller 1973; Kernell 1978; Brody and Shapiro 1989a). The second phase begins in mid-October 1991 and, for our purposes, is considered to have ended when the cease fire was declared in March 1991. The second phase may not be a rally. In nonrallies the public responds to policy outcomes, which is to say, to information that indicates the apparent success or failure of diplomatic and military efforts. Mass media content is crucial to public opinion in both phases. But the type of media content affecting public opinion is expected to be different in the two phases of the confrontation.

The distinctiveness of the two phases of the confrontation is readily apparent in the trend in public assessments of President Bush over the thirty-three weeks from mid-July 1990 to March 1991; this trend is presented in figure 1.[2] It remains to be shown that the trend in support is associated with one type of media content in the "rally" phase of the crisis and with another type of content after the rally phase ended.

This demonstration will take place in the context of research on sources of public support for the president and of related research on the effects of international crises on the structure of public approval of the president.

This chapter will focus primarily on the "rally" phase of the confrontation between Iraq and United States in the Persian Gulf. After looking closely at the rally, we will examine the second—postrally—phase of the crisis.

The Confrontation in the Gulf: Phase I

Confrontation between Iraq and United States in the Persian Gulf arose, without question, from a failure of United States foreign policy but a failure about which the public was, at the time, largely unaware. How did our policy fail? It now appears that, despite a sizable intelligence operation in Iraq and despite an accumulation of evidence that could have signaled Iraq's intention to annex Kuwait, the Bush administration was caught off guard by the August 2, 1990, invasion. Saddam Hussein had

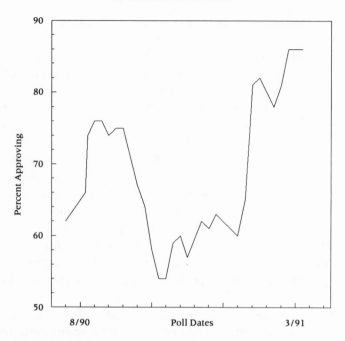

Fig. 1. Bush Approval, July 1990–March, 1991

been issuing public threats to Kuwait and the Gulf emirates from the middle of July but the Bush administration convinced itself that Saddam was simply "posturing." On July 24 the United States carried out a modest air and sea deployment in the Gulf. Ironically, this mobilization took place the day before Ambassador Glaspie met with Saddam to assure him of our friendship. With the benefit of hindsight it appears that the president was more active in trying to convince Congress not to impose economic sanctions on Iraq than in trying to convince Iraq of our commitment to Kuwait and the emirates.[3] In the end, our policy with respect to Iraq and the Gulf failed because it neither placated nor deterred Saddam Hussein.

In the special war commemorative issue of *Newsweek (America at War: From the Frenzied Buildup to the Joyous Homecoming)*, Tom Mathews, in recounting the elements of United States policy in the Gulf, documented our assessments of Saddam's intentions and the degree to which the invasion revealed a failure of our intelligence and policy.[4] From his review of preinvasion diplomatic and intelligence efforts Mathews concluded that "not since 1950, when Dean Acheson announced that South Korea was not within America's Asian defense perimeter, had the State Department left a friendly nation so open to attack." The failure was not the

State Department's alone. The Mathews article makes clear that President Bush, the CIA, the Defense Intelligence Agency, and National Security Council shared the State Department's misreading of Saddam's intentions.[5]

When Iraq went into Kuwait, leaders in Congress knew the key features of our Gulf policy; they were aware that we had misconstrued intelligence information from the Gulf and that, as a result, our policy had failed. *Newsweek* reported discussions between senators and Saddam in the spring of 1990[6] and mentioned precrisis briefings, by the CIA's and DIA's Gulf specialists, of the Senate Intelligence Committee and the House Foreign Affairs Committee. At the time of the invasion the potential existed for opinion leaders to criticize the premises and execution of our Gulf policy. Members of Congress had the basis for informing the American people of the administration's failure to deter Saddam. But with some exceptions credible opposition elites did not provide this analysis to the American people (Entman and Page, Chapter 4 in this volume).

News about the Gulf for the first month was dominated by stories about the deployment of United States troops to Saudi Arabia, the bringing of other nations into the region in opposition to Iraq, United Nations resolutions, the release of some foreign nationals by Iraq, and cooperation between the U.S. and the USSR. Richard Cohen discusses the advantage gained by the Bush administration from the fact that most members of Congress were out of town working in their districts for the first month of the crisis:

> the timing of the Iraqi invasion of Kuwait gave President Bush an unusually free hand and an unchallenged voice, on both the legislative and partisan fronts, in steering what may be the key event of his presidency. Throughout August, few members of Congress were visible in Washington to discuss the crisis with one another or with the American public.[7]

But the mechanical advantage of Congress being out of town is insufficient to explain the assent of members of Congress. Senate and House leadership was openly supportive and praising of the actions. Majority Leader George Mitchell signed onto the initiative: he stated on August 8, 1990, "it is important for the nation to unite behind the President in this time of challenge to American interests." Richard Gephardt's only complaint was that our allies were too slow in matching our response. Congress members returned to Washington on September 4. Hearings were held on September 6, and some cautious criticisms were voiced by Tom

Harkin (D.-Iowa), Terry Sanford (D.-N.C.), and Sam Nunn (D.-Ga.). As chair of the Armed Services Committee, Senator Nunn is the kind of spokesperson to whom the public looks for opinion leadership. But these cautious voices were overwhelmed by praise for the action. The *Congressional Quarterly* describes senators' and House members' reactions to Secretary Baker's testimony, at the first hearings on the Gulf crisis, as "[lavish] praise for the administration's actions when Baker testified before both chambers' foreign affairs panels."[8]

On September 11—six weeks into the crisis—President Bush addressed a joint session of Congress. Richard Gephardt gave the Democratic "response." Andrew Rosenthal described Gephardt's response as highly "supportive."[9] However, Susan Rasky—under the headline "From Congress, Praise and Muted Criticism"—reported concerns expressed by Democratic and Republican members of Congress. Barney Frank (D.-Maine) and Henry Hyde (R.Ill.) were quoted in the piece.[10]

On September 13 more criticism was reported: Dante Fascell (D.-Fla.) mentioned the War Powers Act. This was a switch since Fascell was reported earlier as having silenced Robert Torricelli (D.-N.J.) when he had questioned Secretary Baker's characterization of the War Powers Act as unconstitutional (Cohen 1990). Brock Adams (D.-Wash.) argued that Congress should move to reassert its authority.

By September 20 criticism of the policy became an important theme in reporting. R. W. Apple, Jr., wrote: "Congressional criticism of the Bush Administration's policies in the Persian Gulf, nonexistent in the first days after Iraq's invasion of Kuwait, then muted, is growing louder on both sides of the aisle as lawmakers openly attack the President on several major points."[11]

From this point forward the Gulf crisis appears to have lost its special status for opposition elites. Press attention to the Gulf began to wane and other stories appeared, especially stories about the budget deficit, the bipartisan budget compromise that failed to get support on the Hill, and the possible shutdown of the government. Bipartisan criticism of the president on the Gulf and the budget was the likely source of the rapid decline in public support for President Bush that set in seven to eight weeks into the crisis.

We should not lose sight of the fact that throughout this period U.S. policy in the Gulf was subject to severe criticism from Iraq, Jordan, and from the leadership of the Palestine Liberation Organization. President Bush's policy may have been relatively free from criticism by American opinion leaders, but criticism of the policy by foreign leaders was available to the American people.

Public support for President Bush, in this time period, reached its maximum about four weeks after the invasion of Kuwait. This point in time was coincident with the first stirring of criticism of the policy by members of Congress. The data also suggest that as the pace of critical commentary increased, President Bush's support declined precipitately.

Daily News and the Gulf Rally

In order to systematically explore the sources of the rally in the first phase of the confrontation between Iraq and United States in the Persian Gulf we have defined four measures derived from news of the crisis.

COVERAGE

The first measure is an index of news attention to the crisis in the Gulf ("coverage"). We use two indexes of total coverage. One is derived from our analyses of data found in Vanderbilt University's *Television News Index and Abstracts*. It is the total daily time devoted to the Gulf story averaged for the days between two adjacent polls measuring support for President Bush. The second draws on the *Executive Trend Watch's* National Media Index (hereafter, ETWI). The ETWI "tracks the content of the three networks' nightly broadcast, five major newspapers, and *Time, Newsweek,* and *U.S. News & World Report.* These items are then weighted according to where Americans with at least a high-school degree get information on national issues" (LaMay 1991, p. 45). We have transformed the ETWI to reflect Gulf coverage as a percentage of the top six news stories in a given period. Because it includes newspapers and news magazines, as well as television news, the ETWI is a broader measure of coverage than the one we built from the Vanderbilt data.[12]

The pattern of news attention in the rally phase of the confrontation between Iraq and United States in the Persian Gulf is presented in figure 2. Clearly, media attention is not constant. It waxes early in the crisis and wanes after the initial troop buildup and as the budget deficit story supplants the Gulf toward the end of the rally.

Coverage is a measure of the degree to which public opinion was "primed" to take account of the confrontation in the Gulf as it evaluated President Bush's performance. But priming, per se, does give us an expectation about the direction of the effect on support. We will need measures of "content" rather than simply "coverage" if we wish to explain the impact of Gulf news on support for President Bush. To pursue this explanation we coded three types of news content.

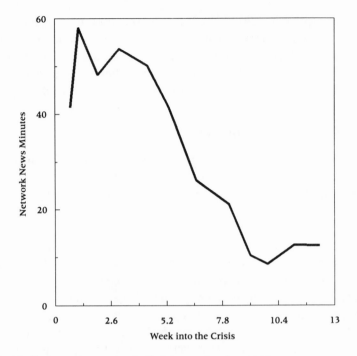

Fig. 2. Media Attention to the Gulf, August–October 1990

RESULTS NEWS

Each news report during the period of the confrontation between Iraq and United States in the Persian Gulf—irrespective of whether or not it was a Gulf related story—was coded as either an outcome or a non-outcome story.[13] "Non-outcome" stories report policy proposals or present ideas or facts about events. "Outcome" stories report system outputs and/or the results of specific actions by the participants in the crisis, or non-Gulf results stories that attain the status of "most important story of the day." Outcome stories are furthered classified as positive, negative, or neutral by the standards described above. Positive— "good"–stories either report outcomes whose desirability is not in dispute (so-called "valence" issues) or outcomes which meet expectations set by the administration. Negative—"bad"–outcomes are the mirror image of positive outcomes; those whose undesirability is not in dispute or which confound expectations set by the administration. Neutral outcomes are those for which there is no societal consensus and for which the administration has set no expectations.

The results news stories, during a period bracketed by two opinion polls, are combined into a news ratio. To model the hypothesized inertia and updating in the impression-formation process the news ratio is summed and averaged. This quantity can be thought of, for the public at large, as the aggregate equivalent of Lodge's individual-level "judgment tally" (Lodge et al. 1989, 401). Previous research suggests that this measure will not be related to support for the president during the rally phase of the crisis but will be a key to understanding presidential support during the second phase of the confrontation between Iraq and the United States in the Persian Gulf.

CRITICISM BY AMERICAN ELITES

Our measure of criticism by American opinion leaders was also built from Vanderbilt data. The individuals who were the sources of on-camera quotations within each story were listed and identified as either supporters or critics of the policy. Supporters were sources in or out of the administration who praised or were not apparently critical of the policy. Critics were elite opposition sources including senators and representatives who were openly critical of administration actions. The measure we employ is the percentage of all American elite sources who were critical of U.S. policy or actions in the Gulf. Our expectation is that this percentage will be negatively related to support for President Bush.

CRITICISM BY FOREIGN ELITES

Foreign opposition sources—usually Saddam Hussein, other Iraqi leaders, leaders of the PLO, or King Hussein of Jordan—frequently criticized the United States' policy in the Gulf. The measure we employ is the percentage of all coverage of foreign elite news sources which was critical of U.S. policy or actions in the Gulf. This measure offers a rough test of the "patriotism" hypothesis in that it reflects the idea that criticism by our adversaries will make it harder for Americans to express negative views and thus symbolically make common cause with our enemies. Although this variant of the patriotism hypotheses has not been found to affect support in previous rally situations (Brody and Shapiro, 1989b), the prominence of foreign critics in this crisis argues for including it in the study. If foreign criticism makes Americans reluctant to criticize the president, we would expect a positive relationship between the relative level of criticism among foreign commentary on our policy and support for President Bush.

Figure 3 displays the trends for these three measures of news content.

Over the twelve weeks of the rally phase of the confrontation between Iraq and United States in the Persian Gulf the cumulative news

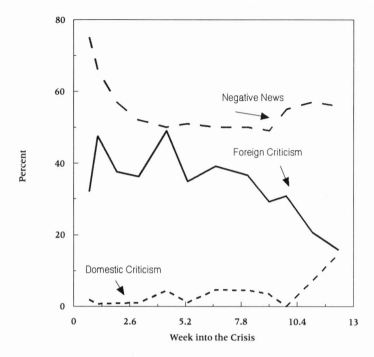

Fig. 3. Media Content Trends, August–October 1990

ratio moved from being very negative to less negative to more negative again. News of the invasion, hostage-taking, forced evacuations, and other "bad" outcomes began to give way to indications of policy success. The news increasingly offered indications that Iraq had been deterred from moving into Saudi Arabia,[14] that the strategy of creating a coalition in opposition to Saddam Hussein was succeeding, and that the United Nations was backing the United States. By the end of the rally period, news of the politics of the federal budget deficit and the failure of the president and congressional leadership to craft a successful budget compromise began to supplant the Gulf as the most important story of the day. The focus on Washington politics brought an increased volume of "bad" news to the American people.

Figure 3 shows that trends in American and foreign elite criticism of U.S. Gulf policy were mirror images during the rally phase. When foreign elite criticism was high, domestic criticism was low. When the proportion of foreign criticism to all foreign commentary declined midway through the rally, criticism by American opinion leaders became more prominent.

Analyses of news content show that public support for President

Bush during the rally phase of the confrontation between Iraq and United States in the Persian Gulf responded to two sources of opinion leadership. Despite policy failures and other manifestly bad outcomes in the Gulf, in the early weeks of the crisis the public seems to have reacted to the absence of criticism of President Bush's policies by American elites and the large volume of criticism by our foreign adversaries. The reaction took the form of the public professing its satisfaction with the president's job performance. The rally persisted until opinion leadership reversed its stance. When foreign criticism declined and domestic criticism increased, the American public appears to have shifted to basing its judgment on news reporting political and policy outcomes. At this point, the "bad" news, which had been there all along, took on a different role in the American people's evaluation of presidential performance. A glance back at figure 3 shows that the apparent shift happened at the point when negative results-news was increasing; at this point the Gulf rally ended. Ten weeks into the crisis in the Gulf, public approval of President Bush's job performance had slipped to 54 percent, eight percentage points below its precrisis level.[15]

Phase II: Public Support After the Rally

The second phase of the Gulf crisis covers the twenty weeks from October 1990 until the end of the war. During the first half of this period, from mid-October to the end of December, support for the president gradually returned to its pre-invasion level. During these ten weeks the United Nations passed three additional resolutions that called on Saddam Hussein to end the occupation of Kuwait, release the foreign nationals (hostages) being held in Iraq and Kuwait, and, in Resolution 678, which was passed on November 29, 1990, that authorized "member states . . . to use all means necessary . . . to restore international peace and security in the area." This period also includes congressional hearings on policy options in the Gulf, the 1990 midterm national elections, and the issuing of presidential orders increasing the number of U.S. forces in the Gulf to half a million. On December 1, 1990, Saddam Hussein accepted President Bush's proposal for talks; but for the balance of the month talks were elusive. However, more concretely, on December 6 Iraq released the foreign nationals being held in Iraq and Kuwait.

In these ten weeks the American people received a mix of favorable and unfavorable news. Prominently featured positive news included the end of the budget crisis with the passage of the budget compromise. But this good news was tempered by the fact that statements by members of

Congress, including the president's partisan supporters, were full of re-crimination and expressions of disappointment over Bush's violation of his campaign pledge not to increase taxes. News about the Gulf included a series of U.N. resolutions supporting the U.S. policy of challenging Saddam Hussein with a wide-ranging international coalition. The release of the hostages held in Kuwait and Iraq was widely interpreted as a victory for United States and United Nations policy. On the negative side, the net loss of Republican seats in the midterm congressional elections was bad news from the president's perspective. Bearing more directly on the Gulf crisis, the tenor of the congressional committee hearings on Gulf policy was unfortunate for the president. In these hearings we find highly credible military figures questioning the wisdom of increasing the size of our forces in the region.

The second half of phase two begins with 1991. The impressive rise in approval of President Bush's "handling of his job as president" evident in this period, was accompanied, *inter alia*, by the other events. The talks between Iraq and the U.S., which Saddam Hussein had agreed to on December 1, began at the foreign-minister level on January 9, 1991; they did not contribute to a resolution of the situation but that did not prevent them from being well received by the American people, at the time. Congress, on January 10, began two days of debate on the question of whether to grant President Bush the authority to use military force against Iraq or to urge him to delay military action until the economic sanctions had been given further time to demonstrate their effectiveness. On January 12, Congress authorized the use of force. On January 15, President Bush issued an order authorizing an attack on Iraq if it failed to withdraw from Kuwait and otherwise conform with U.N. Resolution 660 before the U.N. deadline of midnight that day. On January 16, the air war against Iraq began; on February 23, the allied ground offensive began. On February 28, Iraq announced a cease-fire. And on March 9, 1991, the first American troops returned to the United States, signaling, to an approving public, the end of the war.

During the August-September rally and the last ten weeks of the crisis, news from the Gulf dominated the dynamic of public support for President Bush; early in the second phase news from the Gulf was a smaller element in support for the president. Figure 4 presents a comparison of trends in support for the president and in press attention to the Gulf during the thirty weeks of crisis and war, i.e., from August 2, 1990, to March 12, 1991.[16] These trends indicate that in the ten weeks after the rally associated with the invasion of Kuwait ended, coverage of the crisis and support for the president were on different tracks. The two

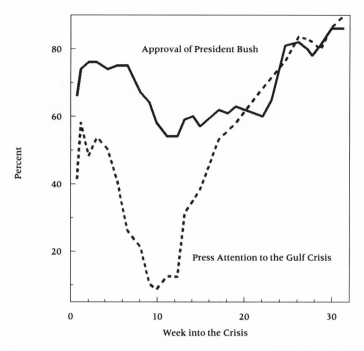

Fig. 4. Coverage and Approval, August 1990–March 1991

trends got on track with each other about the first of the year. Given what we know about the sources of the dynamic in public support for the president, the separation and coming together of the two trends is what we would expect.

At the beginning of the second phase there was no one area of news sufficiently dominant to be considered the central issue informing impressions of President Bush's performance. Eighteen weeks into the crisis Gulf news accounted for more than half of all news but the inertial component of support for the president meant that aggregate opinion was still influenced by earlier news of the budget summit, the federal deficit, high-profile defections from the budget compromise, and concerns about the economy. By December 1, 1990 Gulf news again came to dominate press reports and it continued to do so until the end of the conflict.

To say that Gulf news dominated during the final ten weeks of the crisis substantially understates the case: LaMay reports that, between December 1990 and March 1991, network television news devoted 2,658 minutes to the Gulf crisis and war; during this period the story with the second highest volume of coverage—Soviet politics—got 56

minutes of network news (LaMay 1991, 47). The Gulf consumed 83 percent of all network news time between December 1990 and March
1991. If we want to understand the public's judgment of President
Bush's performance, we will have to look to its reaction to the Gulf War
and/or to its reaction to news of the Gulf War.

The content of daily news was a source of public support for President
Bush during the second phase of the crisis in the Persian Gulf. However,
during this period the news content variables performed differently
than during the August-September rally. By the end of the August rally
the American people were thoroughly familiar with the crisis in the
Gulf. Under these circumstances evaluations of Bush depended less on
opinion leadership and more on responses to reports of policy outcomes
in daily news. News of the success or failure of public policy helped the
public update its assessment of presidential performance. In this respect
the basis for evaluations of the President were no different than evaluations of the previous six presidents (Brody 1991).

In the war phase of the Gulf Crisis criticism of the president's policies
by American and foreign elites was not important in determining support for the president. During this period Bush's support increased on
evidence of successful policy outcomes and from increased media attention to the situation in the Gulf. This phase of the Gulf Crisis was not
strictly speaking a "rally" of public support. To be sure the public in un-
precedented numbers came to support President Bush and his policies
but this resulted from policy success and not from public uncertainty.
Support for Bush grew for the simple reason that the policies succeeded
quickly and without great cost. The war lasted only forty-five days, U.S.
forces encountered very little resistance from Iraqi air forces or air de-
fenses, and the ground war, when it came, ended in one hundred hours
with the Iraqi withdrawal from Kuwait.

Public opinion during this period was dominated by press reports of
policy success. The same process is evident during the last twenty
months of the Bush presidency when economic news came to dominate
press attention and the linkage between news and public evaluation of
presidential performance led to Bush's defeat.

Conclusion

The sources of public support for President Bush during the period of the
crisis and war in the Persian Gulf differ not at all from those that informed evaluations of previous presidents. Policy actions, elite opinion
leadership, and media content affected assessments of Bush's manage-

ment of United States policy. During the first eight weeks of the crisis, public support for the president responded to elite comments about the situation: criticism of President Bush and his policy by such foreign leaders as Saddam Hussein and Yasir Arafat added to his level of approval, but criticism by key American political leaders subtracted from his support. After the August-September rally came to an end, the impact of elite commentary on shaping public assessments of Bush's performance was reduced; the public began to respond to policy outcomes both in the Gulf and elsewhere. News reports of policy outcomes were the main ingredients of public evaluations of the president. When policy led to bad results, such as the budget compromise, public support declined. When the president succeeded in welding an international coalition, in gaining cooperation in the United Nations, and, after the middle of January, in winning on the field of battle his support increased.

News content affected public support for the president in both phases of the crisis and war in the Gulf. The specific content affecting the public's judgment was different in the two phases but in both phases the public apparently used the information brought to it by the media. This means, of course, that the factors affecting news content, discussed elsewhere in this book, indirectly affected public opinion during the crisis and war in the Persian Gulf.

Notes

Thanks are due to Hollis Robbins for her assistance with this project and to R. Douglas Rivers for invaluable advice in the development of this chapter.

1. This study and the studies of media and public opinion on which it is modeled use national network television news as the information source upon which the public draws in forming its assessment of presidential performance (Brody 1991). Hallin and Gitlin (Chapter 7 in this volume) find that local television news supplanted network news in the informing of public opinion on the Gulf. To the extent that this is true across issue areas and to the degree that news content differs from locale to locale, the practice of treating national news as the key to performance judgments may be in error. At present the absence of a comprehensive archive of local television news makes impractical the estimation of the degree of measurement error introduced by this assumption.

2. The data in figure 1 are the averages of twenty-nine sets of surveys carried out between July 7, 1990, and March 10, 1991, as reported in the September/October 1990 to May/June 1991 issues of the *Public Perspective*.

3. There were stories in the *New York Times*, in the fortnight following July 18, 1990, reporting Iraqi threats and the limited response by the United States. The

movement of Iraqi troops to the region of the Kuwaiti border was reported on July 24 and an increase in the deployment was reported on July 26. July 26 is also the day on which it was reported that OPEC had agreed on the 25th to an increase in the price of oil. The debates in Congress over imposing economic sanctions on Iraq were reported on the 27th and 28th. One notes that there was bipartisan criticism of the administration's plan to give Iraq $700 million in loan guarantees.

4. T. Mathews, In *America at War: From the Frenzied Buildup to the Joyous Homecoming*, special issue of *Newsweek* (1991), pp. 32–38.

5. Mathews' view is not singular. A recently published anthology of articles on the war, *The Gulf War Reader* (Sifry and Cerf, 1991), reprints several articles that document the intelligence failure (see, for example, Walid Khalidi's "Iraq vs. Kuwait: Claims and Counterclaims," pp. 57–65, and, from the *Economist*, "Kuwait: How the West Blundered," pp. 99–106). See, also Leslie H. Gelb, "Mr. Bush's Fateful Blunder," *New York Times*, July 15, 1991, p. A-13, and dozens of articles which raise questions about the wisdom of the United States policy toward Iraq before the invasion of Kuwait. The point to be drawn from these commentaries is not that the Bush administration should have recognized the signs of Saddam's intentions but that, given the invasion, the opportunity existed for opinion leaders to blame the administration for not recognizing the signs.

6. See also Sifry and Cerf (1991, pp. 119–22).

7. R. Cohen, *National Journal*, September 8, 1990, p. 2150.

8. *Congressional Quarterly Weekly Reports*, September 8, 1990.

9. *New York Times*, p. A-1.

10. *New York Times*, p. A-20.

11. *New York Times*, September 20, 1990.

12. For the study of this rally the ETWI is less useful than Vanderbilt data since it indexes news in two-week periods that do not match as well with the periods between polls during the first twelve-plus weeks. If we interpolate the ETWI to get a comparable set of data points to the measure derived from Vanderbilt, we find that the two indices are virtually indistinguishable ($r = .966$) and probably substitutable during the rally period. Since we would rather not work with interpolated data, we chose the index derived from the Vanderbilt abstracts.

13. During most of the period of the rally, Gulf news was the most important story. However, after mid-October other stories, especially those about the federal budget, replaced Gulf news. The studies on which this chapter is modeled (Brody 1991, 129ff.) use news which qualifies as the most important story of the day irrespective of policy area. The assumption underlying this coding decision draws on research on the capacity of the media to prime the policy areas in which the president is judged (Iyengar 1991).

15. We of course do not know Saddam Hussein's actual intentions with respect to Saudi Arabia, but from the perspective of expectations set by the Bush administration the troop deployment appears as a successful deterrent.

15. Copies of the statistical analyses that support this conclusion can be obtained from the author.

16. Data for the measure of media attention are drawn from LaMay (1991). They are based on the *Executive Trend Watch's* National Media Index published by

the Conference on Issues and Media. See text above, for a fuller description of this measure.

References

Almond, G. A. 1950. *The American People and Foreign Policy.* New York: Harcourt, Brace.

Brody, R. A. 1991. *Assessing the President: The Media, Elite Opinion, and Public Support.* Stanford: Stanford University Press.

Brody, R. A., and B. I. Page. 1975. "The Impact of Events on Presidential Popularity: The Johnson and Nixon Administrations." In *Perspectives on the Presidency,* ed. A. Wildavsky. Boston: Little, Brown.

Brody R. A., and C. R. Shapiro. 1989a. "A Reconsideration of the Rally Phenomenon in Public Opinion." In *Political Behavior Annual.* Vol. 2, ed. S. Long. Boulder: Westview Press.

———. 1989b. "Policy Failure and Public Support: The Iran-Contra Affair and Public Assessments of President Reagan." *Political Behavior.* 11:353–69.

Haight, T. 1978. "The Mass Media and Presidential Popularity." Ph.D. Thesis, Department of Communications, Stanford University.

Haight, T., and R. A. Brody. 1977. "The Mass Media and Presidential Popularity." *Communication Research.* 4:41–60.

Iyengar, S. 1991. *Is Anyone Responsible? How Television Frames National Issues.* Chicago: University of Chicago Press.

Iyengar, S., and D. R. Kinder. 1987. *News That Matters.* Chicago: University of Chicago Press.

Kernell, S. H. 1978. "Explaining Presidential Popularity." *American Political Science Review* 72:506–22.

LaMay, C. 1991 "By the Numbers, II: Measuring the Coverage." In *The Media at War: The Press and the Persian Gulf Conflict,* ed. C. LaMay, M. and J. Sahadi. New York: Gannett Foundation Media Center, p. 45–50.

Lodge, M., K. M. McGraw, and P. Stroh. 1989. "An Impression-Driven Model of Candidate Evaluations." *American Political Science Review* 83:399–419.

Mueller, J. 1973. *War, Presidents and Public Opinion.* New York: Wiley.

Rosenau, James N. 1961. *Public Opinion and Foreign Policy.* New York: Random House.

Sifry, M. L., and C. Cerf. 1991. *The Gulf War Reader.* New York: Times Books.

The Impact of News and Opinion on Policy-Makers

eleven

Patrick O'Heffernan

A Mutual Exploitation Model of Media Influence in U.S. Foreign Policy

Overview

In 1963 Bernard Cohen concluded from his research that news organizations were to a significant degree the handmaidens of government when it came to foreign policy. The Gulf War offers an excellent opportunity to update this theory—born in an era of print journalism—to match the realities of global, instantaneous television.

Cohen's unit of analysis was the interaction between reporters and their sources, an appropriate focus at a time when both the foreign policy and foreign affairs news communities were part of the same small, congenial Washington establishment. Cohen depicted a symbiotic media-government relationship, with the press as a usually helpful partner in the policy process, advising policy-makers through quiet conversations and reasoned editorials in elite newspapers. He found this relationship understandable because he saw minimal public interest in foreign affairs at the time and few actors outside of Washington and New York power circles.

Critics both in and out of the media and media studies dispute this view now, arguing that the media are either tactically overwhelmed by the public-relations staffs and "spin doctors" at the White House, the Department of Defense, and in congressional offices, or that they are structurally incapable of playing a truly and intelligently critical "loyal opposition" role in American governance. These critiques were especially sharp from within the media itself after the Gulf War and extended to preparations for coverage of the 1992 elections.[1]

But is this true? Are news organizations at a disadvantage when covering politics, wars, and government activities? Has the commercial nature of the American media so distorted its journalistic integrity that it is incapable of providing facts that lower ratings or investigative reporting that draws the ire of popular presidents and provokes boycotts from advertisers? Certainly case studies and content analysis can and have been employed to demonstrate the temerity of the nation's news organizations in face of government intimidation, dissembling, and pressure. But when closely questioned, those in government describe a deeper dynamic within the media-government relationship that cannot be satisfied by a simple bi-polar competition theory based on a contest between reporters' desire for truth and governments' desire for support. In the minds of policy-makers, the reporter-source dynamic of Cohen's day has given way to a multilevel, multidimensional set of evolving, interlocking, and sometimes contradictory relationships.

A picture of these relationships does not emerge readily from case and content studies, but rather requires plumbing the perceptions of those engaged in the relationships themselves. Those perceptions, when joined with evidence from other studies, point to a complex, interdependent media-government relationship best characterized as one of "interdependent mutual exploitation."

This chapter describes the findings and conclusions of two studies of the perceptions of senior U.S. and European official involved in the making of defense and foreign policy, of the role of the mass media in the U.S. foreign policy process. The first study was based on interviews prior to the Gulf War with American and (then) Soviet policy-makers plus earlier survey data of American foreign policy officials.[2] The second, conducted during and just after the Gulf War, involved interviews with American military and civilian security-policy officials, and European military leaders based at SHAPE and NATO.[3]

Results from both studies indicate that those involved in the policy-making, especially security policy, on both a day-to-day and a strategic basis, view media-government relations as interdependent and mutually exploitive, but not necessarily symbiotic, as Cohen and others have described. The interviews from both studies probed deeply the perception of the relationship between government and media; the later study focused on questions raised by the ongoing Gulf War.

Mutual Exploitation

The fraternal, mutually respectful reporters and sources Cohen described have been replaced by two distinct global institutions—the worldwide U.S. foreign policy and diplomatic community, and the global media industry. Both organizations promote their own version of reality around the world; the foreign policy apparatus does so to serve its own policy interests; the media do so because that is what they do. Both are adept at supporting, manipulating, or attacking the other. The relationship is sometimes competitive and sometimes cooperative, but that is only incidental to its central driving force: self-interest.

In this model, the mass media and foreign policy institutions around the world have grown up together, each utilizing the other and learning how to better utilize the other in a dynamic, unending process.[4] This model does not see the cooperative symbiosis of a "subtly composite unity" but a dynamic of two very desegregated, aggressive ecosystems constantly bargaining over a series of "wants" while they manipulate both the structure and output of the other for their own advantage. Sometimes the result is mutually beneficial and sometimes it is not.

This model recognizes that entertainment is actually 80 to 85 percent of all media organizations' output and is an even larger share of their income and profits. As a result, regulatory and opportunistic considerations involving entertainment are often the principal "wants" of media corporations in the ongoing bargaining within the government-media relationship. It also recognizes that media trade organizations continually try to influence the actions of government, especially at the FCC and congressional level, and that government continually tries to influence the outputs of news organizations, particularly at the Washington news bureau level. The result is not an equilibrium, but a constant evolution of the relationship, with the balance of influence changing continually depending upon the issue examined and the point in time of the examination.[5]

Most analysts have overlooked the undercutting impact of the mass media's entertainment outputs on the U.S. foreign policy and domestic policy establishment because the analysts focus primarily on news, which takes up less than 20 percent of the mass media's time and resource use. The entertainment outputs instill perceptions, values, and expectations in the public that are sometimes counter to those promulgated by government.[6]

The findings of the research reveal that security policy-makers perceive the media and government in terms of a co-evolutionary mutual exploitation model which sees a significant element of policy-making involved in using and influencing the media.[7] Policy-makers interviewed perceived that policy-making cannot be done without news organizations and that news organizations cannot cover international affairs without government congruence (but not necessarily cooperation). The media today were seen by the policy-makers interviewed as *part of the policy process,* and that the government has become and must remain part of the media process. The Gulf War was a dramatic example of this mutual exploitation, in which each side tried to control the other and extract what it wanted for its own benefit.

The Television War

Audiences around the world were transfixed by images of a modern technological war as it happened live from the "enemy side." Reporters, generals, and diplomats in the Middle East answered on-air questions from callers around the world while missiles whistled overhead in Jerusalem, Riyadh, and Baghdad. Politicians and ordinary people found that television set the pace of their lives; it determined when they slept, ate, and worked because they could not stop "watching the war." The coverage of the Gulf War was both a metaphor for the medium's role in policy, and a harbinger of what was to come in later event coverage, such as the 1992 American presidential election: it provided vital information and great entertainment, and the line between the two often disappeared. As long as the information supported government policy and was useful to its action, and as long as the entertainment drew audiences that could be sold to advertisers, both parties benefited.

But television coverage of the Gulf War triggered an international debate about the mass media's involvement in the foreign policy of the United States and other nations. President Bush and political conservatives in the United States railed against *Peter Arnett's* broadcasts from Iraq, with Arnett virtually being accused of treason by U.S. Senator Alan Simpson (R.-Wyo.). Media organizations protested against censorship, intimidation, and outright disinformation from the coalition briefer (O'Heffernan 1991b). If both the media and the government benefited from the war's coverage—that is, were able to exploit each other—why the controversy? The answer appears to be that both sides seem to take the benefits of the relationship for granted but rail against the burdens and position themselves to increase their share of benefits at the other's expense in future conflicts.

Following the war, the debate on the media and their influence on or support of policy quickly narrowed to a negotiation on the degree of military restrictions that could be imposed on reporting during wartime—the rules of exploitation. The Radio and Television News Directors Association and representatives of broadcasters squared off with the Pentagon to develop ground rules after much discussion in news columns, conferences, and testy meetings.[8] Lost in this debate over the details of permission slips was the larger void of widely available analysis of the four decades of policy that had incrementally created the conditions

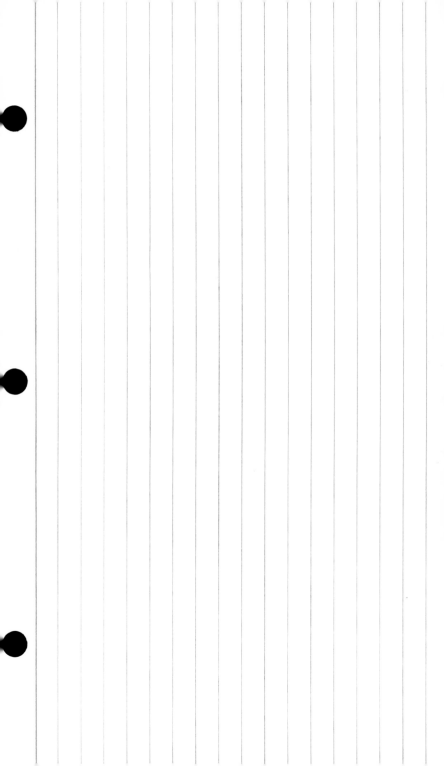

for the war and the mass media's inability to raise the salience of the issue with the public before force was necessary.

Mutual Exploitation: Policy-Makers' Perceptions

Throughout the war and its regulatory and self-critical aftermath, the question of the relationship between the media and the government, especially in foreign policy matters, was raised in many forms, but a few questions dominated the discussion: should the nation's news organizations support the government in any military endeavor, or is the media's role one of a neutral observer; should the nation's news organizations remain at arm's length from the government in foreign policy matters, or should they try to influence government action; does the government control or influence the media, and should it do so during battle? The existing models could not address these questions because they assumed two distinct entities either in competition or in collusion, models that did not fit the observations.

One way to probe the actual media-government relationship is to examine the perceptions of the actors in the relationship by using interview research (Rosati 1984). Illumination of the paradigm within which the players operated may explain some of the controversies and disagreements between the foreign policy establishment and the media. A team from Georgia Tech initiated a series of interviews of senior foreign policy and defense officials during the Gulf War, probing their responses to the coverage, their consumption of media, and their internal paradigm of the media-government relationship and of the impact of media on their paradigm of national security. This followed an earlier set of interviews with journalists and officials in the United States and the former Soviet Union probing the same questions in the context of U.S.-Soviet relations.

When data from both sets of studies were examined together, the mutual exploitation theme quickly emerged.[9] Both sets of actors acknowledged attempting to use, or using, the other. Both sets of actors could readily detail incidents in which media and government exploited each other with policy impacts, and both sets of actors described their perception of the relationship as one of both sides using each other for their own benefit.[10] The questions asked focused on the following points:

- Did the Gulf War coverage change policy-makers' perception of the use of the media in the policy process?

- Did the Gulf War coverage change their perception of the media's impact on public opinion and the decisions of other nations' governments?
- Did the Gulf War coverage affect how policy-makers used the media?

Did the Gulf War coverage change policy-makers' perception of the use of the media in the policy process?

While this specific question was not asked in the two studies used, policy-makers use of the media, their perception of its usefulness, and their ranking of various media by their utility were probed, and the responses can provide insight into their perception of the mass media as a tool available to foreign policy elites. In terms of policy-maker perception of the media as a useful source of information, the Gulf War reinforced perceptions found to exist prior to the war.

Eighty-seven percent of the interview respondents could recall cases when the media were the only source of information available for decision-making, and 65 percent agreed that the media were frequently the fastest source of information for policy-making. This was true in both the prewar study and the study conducted during the Gulf War. Policy-makers perceived that the media played distinctive, active roles in the setting of policy agendas, determining the information environments in which policy is made, and providing a "front channel" of diplomatic communication outside of routine diplomacy. During the Gulf War, both military and civilian policy-makers complained that the media were in fact diplomatic communication instruments operating out of control. But they also admitted that they themselves used the media for various purposes, including diplomatic communication.

A majority, 63 percent, of the policy personnel interviewed prior to the War indicated that the media were frequently the most rapid source of information in crisis situations. Many told of earlier situations, like the 1985 highjacking of TWA Flight 847 in the Middle East, in which the media were the only source of information at the beginning of a crisis. Virtually all of those interviewed before and during the Gulf War offered an anecdote or observation from their personal involvement on the utility of the media in a crisis.

Eighty-seven percent of those interviewed prior to the war could recall situations wherein the media were the only source of information for policy-making in fast-breaking crisis or terrorist incidents. If anything, this perception was strengthened by the Gulf War and the war's

TABLE 1.   Policy-Maker Use of Media Over Time

Time Spent with Media to Gain Information	1991[1]	1988[2] (Percent of Sample)	1984–85[3]
2 hours or more per day	54	27	15
1–2 hours per day	30	43	27
Less than 1 hour per day	5	30	53

1. N = 35; interviews January–February 1991.
2. N = 25.
3. N = 93; written survey with response of 900 senior policy-makers; 93 responses were isolated as foreign policy decision-makers and tabulated.

coverage in the mass media (see table 1 on policy-maker use of the media over time). The post-Gulf interviews also revealed that policy-makers saw nothing unusual about using the media as a communication instrument to address other national leaders and populations. While the earlier research indicated that policy-makers recognized this media role as possible and as occasionally used by heads of state, the post-Gulf respondents demonstrated an attitude that this was routine and expected.

This was true equally in SHAPE and NATO headquarters, the Pentagon and the State Department, and in the offices of a (former) Communist Party Central Committee member and (former) high-level Soviet policy-makers. Many volunteered statements such as that by Supreme Allied Commander (SACEUR) General John Galvin, who said during the war: "Today the first indication sometimes—sometimes, I would underline—that guides intelligence and reconnaissance and acquisition of information is something that appears on television." Television is also not a purely American habit. Captain Ulrich Frike of the German Navy, assistant to the chief of staff of NATO's Military Committee said: "Today, under the present circumstances, I'm probably looking at TV for 4–6 hours a day. . . . I have to monitor the media. . . . we get the most up-to-date information by TV, so that's the first source. . . "

Did the Gulf War change policy-makers' perception of the influence of mass media on world events and world politics?

Did the Gulf War coverage change policy-makers' perception of the media's role in influencing public opinion and input into foreign policy decisions?

While the prewar research did not ask these questions, the 1991 interviews did ask them and the results were overwhelmingly positive, although with warnings and qualifications. Policy-makers saw the media as the leading shapers of public opinion and influence on world politics and world order, and foresaw a major role for the mass media in a new world order.[11]

When asked if a new world order has emerged or is emerging, without being required to specify exactly what it might be, 82 percent of the sample answered in the positive. When asked if the mass media played a role in that new world order, 82 percent of the sample answered in the affirmative (there was a slight variation among the respondents to these two questions). Many volunteered answers to the effect that the new order would not have emerged without the mass media, and that the mass media will continue to play a central role in an evolving world system. When asked if the public around the world played a role in setting security (foreign policy) agendas of their nations and of the world in general, 100 percent responded that the public was involved to some degree. When asked what the most important influence on the public was, 75 percent indicated that the media were the strongest influence, followed by the head of state, which was selected by 21 percent. Interestingly, 21 percent also volunteered that, among all media, television was the strongest influence on public opinion (some variation among respondents to these two questions).

The interview responses showed a strong perception, especially during the Gulf War, that the media and government manipulated one another for self-interest. Council on Foreign Relations vice president Alton Frye:

> Presidents do not control the debate in anything like the degree they did even when we relied only on radio, and Franklin Roosevelt did the fireside chats. It's now a market place of competitive ideas with the Congress and private critics on display very broadly. I think the public, unlike myself, does see it on television very heavily. . . .

General John Galvin saw the public as the prime force of a new world order and ultimately of foreign policy, with the media an adjunct and amplifier of public demands:

> The media responds to a public pulse, a public orientation, for example, Vietnam. It was not so much the media changing as it was the public changing the media. . . . There is, of course, an independent aspect of the media that has its own editorial production which it also—but I feel the media reflects rather well public thinking, public thrust, public changes. . . . I believe anyway that the message comes from within the public. It is fathomed by politi-

cal leadership, by media people and by others. The public itself fathoms its own message.

Former defense advisor to the U.S. permanent representative to NATO, Richard Stanley:

> Media will play a role in foreign policy that is probably greater. I think it will de-polarize and, hopefully, the media will be a vehicle for consciousness raising. . . . . The media is a communicator to a lot of people who are going to have to take actions against their short term interests. It has a good, positive, constructive role, a big role to play.

The Gulf War coverage appears to have reinforced the interdependence theme. Media use increased and perception of the usefulness of the media increased. Whether or not the government was dependent on the media during the Gulf (it was not dependent for information, but it used the media as part of the ground-attack strategy), one tentative conclusion that can be drawn from the interviews is that policy-makers used the media more during and after the Gulf War than before it, and now perceive the media as more useful and more necessary in their work.

The interpenetration theme was present but not strongly reflected in these findings, since the questions were not designed to probe that particular aspect of the media-government relationship. Some of the comments, however, especially those regarding the president's use of the media, indicate that at least some policy-makers see the media as a tool to be grasped and used as needed to implement policy.

The theme of mutual benefit was obvious in all the findings, although the responses to the questions regarding media influence on public opinion reflected a strong respect for the media's independent agendas, as well as its susceptibility to use by policy-makers.

Possibly the strongest finding of these interviews was the recognition that media use in general and television use in particular have increased among policy-makers. What this means in terms of simultaneous distribution of common images and information to policy-makers around the world remains to be seen, but it is apparent that the elite who shape international politics on a day-by-day basis, as well as those who make the grand decisions and those who are affected by those decisions, are increasingly operating from the same set of perceptions and images, if not of facts.

The Policy Process

The policy-process picture that emerged from these interviews is that foreign policy in the United States and other countries is much more than a meeting between the president or prime minister, the secretary of state or foreign minister, the secretary of defense or defense minister, and the head of the CIA or international intelligence service, even during war. It is the end point of a long chain of events, people, and institutions that collect and shape information, options, and political leverages, and it very specifically includes a self-interested media.

Mass-media influence on foreign policy is issue-specific, with certain categories of issues more likely to successfully utilize the media to develop policy elite support. Environmental issues, those involving human rights or human suffering, and issues that touch Americans or United States residents are far more likely to move forward on the foreign policy agenda as a result of media exposure than more abstract or complex "high politics" issues such as arms control or trade terms (O'Heffernan 1990b, 1991a). Media coverage of human-interest stories during the Gulf War exemplified the media's exploitation of issues that play well with large audiences—in this case, with issues the government wanted to play up. These included the "Hi Mom" stories, mostly run by local television stations and newspapers, about homeboys on the battlefield; the "gee whiz" stories about super high-tech weapons—toys with high entertainment value, especially for male audiences; and the nonstory, made up of press releases and fact-laden but contextually meaningless pronouncements by the Joint Information Bureau.

These three Gulf story categories point up an increasingly important and visible condition in the government-media relationship: the growing media savvy of the policy institutions involved. A media-sophisticated organization, like the Joint Information Bureau of the military forces in Saudi Arabia, can mitigate or even reverse the influence of the media on an issue. Media-sophisticated elites can redirect media attention away from unpleasantness, like the poor operational record of Apache helicopters in the desert, and toward less dangerous fare such as the menus of troops in the Saudi desert. Other public-relations techniques used by media-sophisticated foreign policy decision-makers and the institutions within which they operate include:

- thwarting national media from examining the basis for a policy—or the lack of it, as in the early stages of the Gulf War—by configuring its public relations to appeal to local stations and newspapers that are more subject to public demands for local human-interest, while intimidating the deeper-digging network news teams with phone calls to network business offices questioning the patriotism of skeptical reporters;

- releasing powerful visuals which co-opt TV news agendas, such as the smart-bomb video tapes and the images of Patriot missiles appearing to knock out incoming SCUDS;
- providing a daily mountain of insignificant details in press releases and background reports that overwhelm hard-press reporters; this technique also worked well in the Joint Information Bureau's daily briefing;
- policing agency employees to control information flows and to stop leaks, as was done both in the Joint Information Bureau and in the field during the war;
- stonewalling—refusing to provide information through normal press-distribution channels, knowing that only a small percentage of the reporters have the time, expertise, or funds to dig out a story while it is relevant.

A condition that can be even more important is the cohesion of the executive. Mixed messages or disagreement from within the executive that makes its way to the media seriously undermines public-relations efforts and enhances the opportunity and likelihood of adversarial media treatment of real policy positions. The early stages of the Gulf War saw a lack of consensus, both from General Powell and from the Congress. But the administration was able to use the media and the government's (its) internal political muscle to construct a consensus and deny the doubters a broad forum, guaranteeing a positive press support for the eventual policy.

Into this mix of influence mechanisms and conditions must be added countervailing forces, forces which tend to dilute media's influence on foreign policy makers and on foreign policy outputs. Major overt countervailing forces present in the Gulf War included:

Systems of state secrecy.   All nation-states, governments, governments in exile, and insurgent groups trying to become governments have secrecy systems. These systems range from the elaborate classification "Q" process of the United States, to similar processes in the former Soviet Union and most Western nations, to virtual blackouts on any foreign-policy relevant information in states such as Iran, Iraq, Albania, and Syria. During the Gulf War, information was not so much protected by systems of state secrecy as it was withheld or provided late. Categories of information not completely provided included the actual performance of weapons, the location and amount of damage from missile and bomb hits in both Coalition and Iraq territory, and extent of civilian injuries.[12]

Overt censorship.   This was seen in the Gulf War at the Joint Information Bureau and the Ministry of Information of Iraq, and similar ministries in Israel, Jordan, Syria, Iran, and Turkey. Ironically, for a period at the beginning of the war, CNN broadcasts from Iraq were probably less censored than any news from the JIB because the Iraqi Ministry of Information had not yet organized itself to deal with Peter Arnett and his satellite phone. Overall, all sides in the Gulf War were effective in censoring reporting they opposed. While the *news* organizations involved objected, they failed to join the litigation by magazines, because from a business standpoint the networks were obtaining large audiences that did not want negative reporting or stories contrary to the administration's line.

Elite consensus.   Foreign policy elites often do not agree on the details or even the thrusts of policies at the early stages of policy formation, but, in the United States, the role of the White House chief of staff and his aides is to build a consensus around a desired policy (Allison 1971). When this effort is successful, as it eventually was in the case of Gulf War policy, the ability of the media to obtain critical or policy-negative information is drastically reduced. In the case of highly popular policies like the war against Saddam, the media's ability to report such information is almost eliminated (O'Heffernan 1991b). Few sources will talk regardless of their position on the issue at hand, and the next day the administration will launch an investigation of who talked and an attack on the credibility of the reporter and company.

The objections in the Pentagon were eventually silenced and the vote in Congress put an end to congressional criticism.

Physical danger to reporters.   Reporting from Peru, the former Yugoslavia, Lebanon, and a handful of other countries places journalists in extreme physical danger of death, kidnapping, or torture, either from the government or government-hired hit squads, or one or the other side of an internal conflict. Not surprisingly, these locations are covered either very lightly by a few journalists willing to take the risk, from afar through interviews with travelers, from domestic broadcast monitoring, rumors, handouts. Reporting from the Gulf War carried little physical danger except to "enterprise" reporters who evaded or ignored government orders and went to the front to gather news directly. While the danger was most likely not a factor in the small number of journalists who did venture afield, it did give the Joint Information Bureau a good excuse to forbid journalists from doing so.

Technological limitations on news gathering and transmission. It is not correct to assume that anything can be beamed from anywhere to anywhere via uplinks and satellites. Television crews must often utilize government-owned uplinks which can be denied for political reasons, or which can be given only after review and editing of copy. This was the case in the Gulf War for many reporters who did not have flyaways (portable uplinks). Even when a broadcaster is allowed (or pays bribes) to bring in a flyaway free of government control, satellite time-availability, costs, and the location of news events can impede transmission.

The Gulf War was a showcase of new technology for bringing live news direct to viewers, but it must not be assumed that because this technology exists everyone has it, or that governments have lost their ability to control it. In reality, it showed that live SNG (satellite news-gathering) technologies can be exploited by governments as readily as they can be used by media to exploit governments for high-ratings stories. Technological limits are constantly being eroded by new generations of equipment and new transmission methods, but governments can still retaliate against journalists who smuggle objectionable tape or signals out of a country for global or national broadcast. What the Gulf War demonstrated is that it is technologically possible for commercial news organizations to cover a war from both sides. The product of that technological capability can be and was as exploitive as the actors were able to make it.

Complex Reality and the Media in War

War and coverage of war is a very complex reality. The relationships among the actors in the Gulf War were not well understood, even by the actors themselves. In the process of mutual exploitation, both the media and the government and military did not clearly understand their goals and objectives, their roles and relationship, and the rules of engagement and cooperation. Live broadcasting of a war from both (all?) sides of a battlefield was simply new territory for everyone involved. Both sides continued to follow the old rules of exploiting the other for self-interest and immediate gain, using the vacuum of policy about live war-reporting to their advantage. The media wanted access, stories, audience appeal. The JIB and the governments on both sides wanted public support and enemy confusion. The output was a media that got record ratings, a government that got public support and little criticism and investigation, and a public that was well entertained, but not always well informed.

But given the limitations on the media side of the equation during a war described in various chapters in this volume, and the media's predilection for marketable information over critical information, isn't this the best we can expect? Isn't it unreasonable to ask more than that both sides exploit the other and the public takes what the government wants it to have and what the media thinks the public wants to have?

Not necessarily. While the culture of the media organizations is ratings-driven, the culture of news divisions, and especially of CNN, is story-driven. Reporters who are educated about war and its technology can provide insight and context to the live feeds, bypassing censorship in many cases. For instance, reporters who were knowledgeable about the Patriot missile systems would not have reported hits when they saw explosions in the sky that later research showed were misses.[13] And news organizations familiar with military tactics and history would have seen in advance the feint General Schwarzkopf was planning when he allowed them to film the practice 'assaults on the Kuwaiti coast when in fact the main attack was planned over the western Saudi-Iraq border.

This does not address the larger questions of a national media organization's obligation to cooperate in a national war effort, or at least not undermine it. Nor does it address the question of government control and exploitation of the media to influence public opinion, and of media use of government information to boost ratings, to the exclusion of investigation and context. As long as the paradigm of the government-media relationship, at least in the minds of government representatives, is one of mutual exploitation, the goal of clear and complete objective reporting of hostilities will be subordinated to other interests of the institutions involved. The resolution of the questions raised by the exploitive nature of the Gulf War coverage will come within the framework Allison used to characterize the U.S. foreign policy process—continual bargainings among separate constituencies, some inside the media, some inside government, some among media and government representatives. The process will be ongoing, with new situations raising new questions, but often avoiding old questions. The model of mutual exploitation drawn from the Gulf War provides a framework for understanding the workings of these bargainings in wartime, so that the stakes, the stakeholders, and the possible outcomes are clearer, as well as the driving forces. Unfortunately, the framework tells us that the dominant driving force is rarely clear public understanding.

Appendix

POST-GULF INTERVIEW SUBJECTS*

Gordon Adams
Director of Defense Budget Project
Washington, D.C.

Harold Baumgarden
Press Officer
NATO Information Services
Brussels, Belgium

W. Tapley Bennett, Jr.
Washington, D.C.
(former U.S. ambassador to NATO)

Barry Blechman
President, Defense Forecast Inc.
Washington, D.C.
(former assistant director, ACDA)

Kent Brown
Internal Affairs Advisor
SACEUR
SHAPE, Mons Belgium

Richard E. Darilek
U.S. Army Concepts Analysis
Agency
Washington, D.C.
(former director, Mutual and
Balanced Force
Reduction Task Force,
Department of Defense)

General Russell E. Dougherty
(Ret.), USAF
Washington, D.C.
(former commander-in-chief,
Strategic Air Command)

General Vigleik Eide
Norwegian Army Chair,
NATO Military Committee

Captain Ulrich Frieke
German Army
Assistant to General Eide,
Public Information Officer, NATO
Military Committee
Brussels, Belgium

Alton Frye
Vice President, Council on Foreign
Relations
Washington, D.C.

General John Galvin
Supreme Allied Commander
Europe (SACEUR)
SHAPE, Mons, Belgium

Raymond Garthoff
Senior Research Fellow,
The Brookings Institution
Washington, D.C.
(former U.S. ambassador to
Bulgaria)

Charles W. Groover
Advanced Technology
Development Center
Atlanta, Ga.
(former deputy assistant secretary
of defense)

John Hardt
Library of Congress
Washington, D.C.

*Affiliations at time of interview. Prewar interviews described in O'Heffernan (1991a).

Lt. Colonel Jim Holcomb
SACEUR staff
SHAPE
Mons, Belgium

Colonel John Hughes-Wilson
Basic Intelligence Branch
SHAPE
Mons, Belgium

General Sir Brian Kenny, A.O.U.K.
Deputy SACEUR
SHAPE
Mons, Belgium

Lawrence Korb
The Brookings Institution
Washington, D.C.
(former assistant secretary of
defense for manpower,
installations and logistics)

Jenny Lincoln
Special Advisor to President Carter
Carter Center, Atlanta Ga.

Major General Lutgandorf,
Belgium Army
SHAPE, Mons, Belgium

Patrick Moon
Assistant Secretary, Conventional
Arms Delegation
United States Mission
Vienna, Austria

Robert Pastor
Carter Center, Atlanta Ga.
(former staff member, National
Security Council)

Colonel Charles Ricks, E7
Chief of Public Information and
Policy
SACEUR
SHAPE, Mons, Belgium

Major General Alan Rogers
Assistant Chief of Staff for
Operations
SHAPE
Mons, Belgium

Eugene Rostow
Washington, D.C.
(former director, Arms Control and
Disarmament Agency)

Rene Schaelbroek
Director, News Analysis Section
SHAPE, Mons, Belgium

General John Shaud, USAF
Chief of Staff
SHAPE, Mons, Belgium

Don Snider
Center for Strategic and
International Studies
Washington, D.C.
(former staff member, NSC)

Helmet Sonnenfelt
The Brookings Institution
Washington, D.C.
(former staff counselor,
Department of State, member of
the NSC)

Timothy Stanley
President, IESI
Washington, D.C.
(former defense advisor to the U.S.
Permanent Representative to NATO)

Leonard Sullivan, Jr.
Systems Planning Corporation
Arlington Va.

Peter Wilson
Washington, D.C.
(former member, Policy Planning
Staff,
Department of State)

Air Vice Marshall
Antony Woodford, RAF
Assistant Chief of Staff for Policy,
SHAPE, Mons, Belgium

John Woolsey, CFE
United States Ambassador,
Conventional Arms Talks
Delegation
United States Embassy, Vienna

Notes

Research for this article was underwritten by the Social Science Research Council, the National Science Foundation and the Center for International Strategy, Technology, and Policy of Georgia Tech. I am also indebted to Dr. Daniel Papp, director of the Georgia Tech School of International Affairs and Lynn Gutstat, director of Research for CNN for their patience and assistance.

1. In an unusually blunt roundtable in New York City the day before the opening of the Democratic National Convention, national news anchors, executives, and producers from the broadcast networks and PBS vied with one another in criticizing their manipulation by public officials in their coverage of the Gulf War and the 1988 election, vowing to provide more substance, investigation, and issue coverage and less horse-race reporting in the 1992 election.

2. For the full text of this research, see the Appendices in O'Heffernan (1991a).

3. For the full text of this research, see O'Heffernan (1991b).

4. In this model, the word "media" includes entertainment and business elements of the organizations that produce wholesale and retail mass-distributed information.

5. The public is also a player in this relationship. For instance, the media prevailed until 1992 in the question of telephone-company access to the cable industry despite heavy pressures from an extremely well financed telephone lobby; but the public has prevailed in the move to limit children's television advertising. Since it is difficult to tell what the government's "wants" are in such issues as who pays and receives royalties for reruns and syndicated programs, when both government and media elite are divided, neither media nor government nor public has prevailed.

6. And which can themselves be manipulated, as then candidate Clinton did in his appearances on the "Arsenio Hall Show," "Larry King Live," and "MTV."

7. Co-evolution is an ecological process in which two species exploit each other so tightly that they evolve together, each affecting the direction and pace of the other's evolution. Co-evolution differs from symbiosis in that the symbiotic species, while they may derive benefits from their association, do not exploit each other and do not necessarily influence the direction of each other's evolution. See Odum (1983).

8. The author conducted one of these meetings, off-the-record, in February

1991, at SHAPE Headquarters in Mons, Belgium, between a representative of CNN and command officers of SHAPE/NATO. While the dozen or so individuals involved showed respect for one another, some positions were tenaciously held by both sides and the discussion occasionally got quite heated.

9. Data were also obtained from Linsky's survey (1986) and analyzed.

10. Rigorous research on these questions undertaken at policy-maker level of analysis would require new elite survey research, a daunting undertaking, methodologically, in the construction of the universe and deriving a representative and statistically valid sample, and in recruiting and working with very busy subjects. While not all the questions in the ongoing research and the earlier interviews were exactly comparable, some were and the thrust of the two studies were quite similar so that a demonstration of perception change, or lack of it, can be indicated on these questions.

11. I will not engage here in the semantical and political debates surrounding this term. Suffice it to say, to the degree that international politics is vastly different today than it was 5 years ago, there is a new world order. Whether or not it is a "better" world order is another issue.

12. As later analysis has shown, the Patriot missle was 94% ineffective, not 94% effective, as claimed by the military and its contractor, but this information was not made available. See Postel (91).

13. Postel (91, 91–92).

References

Allison, G. 1971. *The Essence of Decision*. Boston: Little, Brown.

Cohen, B. C. 1963. *The Press and Foreign Policy*. Princeton: Princeton University Press.

Cutler, L. N. 1984. "Foreign Policy on Deadline." *Atlantic Community Quarterly* 22: 223–32 (reprinted from *Foreign Policy* 56 (Fall 1984).

Linsky, M. 1986. *Impact: How the Press Affects Federal Policy Making*. New York: W. W. Norton.

Odum, E. P. 1983. *Systems Ecology: An Introduction*. New York: Wiley.

O'Heffernan, P. 1991a. *Mass Media and American Foreign Policy*. Norwich, N.J: Ablex.

———. 1991b. "TV and Crisis: Sobering Thoughts on Sound Bites Heard 'Round the World." *Television Quarterly* 24: 6–21.

———. 1990a. "Policy Maker Perception of Mass Media Roles in Foreign Policy." Paper presented at the Annual convention of the International Communication Association, Dublin, Ireland, June.

———. 1990b. "Mass Media and Foreign Policy: An Inside-Outside Model." Paper presented at the Annual meeting of the American Political Science Association, San Francisco, September.

Postel, T. 1991–92. "Lessons of the Gulf Experience with Patriot." *International Security* 16:3 (Winter 91–92): 119–71.

Postel, T., and R. Stein. "Correspondence: Patriot Experience in Gulf War." *International Security* 17:1 (Summer 92): 199–240.

Rosati, J. A. 1984. "The Impact of Beliefs on Behavior: The Foreign Policy of the Carter Administration." In *Foreign Policy Decision Making,* ed. Donald A. Sylvan and Steven Chan. New York: Praeger.

Vanderbilt Television News Archive. 1976–80. *Television News Index and Abstracts.* Nashville: Vanderbilt University.

twelve

John Zaller

Strategic Politicians, Public Opinion, and the Gulf Crisis

I know whose backside is at stake and rightfully so. . . .
George Bush, on chances of victory in the Gulf War

Past studies of the mass media and public opinion, strongly corroborated by the experience of the Gulf War, make two key points: At least in the domain of foreign affairs, the media normally take cues from government officials, "indexing" coverage to the range of opinions that exist within the government.[1] Further, mass opinion tends to follow elite opinion, with the most politically attentive members of the public following elites most closely.[2] These results imply a stark political world in which elites lead, masses follow, and the press does the bidding of the government.

This top-down model of political influence can be defended as a useful first approximation of what occurs in foreign policy decision-making, especially in foreign policy crises. Nonetheless, reality is always quite a bit messier than social scientific models make it out to be. The major limitation of the top-down model is that, even in situations in which elites appear to be firmly leading mass opinion, the public can have substantial influence over its leaders. This influence arises from the fact that political leaders, most of whom are under threat of electoral retribution, take great care to lead public opinion only toward goals that the public will, in retrospect if not always in prospect, applaud. Thus, politicians attempt to be responsive to future opinion at the same time they are trying to shape current opinion.

An illuminating example comes from the Vietnam War. There is no evidence that the American public in 1964 was eager for a fight with communist guerrillas in Vietnam. But President Lyndon Johnson clearly feared that if he failed to prevent a communist victory, the public would repudiate him and his party for "losing Vietnam." Hence, he *followed* public opinion by *leading* it into a war that neither he nor the public wanted.

V. O. Key, Jr., gave a general account of such cases in his classic study of *Public Opinion and American Democracy.* The only public opinion that really counts in American politics, he contended, is the public opinion that politicians hope they might be able to create by their own actions, or fear might be created by the attacks of opponents in the next election. As a result, politicians' estimates of possible states of future opinion have more effect on policy-making than current opinion, which, as the politicians know, may evaporate overnight.

There are, as the reader will soon see, formidable barriers to rigorous demonstration that anything so slippery as "anticipated future opinion" affects foreign policy decision-making. However, the phenomenon is too important to be neglected because fully adequate evidence and analytical techniques are unavailable.

Method

This chapter examines four key decisions in the process by which the United States was led into the Gulf War, showing, to the extent possible, how calculations concerning current and future public opinion influenced each decision. The events I examine are:

- President Bush's decision to stake his political reputation on the expulsion of Iraqi troops from Kuwait, which he did when he declared the aggression "will not stand."
- The decision of congressional Democrats to give virtually unanimous support to Bush's decision in August to send 200,000 U.S. troops to Saudi Arabia.
- Bush's decision in November to send an additional 200,000 troops to the Gulf. In so doing, Bush was, in effect, choosing to forgo reliance on economic sanctions and to rely instead on either the threat of force or the application of force to resolve the crisis.
- The vote of Congress in January 1991 to authorize the president to use "all necessary means" to force the Iraqi army to withdraw from Kuwait.

For evidence I rely primarily on published accounts of decision-making, which are mostly journalistic, and my own interviews of top staff aides to key decision-makers. Those interviewed included aides to most congressional leaders on this issue in both parties and in both houses. The only important exception is Senate Majority Leader George Mitchell, whose office refused to allow me access to any members of his staff. I also spoke to two executive branch officials, namely, a top staff member from the National Security Council and a top military official in the Pentagon. Interviews were conducted in winter 1992–93.

The obvious difficulty with these kinds of data is that sources tend to stress motives they regard as legitimate, such as "making good public policy," and to downplay political motives, which they see as tainted. The appropriate response to this natural bias in interview data is not, I believe, to ignore indications of concern about public policy, but to make inordinate efforts to discover what political motives may have made some visions of good policy more attractive than others, so as to present a more balanced picture of what occurred.

Four Key Decisions

"THE LINE IN THE SAND"

Four days after Iraq's invasion of Kuwait, Bush declared in an impromptu news conference, "This will not stand, this aggression against Kuwait."

There is little doubt that when the president uttered these words he was staking his political reputation on the removal of Iraqi troops from Kuwait. "A President Puts Himself on the Spot" was the how the *New York Times* described Bush's action in a headline the following day.[3] "If Mr. Bush is blustering during an international crisis," added columnist William Safire, "he will be the one who 'will not stand.'"[4]

What *political* reasons might a president have had for taking the fateful and politically risky step of pledging himself to force Iraqi troops from Kuwait?

One possible explanation for Bush's actions can be quickly dismissed: He was *not* responding to any overt pressure from public opinion or the media for a tougher stand. Polls did not yet exist in what still seemed a minor crisis, and media coverage of the president's initial actions—a strong condemnation of the invasion coupled with winning U.N. support for an economic embargo against Iraq—was wholly favorable without suggesting that the president should do either more or less than he had. As the *New York Times* editorialized: "The U.S. has no treaty obligation to come to Kuwait's aid. But the Gulf states still look to Washington for leadership and help in organizing action. President Bush has responded with the right lead—a strong national stand and a strong push for collective diplomacy."[5]

It is, however, easy to infer domestic political rationales for Bush's stance. First, success against Iraq would obviate criticism that Bush had responded weakly to an aggression that was certain to drive up oil prices, exacerbate the impending U.S. recession, and perhaps even bring on a new energy crisis. (The effect of higher oil prices on the weak U.S. economy was discussed in a key decision-making meeting, but there is no indication Bush considered this point important.)[6] In light of the Bush administration's efforts to build up Iraqi power in the 1980s and its weak diplomatic response to Iraq's threats against Kuwait prior to invading it, it was likely that Democratic criticism would be especially sharp.[7]

Second, a rollback of the Iraqi invasion could constitute an important part of the president's record in the 1992 election. In his first two years in office, the president had accomplished little he could take credit for.[8] His most notable action so far had been to abandon his famous pledge of "Read my lips, no new taxes," which he did in June 1990.

Finally, the crisis afforded the president an opportunity to overcome long-standing criticism that he was a weak and unprincipled leader, a moral "wimp." Gary Trudeau detailed the nature of the allegation during the 1988 campaign. Bush, he maintained, is "not a wimp in the sense of lacking physical bravery."

> The issue is rather one of moral courage, the willingness to place oneself at risk for one's principles. . . . The unfailing inclination to hold everybody else's coats during the great conflicts of our times has led to a persona of shimmering translucence—hence the No-where man. . . . President unDukakis . . . the classic cipher.[9]

Such complaints were widespread in the summer of 1992 and continued into the Gulf Crisis. Commenting on Bush's acceptance of a budget agreement with Congress that included big tax increases, columnist David Broder wrote:

> The budget fiasco in the capital has left few politicians untarnished, but the damage to President Bush is particularly serious—for good reason. The president has revealed to the nation's voters that you can't have the courage of your convictions if you lack any convictions. He—and we—will be fortunate if the lesson is not seized upon by Saddam Hussein and other foreign antagonists.[10]

Elizabeth Drew reported in the *New Yorker,* "A Senator said to me recently, reluctantly, 'We all know instinctively that this is not a strong man. It's greatly disturbing. I try not to think about it. I don't know anyone who's honest with himself who doesn't think this.'" It is hard to imagine a president who wouldn't be personally disturbed by such criticism and eager to put it to rest. But psychology aside, a president with Bush's reputation for moral indecision who stood by while U.S. interests were damaged, and who had the misfortune of a bad economy at the same time, would be risking mortal political damage. It is notable, therefore, that as soon as Bush pledged to liberate Kuwait the media reached a consensus verdict that the promise, if redeemed, "could virtually assure reelection."[11]

There was, of course, also great risk in attempting to liberate Kuwait. But if our concern is what political incentives the president could have had for taking this risk rather than standing by, it is easy to find some rather strong ones.

All of the preceding is, of course, pure inference. What actual evidence exists on the question of whether Bush was motivated by political concerns?

Two kinds of evidence exist: testimonial evidence from those who dealt with Bush in the crisis; and statistical evidence on when, in general, presidents take military action.

Testimonial accounts of Bush's motives for making the pledge stress the president's own beliefs about the need to stand firm against aggression.[12] By many reports, Bush was determined to stop Saddam before he could, like Hitler after his takeover of Czechoslovakia in 1938, use the fruits of aggression to become even more dangerous. Bush was further concerned that, coming at the beginning of the "new world order," the conquest of Kuwait could invite similar aggression by other countries unless dealt with effectively.

The national security official to whom I spoke also underscored the importance of Bush's own view of the crisis. "This president to an extraordinary degree said, 'This is right and I'm not going to be influenced by the polls if I'm confident on the right course.'"

Before concluding from this testimonial evidence that no calculation occurred, one must ask how likely it is that one could uncover evidence of calculation even if, in truth, Bush had been politically motivated. For one thing, discussion of political considerations, if any occurred, would probably have been limited to Bush's closest aides, who would then remain loyally silent. For another, decision-makers need not be aware of their real motives—need not, that is, say to themselves or anyone else. "I am going to take this grave action to bail myself out of a political mess"—in order to have been influenced by politics. They can simply allow themselves, possibly unconsciously, to be persuaded by reasons that someone else, in different political circumstances, would not find persuasive.

It is worth noting, in this connection, that Bush's publicly stated goals are not really so far from the political goals I have suggested. After all, a president who leads an effective international response to, as Bush sought to convince the public, the greatest threat to world peace since Nazi Germany, thereby playing Churchill to Saddam's Hitler, would obviously avoid criticism for "losing Iraq" or being a wimp. Lofty international goals may thus satisfy down-to-earth political needs, and may be pursued or even created for this reason.

Yet how, in view of these concerns, could a researcher *ever* show that politicians have taken grave political decisions for reasons of political interest?

Actually, quite easily: by gathering data on whether, over many diverse cases, politicians facing a certain situation act consistently in accord with their supposed interest.

For the present problem, such data have already been gathered. According to three studies, U.S. presidents from Truman to Reagan have, in fact, been more prone to use force at times when the country was in economic difficulty.[13] Thus, President Bush, in launching the Gulf War in the midst of the 1990–91 recession, conformed to the general pattern.

The correlation between use of force and economic difficulty is, I should add, far from perfect. Nor do the data alone explain why the correlation exists. Yet the data do show a connection between the political vulnerability and decision-making that bears scrutiny.

I will have more to say about these data after some additional data have been reviewed. In the meantime, discussion may be summarized as follows: All of the testimonial evidence concerning Bush's behavior in this phase of the Gulf Crisis depicts a president who acted on the basis of his conception of U.S. interests. Yet a parallel explanation for this behavior, based on Bush's political vulnerabilities, can be readily constructed, and there is quantitative evidence that one of Bush's vulnerabilities—a weak national economy—has affected foreign policy decision-making in past administrations.

THE CONGRESSIONAL RALLY BEHIND THE PRESIDENT

A few days after declaring that Iraqi aggression against Kuwait would not stand, Bush announced that he was sending combat troops to Saudi Arabia to protect that country from invasion by Iraq. Congressional support for this decision was immediate and clear. As Senator George Mitchell, Democratic leader in the Senate, told the press: "American interests and our long-standing ties with Saudi Arabia make the president's decision to help defend Saudi Arabia the correct one. . . . It is important for the nation to unite behind the president in this time of challenge to American interests."[14] Many members of Congress made similar supporting statements and no member of Congress publicly opposed the initial decision to commit U.S. ground forces to the region.[15]

Congressional support for Bush in this phase of the crisis appears to have been politically important. With Congress supporting the president, the media were deprived of oppositional sources, which constrained them to be supportive, which further enhanced public support for Bush. With strong support for his policies at home, the president's threat to use force gained credibility abroad, which strengthened his hand in pulling together an international coalition against Iraq. The initial congressional and public support for his policies may also have encouraged Bush to escalate the level of military confrontation later on.

Elite support which generates mass rallies for presidential policies is common in foreign policy crises (see Brody, Chapter 10 in this volume). How can it be explained in this case?

When I asked a senior foreign policy aide why congressional leaders rallied behind the president's decision to send troops to Saudi Arabia, the question struck him as silly. "Why not support the president when he stands up for American interests? You can always withdraw your support later if you want to. In the meantime, go along." This aide also said that he had seen intelligence reports suggesting that Iraq intended to invade Saudi Arabia. "I've seen lots of this kind of data in other cases, and not all of it showed what the president said it showed. But this time, the evidence was strong."

These factors came up in other interviews and were never contradicted. Iraq's aggression was perceived in Congress as a real threat to American interests, and there was little political cost to supporting the president, so why not go along, at least for now.

It should not be assumed, however, that Congress would acquiesce in any presidential action in a crisis. Although some legislators doubted that the U.S. interest in Kuwait was strong enough to justify war, few doubted that the U.S. had an important interest in the region. Such judgments are best understood as reflections of reigning conceptions of geopolitics, and were the only apparent motivation of the congressional rally in August.

It appears especially unlikely that congressional leaders were toadying to public opinion in their support for Bush's policies rather than expressing their own feelings. For one thing, congressional endorsement of Bush's decision to send troops to the Gulf began in the same news cycle in which the policy was announced, before public reaction was known. For another, some congressional leaders who praised the president in August criticized him in November when he announced a policy they disliked. Although polls had by then shown Bush's Gulf policies to be popular, these leaders (though not necessarily all member of Congress) showed little hesitation in lambasting the president.

So here it appears that Washington elites took an action—public endorsement of Bush's Gulf policy—on the basis of their own convictions. In so doing, they were not, in any discernible way, responding to public opinion but helping to shape it. They did so, however, in the comfortable knowledge that if Bush's policies failed, they could bail out without incurring political damage to themselves.

THE NOVEMBER TROOP DEPLOYMENT

The August deployment of 200,000 troops to the Gulf was too small to take offensive action against the 400,000 Iraqi troops in Kuwait. The purpose was simply to defend Saudi Arabia. But on November 8, Bush announced the deployment of enough additional troops to give the United States and its allies the capacity to launch offensive actions.

The additional troops profoundly transformed the crisis. The initial expectation was that events would play out over many months or perhaps years while sanctions and diplomacy ran their course. But the American force was now too large to wait in the desert while sanctions ran slowly on, so the timetable for resolution of the crisis speeded up. Either Iraq would withdraw within three or four months, or the U.S. would go to war.

Congressional Democrats were furious about the new troop deployment, claiming that it "boxed us in" to a position in which they would have two bad choices: acquiesce in a presidential decision to use force, which most Democrats thought was bad policy, or breach national unity by "taking on" Bush in the midst of crisis, which was political dynamite.

Republicans, however, sympathized with Bush's decision to speed up the crisis. If U.S. troops were kept in the desert for an extended period, said a Republican Senate aide, "we would start getting letters from families with loved ones overseas, stories about little babies who had never seen their fathers, then the inevitable accident in which lots of GI's are killed . . . then pictures of children in Iraq starving from the boycott." Congress, he said, responds to this kind of thing. "I think you would have seen a process of weakening of American resolve" which would have made it hard to start a war if sanctions failed to work. "This is a classic case of the 'best' policy [i.e., trying sanctions first] being politically impossible."[16]

Another aide to a Republican senator saw the same nightmare. "It would have been a delight to the Democrats," who would be constantly "sniping at Bush" and "eroding support for his policy" with the public. And then, once the public support was gone, the Democrats would want Congress to vote. "This is a very partisan place . . . a sick place," he said.

In my interview with the National Security official, I asked whether the domestic political effects of the second troop deployment—boxing in the Democrats, and avoiding a drawn out affair in which public support would erode—had been intended by the administration, or were merely fortuitous coincidence. The latter, he said; military concerns entirely determined policy. "Without additional troops, we had no chance of persuading Saddam to leave Kuwait," he said. "Why should he leave if we couldn't make him leave?"

I also asked whether the decision to send extra troops had been affected by the Vietnam War, in which flagging public support made it politically impossible to send more troops when they were needed. Perhaps troops were sent early because public support wouldn't exist when they came to be needed. "That's the same question you just asked," he replied. "We weren't thinking about domestic support when we decided to send more troops." He agreed that public support might wear thin during an embargo, but "we always assumed that we'd have the support to do what needed to be done."

At this point I asked whether the Bush administration had paid *any* attention to public opinion during the crisis. Certainly, the official replied, "In order to make our threats credible to Saddam and to hold our international coalition together, it was tremendously important for us to demonstrate that we had national unity in support of our policies."

What practically was done to assure such public support, I asked. "We worked a lot harder than usual on putting out statements, getting the president out there explaining the policy, sending people out to speak to groups." Seeking U.N. approval for the use of force, he added, was also part of a strategy to bolster domestic public opinion.

"Public relations was not a strength of this administration," in large part because Bush didn't like having to make speeches, the official said. "But on this we really tried."

Again, then, testimonial evidence indicates that political considerations and public opinion played no role in the Bush administration's decision. The administration was concerned about public opinion, but this concern manifested itself in efforts to convince the public to accept the policies that the Bush administration judged to be the best.

But as before, there are reasons to doubt this conclusion. First, the decision was taken in a context in which the public had supported Bush initiatives so far. For example, 66 percent said in a CBS-*New York Times* survey just before the troop announcement that it was the "right thing" to send troops to Saudi Arabia. As can be seen in table 1 of my earlier essay (Chapter 9 in this volume), there were clear indications that the public, though not clamoring for more aggressive policies, would go along with stronger action if so urged. So if the Bush administration didn't worry much about public opinion in deliberating over the second troop deployment, it was because it had learned it didn't have to. It could anticipate that a public that had supported its initiatives up to that point would respond favorably to new initiatives as well.

There is, in addition, indirect evidence of a more fundamental political influence. In a study of wars since 1815 that involved democracies, Gaubatz (1991) found that nations were less likely to become engaged in wars at election time than at other times.[17] Although the reason for this was not clear, avoidance of political risk appeared a likely possibility.

Although neither Gaubatz's study nor the studies I cited earlier use data from the Bush years, the patterns they find correctly anticipate Bush's two key decisions in the Gulf crisis: As the country was slipping into recession, Bush sent troops to the Gulf and pledged to force Iraq to leave Kuwait; and, in a separate decision, he dispatched enough extra troops to make sure that, if war did occur, it would occur in 1991 rather than in 1992, the election year.

How does one evaluate this evidence? Although the coincidence of the particular case of the Gulf War with a general pattern cannot prove anything about the one case, it can certainly raise suspicion. If that suspicion still seems unwarranted, consider the following: If Iraq had invaded Kuwait at the beginning of 1992, and if the U.S. economy had been booming at the time, would the president have been as likely to risk war as soon as troops could be readied for assault, as Bush did in the Gulf crisis? Or would he have been more likely to rely on sanctions until after the election, even if that meant waiting a year or more?

These questions, though obviously unanswerable, make clear, I think, that the suspicion raised by the correlational data is reasonable, and that the general issue under examination—whether presidents take account of the likely political impact of their foreign policy decisions—must be taken seriously even when, as in the case of Bush and the Gulf War, there is no testimonial evidence that the president did so.

CONGRESS AUTHORIZES THE USE OF FORCE AGAINST IRAQ

On January 12, Congress voted on resolutions authorizing the president to use "all necessary means" to drive the Iraqi army from Kuwait. After a decorous debate, the resolutions passed by votes of 52–47 in the Senate and 250–183 in the House.

These vote margins were roughly in line with contemporary opinion polls, which showed the public divided but leaning toward war.[18] The votes of individual House members tended, in addition, to line up with opinion in their districts: The stronger Bush had run in a district in 1988, the more likely its representative was to vote for use of force (Jacobson 1993). Taken together, these facts strongly suggest that the congressional vote on the war was a well-calibrated response to the public opinion that existed at the time of the vote.

Yet to take this as the whole story of the public's influence on the Gulf War vote would be greatly misleading. Members of Congress are deeply strategic players whose visible actions often obscure their real intent. Consider this example from the Gulf Crisis: Senate liberals, as I was told by a well-placed source, initially wanted Congress to vote in September on a resolution that would both approve Bush's decision to send troops to the Gulf and set strict conditions on the use of those troops in an offensive operation. Liberals put aside this plan, however, after concluding that, in the flush of public support for the president that existed in September, and with a congressional election coming up in November, Republicans might be able attract enough support from electorally vulnerable Democrats to reverse the intent of the resolution. Rather than voting to restrict Bush's authority to take military action against Iraq, as liberals wanted, Congress might pass an amended resolution that would permit Bush to use force at his discretion. It was, the liberals therefore calculated, safer to wait until after the election and after public support for Bush had begun to erode, since that would increase chances of a dovish vote in Congress.

Such strategic maneuvering, which routinely occurs in Congress, can turn evidence of apparent responsiveness on its head. What looks at first like Congress doing the bidding of the public becomes instead congressional leaders manipulating events so that they can use public opinion as a cover for doing what they want to do anyway.

This problem is key to interpreting the action Congress finally took on the Gulf War. When Congress reconvened after the election, public support for Bush's gulf policies had, as liberals had anticipated, declined. By quite lopsided margins, the public also appeared to favor congressional debate, as this CBS News–*New York Times* poll item shows:

President Bush and his advisers have said public debate over whether we should fight Iraq will hurt the effort to persuade Iraq to get out of Kuwait. Others say Congress should be able to debate the issue openly. What do you think? Will debate hurt the effort to get Iraq out of Kuwait, or should Congress be able to debate the issue openly:

Hurt effort	25%
Debate openly	65
Both (volunteered)	3
Don't know	8

In view of this, many liberals wanted to vote on a resolution to restrict Bush's powers to go to war, and to do so in December. The reason for moving quickly was fear that, as the U.N.'s January deadline for Iraq to withdraw from Kuwait approached, public pressure for a prowar vote might become too strong to resist.

Yet the Democratic leadership, though wanting to limit Bush's powers to make war, nonetheless put off scheduling a vote until January. Why it did so, and how public opinion affected its decision, is what I shall now try to explain. Since, however, the leadership's actions must always fit the needs and preferences of its followers (see Cox and McCubbins 1992), I begin with the views of ordinary members of Congress.

Ordinary members. In the middle of November, as war was growing more likely, Defense Secretary Dick Cheney gave a briefing to about a hundred members of the House. As Bob Woodward described the scene in *The Commanders,*

After an hour, Cheney said, "I assume all of you guys want to vote up or down on the proposition."
The room erupted. There were shouts of no and yes (p. 311).

Many members of Congress did not initially want to vote on whether the U.S. should go to war against Iraq. Some legislators, most commonly from very safe seats, were eager to play the role of partisan gladiators. But the majority of members were more hesitant. They would get little credit no matter how the war turned out but might face retribution if they either opposed a successful war or supported a disastrous one. In this situation, many members saw no reason to commit themselves to a position any sooner than necessary, and a few, as I was told, wanted to avoid taking a position even at the very end.

Such reticence is normal in Congress. Although members may have particular issues on which they are always prepared to do partisan combat, few are eager to take on issues that are both highly conflictual and highly salient to the public (Arnold 1991).

Eventually, however, congressional leaders scheduled a vote, thus forcing members to take a public stand. When I asked staff aides how members decided to vote on the war, virtually all said public opinion had been a modest influence on decision-making and that the members' own judgments about "the right policy" to follow were paramount. The vote was, in a phrase that came up repeatedly, a "conscience vote," one that many members had anguished over more than any they had ever cast. "When you're voting whether to send soldiers into battle, you don't think about politics," I was told many, many times.

One could, however, just as easily make the opposite argument: "When you're voting whether to send soldiers into battle, you had better think about the politics, because if you take the wrong side of the issue, your constituents are likely to notice." And, in fact, a few legislative aides went on to observe that the vote was a conscience vote mainly because current public opinion was split and the most politically relevant aspect of the decision, the outcome of the war, was unknown. For example:

> [O]ne congressional aide explained to me after . . ."The vote was a potential career-killer—either way." The members of Congress knew that they could be caught on the wrong side of history—but when they voted there was no telling which side that would be. (Drew 1991, p. 86).

An aide with many years of experience on Capitol Hill put it this way:

> You're talking about a body of politicians about as good as any in the world, and suddenly they're not getting a clear message from the public. Some guys, of course, are all conscience on every vote, but most members wanted to make a political decision and couldn't.
> . . . A lot of the anguish you heard so much about was just because members couldn't get a clear message from the public.

The notion that many members voted their conscience only because they were forced to do so by circumstance was, as I indicated, volunteered only a few times. But after the idea was suggested, I raised it many more times myself, and in only one case did someone disagree, this person saying it was "too cynical." In the other cases, I got a silent nod, a statement of "well, of course," or some other form of assent.

We have, then, a convergence of two powerful forces: The normal reluctance of members of Congress to risk their careers on salient and controversial issues, and members' uncertainty over how the action they took would appear to the public in light of future events. Both encouraged a low-profile approach to the issue.

Two other features of the congressional vote are noteworthy. The first is the solemn manner in which it was conducted. Partisan acrimony was put aside as member after member went before colleagues—and, of course, the television audience—to offer heartfelt and thoughtful accounts of their votes. The occasion was, as several aides still proudly recalled, one of "Congress' finest hours."

These decorous trappings had great importance to members. In dangerous circumstances, it is essential to cast what in Congress are called "explainable votes"—votes that appear well-reasoned, well-informed, and sincere.[19] And this is what the long, dignified debate on the war, which was not really a debate at all but a series of unrelated monologues, permitted members to do.

The other notable feature of the vote was its partisan composition. Essentially all of the Republicans and 70 percent of the Democrats cast party-line votes. Such voting is by no means unusual. Legislators come from districts that differ in partisan orientation and tend to reflect those differences in their voting. Whether one counts this as the influence of public opinion, since different publics select different types of members, or the influence of conscience, since members, once elected, may cast ideological votes that are akin to conscience votes, is not clear. Undoubtedly, both factors contributed to the partisan coloration of the war vote.

As in the examination of decision-making in the White House, then, one can identify two quite different explanations for why key decisions were made. One stresses that, after much soul-searching, members of Congress voted their consciences. This explanation came up in most interviews, and in some it was the only one given much credence. The other explanation stressed political calculation—that any vote was risky, that members were frustrated by the difficulty of anticipating how future opinion would judge the war, and that little could be gained and much possibly lost by high-profile involvement in the issue.

The Democratic leadership.   As in any foreign policy crisis, the president set the agenda to which Congress had to respond. The essence of Bush's policy was to "threaten war to prevent war"; that is, make a credible threat to force Iraq from Kuwait in the hope that it would then withdraw on its own accord. The president further asserted that his role as commander-in-chief gave him all the authority he needed to make good on this threat.

The Democratic leadership of Congress—in particular, Speaker Thomas Foley and Senate Leader George Mitchell—had two fundamental objections to this agenda. They opposed war until sanctions had been given a long try, and they objected to the assertion that the president could start a war without authorization from Congress. "Under the American Constitution, the president has no legal authority—none whatsoever—to commit the United States to war," asserted Senator Mitchell. "Only Congress can make that grave decision."[20]

From the president's side, disagreement with Congress was a source of concern but no apparent anguish. The president, according to published accounts and my interviews, worried that congressional opposition might give encouragement to Iraq but felt confident that he had both the moral right and sufficient political support to go to war without Congress. "Nobody cared about Congress," as a military official bluntly stated.

Public opinion was more important to the administration, but here Bush was confident. "Low levels of public support for war before the war started were no problem," explained the same military official. "We felt the country basically supported the military effort, and that as soon as the fighting started, there would be a surge of increased support." Then, if the war could be won quickly enough, public support would never become an issue.

The complement of presidential confidence was congressional trepidation. The leadership's problem was how to oppose the president without asking too much of politically cautious party members or risking public backlash. This was no easy task. Real opposition would draw Democrats into a partisan crossfire many would prefer to avoid. It could also undermine the strategy of threatening war to avoid war, thereby making Democrats liable to the charge that, in opposing Bush's policy, they were making war more likely. Why, after all, should Iraq back down peacefully if Democrats were going to tie Bush's hands?

Hence, when Bush announced the second troop deployment, the leadership faced a dilemma. It could, as many liberals wished, take advantage of weaker public support for Bush to press for limits on the president's unilateral ability to use force. Or it could hold back, see how events unfolded, and hope for more favorable conditions later on.

Republicans made sure Democrats were acutely aware of the political dangers of confrontation. Republican Senator Trent Lott said in November that if Congress allowed a debate to become "a backing away from the [administration's] policy, it could be giving aid and comfort to Saddam." In using language from the constitutional definition of treason, Lott sent a message that some Democrats were still angry about more than two years later. Bush made the same point by showing a group of legislators a clipping from an Iraqi newspaper purporting to describe congressional opposition to war.

With these incidents in mind, I asked an aide to a leading Senate Republican whether Democrats might have faced attacks questioning their patriotism if they had vigorously opposed Bush's policy. "That's not a possibility," he replied. "That's a fact." Democratic aides to whom I spoke made little effort to conceal their fear of such attacks.

Further, it was not clear that Bush would respect a vote that went against him. This was perhaps the most sensitive point. "There was," an aide said, "a fear that Bush would go ahead no matter what Congress did." The prospect of U.S. troops poised for battle, or perhaps going into combat, fighting and dying, while the courts refereed a dispute between Congress and the president was regarded as "horrendous." It could give the whole government, but especially congressional Democrats, a black-eye in public opinion that would last for decades. And there was no guarantee it would stop the war.

In these circumstances, a Democratic push to limit Bush's war-making power seemed risky no matter how it might come out. Antiwar Democrats might find themselves branded as traitors, abandoned by their more cautious colleagues, and ultimately defeated in their bid to restrain the president. Or, equally perilous, Democrats might win the vote, plunging the nation into "a constitutional crisis within a foreign policy crisis" that would upset everyone.

So, faced with a potentially lose-lose proposition, Democratic leaders decided not to press for an immediate vote on Bush's war-making powers, and to rely instead on public hearings to make the case against war (see Entman and Page, Chapter 4 in this volume). As Representative Lee Hamilton accurately forecast in early December, "Congress is going to be on the margin of any decision to use force."[21]

The leadership did not, however, abandon all effort. There was one type of congressional vote that Bush could perhaps be compelled to honor, namely, one that he himself had requested. There was, of course, a Catch-22 here: the leadership knew that Bush would never request a vote unless he was certain in advance he would win, but it nevertheless began trying to induce the president to request such a vote. As part of this effort, Foley reportedly assured the president in meetings with him that he would not invoke party discipline to pressure Democrats into voting as a bloc against the president.

Why, if the leadership knew it was likely to lose a vote that Bush requested, did it care about having one? Because it felt that a presidential request would create a precedent that would strengthen the role of Congress in the foreign policy-decision-making process. That, apparently, was the most that the House leadership felt it could get from the crisis.

But Bush would not concede even that much, ignoring pleas from both Democratic and Republican leaders that he request a vote. Finally, amidst charges of political cowardice,[22] Foley and Mitchell decided on their own to schedule a debate on a war resolution to begin January 10, with a vote to follow immediately. This meant that debate would occur after diplomacy between the U.S. and Iraq had ended, so Congress could no longer be accused of undermining the policy of "threatening war to avoid war." But it also meant that the vote would occur just before the U.N. deadline, at which time many expected fighting to begin. This made opposition to the war resolution seem like voting against the troops who would fight it, a perception that, by many accounts, made it harder to vote against war.

It is striking that Foley, in announcing his decision to hold a vote on the eve of war, announced at the same time that he expected the president to prevail. In keeping with his earlier assurance to Bush, Foley also said the vote would be a "conscience vote" in which the leadership would make no attempt to line up votes against the war. Mitchell, in announcing the Senate vote, made no prediction about who would win in that chamber, but two other Senators predicted the war resolution would pass.[23]

Shortly after Foley and Mitchell announced that a vote would be held, the president wrote a letter asking Congress to support the war. As the *New York Times* noted at the time, "Bush made the request only after Congressional leaders said in recent days that he was almost certain to receive Congressional endorsement"—provided that he worked hard for it.[24] So, in contrast to the House Democratic leadership, Bush did not declare a conscience vote. Rather, he led an all-out lobbying operation, which complemented the large and well-organized prowar whip organization that had been working unopposed in the House for several weeks under the leadership of Representative Stephen Solarz.

Under these rather advantageous conditions—a huge U.S. force transported to the Gulf and poised for battle; all diplomacy at an end and the clock ticking down on the U.N. ultimatum to withdraw; the Democratic party mounting no organized opposition to the president's policies and, in fact, remaining mostly silent for over a month; and the Democratic House leadership declaring a "conscience vote" and conceding victory to the president—Congress voted a green light for offensive action in the Gulf.

It is essential to realize that it was no accident that Congress voted under these particular circumstances. The time of the vote was chosen, after much deliberation, by the Democratic leadership.[25] The decision-point appears to have come in December, when leaders decided against a galvanizing partisan vote. This was, as indicated earlier, a time when polls showed the public lopsidedly favoring congressional debate, when public support for Bush's policies had declined some 10 to 15 percentage points from its summer peak, and when the public was divided over the prospect of using force. It is thus hard to argue that public opinion, at least as expressed in polls, determined the outcome.

Then what did? I pressed hard in my interviews to find out and, as usual, everyone's initial responses stressed concern about good public policy. One aide, a political scientist who has since returned to academia, said the leadership was motivated by the belief that conflict with the president—that is, a constitutional crisis—would be dangerous for the troops in the field and bad for democratic government generally. He said he was "astounded" by the extent to which the leadership ignored partisanship and tried to do what was right for the country. "In my time on the Hill I saw nothing as apolitical as this vote," he said. "There was a strong feeling of moral righteousness." Another aide said over and over that the issue was just not "ripe" for a vote until January. And another staffer stressed Foley's concern both to do what was right for the country and—in a franker acknowledgment of political factors than the others—to protect the reputation of Congress. Instigating a vote that might well lead to a constitutional crisis would accomplish neither of these goals. Was Foley, I asked, not also concerned about what was good for the Democratic party? "This was a case when good policy was good politics," the aide replied.

I would draw particular attention to the last remark, except that I would restate it as, "This was a case when national unity was good politics." Despite their opposition to an early war, Democratic leaders were clearly reluctant to undercut the president or disrupt national unity. There were apparently two reasons for this reluctance. One was that, as described in the last section, many Democrats whose votes would be needed in an all-out fight were disinclined, whatever their preferences on the war, to be dragged into such a fight. The other was the leadership's judgment that, whatever the polls seemed to say, the public didn't really want to see Congress vying with the president to see who could control foreign policy. It wanted a smooth, confident national effort, and if it got a partisan mess instead, it would be more inclined to blame the Democrats—with their long-standing vulnerability as weak on foreign policy—than to blame the president. Nobody would win, but Congress as an institution and the Democratic party would be the biggest losers. Thus, when I asked a veteran Democratic aide what would have happened if Congress had voted in December against allowing Bush to go to war on his own authority, he was hardly able to take the question seriously: "We would have been accused of appeasement, of playing into Iraq's hands. . . ," he exclaimed. "We'd never do that, it would be a disaster. . . . It couldn't happen."

The stress on national unity was never more apparent than in Foley's speech during the House debate. He spoke strongly against war, but ended with the plea that "however you vote. . . . let us come together after the vote with the notion that we are Americans here, not Democrats and Republicans, all anxious to do the best for our country. . . . without anything but the solemn pride that we voted as our conscience and judgment told us we should."[26]

These are the words of a man standing against a measure he knew would be extremely popular in a few days, when the fighting began, and who didn't want himself or his party, despite their antiwar beliefs, to be guilty of anything that could be called obstructionism. Foley was speaking his mind, but he wasn't getting in the way of those who wanted war.

Clearly, not everyone in Congress was so worried about a galvanizing partisan fight. Some members of both parties began demanding a vote on the Gulf War as early as October. I was especially curious about Republican Senate leader Robert Dole, a loyal supporter of the president who was among the earliest and most insistent in demanding a congressional vote. When I asked an aide familiar with Dole's thinking why the senator had taken this position when it might precipitate a constitutional crisis, he replied that Dole thought the Democrats were trying to "have it both ways"—engaging in cheap partisan criticism of Bush without being willing to go squarely on the record in favor of an alternative policy. Thus, he said, congressional maneuverings on the war were essentially "a political exercise between warring parties trying to set each other up. That's the way it works here, and Dole wanted to draw the lines clearly." Meanwhile, on the other side of the aisle, some Democrats felt equally strongly that the party should go all-out and let the chips fall where they may.[27]

It is notable that none of the partisan gladiators on either side of the issue suffered politically from the war, and some may have slightly increased their national visibility. Indeed, in the end, almost everyone had something to be grateful for in the way the war vote was handled. The gladiators were able to make principled declamations on national television; the cautious were given ample opportunity in a dignified setting to cast explainable votes; Congress enhanced its popular standing because of the manner in which it conducted its "debate,"[28] and enhanced its institutional status because Bush finally sought its approval for war; and, not least important, the country was spared an ugly constitutional crisis. The leadership had done its job, not by following public opinion, which did not really exist on the critical questions of how and when a congressional vote should be taken, but by thinking carefully about how the public would likely react to future events.

One other point is worth pondering. As has been widely noted, victory in the Gulf War, although a boon to Bush's short-term popularity, failed to help much in the 1992 election. The usual explanation is that the public turned its attention to a more salient matter, the economy. Another factor, however, may be the way the war vote was handled. Although many congressional Democrats felt and spoke strongly against the war, their opposition was so carefully modulated and packaged that it hardly penetrated to much of the public. This is apparent in the results of a June 1991 survey by the National Election Studies:

Before the war actually started, do you think one political party was more in favor of using military force in the Persian Gulf than the other party was, or do you think they were about equal in their support for using force? [emphasis in the original]

Democrats favored force more	1%
Both supported force equally	60
Republicans favored force more	38
Don't know	1

With most Americans unable to remember the Democratic party's position on the war just five months after it occurred, it is hardly surprising that Bush had trouble capitalizing on it in the election. But what if the Democrats had succeeded in defeating the war resolution and provoking a constitutional crisis? That, surely, would have been memorable, and memorable in a way that would have hurt the electoral prospects of the Democrats.

Conclusion

Social scientists are properly skeptical of studies, like this one, that rely on unsystematic data. It is too easy for someone with an active imagination and any talent for writing to spin out alluring stories. Yet, especially in the early stages of inquiry, studies using such data can be useful. In this paper, I have sought to contribute in two areas: the role of domestic politics in foreign policy decisions, and the role of elites in shaping mass opinion.

PUBLIC OPINION AND FOREIGN POLICY

Scholars of foreign policy have traditionally paid little attention to domestic politics. Decisions to go to war, in particular, have been thought far too important to be susceptible to influence by mere politics. That presumption, however, is changing. Chagrined by quantitative studies showing that a variety of domestic and political factors are correlated with foreign policy decision-making, scholars are now scrambling to develop a better understanding of how exactly domestic factors influence the international behavior of states.

One question for foreign policy specialists is how states can behave as "unitary actors," that is, develop and stick to a set of coherent policy goals. Certainly the United States managed an impressive degree of national unity during the Gulf Crisis. So the question is how, despite the fact that Congress and the presidency were controlled by different parties in the Gulf Crisis, it did so.

The basis of national unity, as I have suggested, was in elite perceptions of future public opinion, perceptions that were probably quite well-founded. President Bush, fearing the fallout of a do-nothing policy in the midst of a recession and judging that the public would follow and ultimately approve strong leadership, steered a firm, straight-ahead course. The leaders of Congress, judging that the public would be repulsed by the effects of a strong challenge to Bush's leadership, declined to go all-out against it. One can certainly imagine conditions under which elite solicitude for mass opinion would have different implications for national capacity to behave as a unitary actor, but it is noteworthy that domestic politics can, under at least some conditions, support such action.

Another question in the foreign policy literature is whether mass

opinion tends to be pacifist or warlike. This classic question does not resonate well in the Gulf Crisis. If we assume, for the moment, that my
analysis of elite calculations is correct, and assume also that the anticipa-
tions of public opinion formed by successful politicians are likely to have
a realistic basis, American mass opinion can be characterized as follows:
warlike in its presumed readiness to punish Bush for losing Kuwait;
warlike in its presumed unwillingness to brook messy challenges to
Bush's assertive leadership; but pacifist in its presumed dislike of bloody
wars and costly holding actions, which is what induced Bush to get the
fighting over quickly and well before the election. In other words, the
public wanted to have its cake and eat it too—to enjoy the benefits of an
assertive national policy but not to incur the costs. So to ask whether a
democratic mass public is pacifist or warlike may be like asking whether
a public prefers a high level of government services or low taxes: It prefers both, of course, and will offer politicians every incentive to give it
both.

Finally, a factor that seemed important in my analysis but has not received attention in quantitative studies of decision-making is a politician's *domestic* reputation for toughness in dealing with foreign
adversaries, which appears to be highly valued among U.S. politicians.
Democratic aides conceded that their party's reputation for weakness
was a constraining factor in the calculations of the House leadership. In
my interviews with executive branch officials, I did not feel it would be
fruitful to ask whether Bush was also concerned about his reputation as
a strong leader in foreign affairs, but I tried earlier to show why anyone
in his position would have had reason to be so concerned. Eisenhower's
willingness to allow France to be defeated in Indochina; Kennedy's
hyper-tough responses to Khrushchev's provocations; Johnson's fear of
being responsible for "losing Vietnam"; and Nixon's freedom to be the
one to "go to China" seem additional, well-known instances in which
domestic reputation may have been a factor in foreign policy decision-
making. It would therefore seem worthwhile to find some way of quan-
tifying domestic reputation and testing its presumed effects.

ELITE LEADERSHIP OF MASS OPINION

The primary conclusion of this chapter is that, many exaggerated reports
of its demise to the contrary, the democratic interplay between leaders
and followers was alive and well in the Gulf Crisis. Politicians of both
parties were, as past studies have shown, active agents in shaping public
opinion, but they took care to lead toward goals the public would ultimately approve; or, in the case of congressional Democrats, to avoid

leading toward goals the public would not approve. In both cases, the threat of electoral retribution gave pause to the wielders of power. As the president himself expressed it, "I know whose backside is at stake and rightfully so. . . ."[29] Congressional Democrats, thinking of their own posteriors, felt the same way. The interplay between leaders and followers did not turn on the mechanical translation of poll results into public policy, but the officials who took the nation to war were nonetheless vividly mindful that the public they were leading would hold them accountable for their leadership.

Notes

I am grateful to Lance Bennett, Stanley Heginbotham, and David Paletz for encouraging this unusual (for me, anyway) research; to David Flanders for essential advice and logistical support in Washington; and to Larry Bartels, Kathy Bawn, Tim Cook, Barbara Geddes, John Geer, Elizabeth Gerber, John Petrocik, and Nelson Polsby for helpful comments on earlier drafts. Since I did not take all their advice, I stress that I am responsible for the final result.

1. The "indexing hypothesis" was proposed by Bennett (1991), who based his study on earlier work by Cohen (1973), Sigal (1973), and others.

2. See Gamson and Modigliani (1966), Mueller (1973), Brody (1991), and Zaller (1992). Studies by Brody, Iyengar and Simon, and Zaller (Chapters 10, 8, and 9 in this volume) also corroborate this view.

3. Article by R. W. Apple, Jr., *New York Times*, August 6, 1990, p. A7.

4. "Now or Later," *New York Times*, August 7, 1990, p. A19.

5. "Iraq's Naked Aggression," *New York Times*, August 3, 1990. Editorials in the *Washington Post, Los Angeles Times, Chicago Tribune*, and *San Francisco Chronicle* take similar positions; the *Wall Street Journal*, was a bit more hawkish, but by no means urged military action.

6. U.S. News and World Report (1992, p.50).

7. A basis for criticism was present from the start; see Dorman and Livingston (Chapter 3 in this volume); David Hoffman, "U.S. Misjudgment of Saddam Seen: Early Evidence of Bellicosity, Drive for Dominance Noted," *Washington Post*, August 8, p. A1.

8. The Soviet empire was crumbling, but a *New York Times* headline during the unification of Germany indicates Bush's difficulty in claiming credit for it: "Bush Declares He Does Not Feel Left Out by Gorbachev and Kohl," July 18, 1990, p. A1.

9. "Still a Wimp," *Washington Post*, November 4, 1988.

10. "An Absence of Guiding Principle," *Washington Post*, October 12, 1990, p. A21.

11. Jack Nelson, "Conflict in Gulf Is Make or Break Test for President," *Los Angeles Times*, August 9, 1991, p. A8. Also David Shirbman, "Iraq Crisis Presents

Bush with Crucial Opportunity to Define His Presidency, Determine His Future," *Wall Street Journal*, August 7, 1990, p. A18.

12. See Smith (1992) and *U.S. News and World Report* (1992) for summaries of available accounts.

13. Ostrom and Job 1991; James and Oneal 1991; Brace and Hinkley 1992.

14. Karen Tumulty, "Bush Gets Solid Backing from Congress," *Los Angeles Times*, August 9, 1990, p. A8.

15. *Congressional Quarterly 1990 Almanac*, p. 727.

16. See also "A Dangerous Mirage," *Washington Post*, November 1, 1990, p. B7, where Henry Kissinger writes that "by the time it is evident that sanctions alone cannot succeed, a credible military option will probably no longer exist."

17. Gaubatz's study involves 17 democracies and 45 wars between 1838 and 1973. Three other studies, examining use of force rather than war initiation and focusing on the U.S., muddy this picture, finding positive, negative, and null relationships between electoral calendar and use of force (Ostrom and Job 1991, p. 315 and passim). The expected political effects of a minor use of force (e.g., Johnson's air raids on North Vietnam after the Tonkin Gulf incidents of August 1964) would likely be different than those of actual war.

18. For analyses, see Mueller, forthcoming; William Schneider, "Public Backs Gulf War as Last Option," *National Journal*, January 5, 1991, p. 5; Richard Morin, "Two Ways of Reading the Public's Lips on Gulf Policy," *Washington Post*, January 14, 1991.

19. See also Fenno (1978) and Kingdon (1989).

20. *Congressional Quarterly Almanac*, p. 736.

21. Cited in C. Madison, "Sideline Players," *National Journal*, December 15, 1990, p. 3024.

22. See Jeffrey Birnbaum, "New Congress, Full of Sound and Fury Over Iraq, Fuels Bipartisan Outrage by Signifying Nothing," *Wall Street Journal*, January 4, 1991, A8.

23. See Adam Clymer, "Votes Backing Use of Force Are Predicted in Congress," *New York Times*, January 7, 1991, p. A7.

24. "Bush Asks Congress to Back Use of Force," *New York Times*, January 9, 1991, p. A6.

25. Aides to the top House leadership said the leadership felt it had a good but not certain chance of winning a vote in November or December, and contemporary journalistic accounts bear out this view (see R. Jeffrey Smith, "Capitol Hill Hearings Seen to Be Setback for Bush's Policy," *Washington Post*, December 1). Bush, by published accounts, also feared he would lose a fall vote. Yet most aides to less well-placed members, perhaps influenced by intervening events, thought the prowar position could have carried at any time. By all accounts, however, support for war in Congress grew stronger by January, when the vote was finally taken, than it had been in November.

26. *Congressional Record*, January 12, 1991, pp. 441–42.

27. There were, however, signs of restraint. A Nunn aide said "no one contemplated there would be a constitutional crisis because Bush would abide by Congress' decision, having asked for it." But what if Congress voted against war *without* having been asked by Bush? "I don't think there was ever any dwelling on that possibility," he said, because few favored that.

28. According to the CBS-*New York Times* polls, the percentage saying Congress was doing a fair or good job went from 23 in the fall of 1990 to 48 in February, 1991.

29. Woodward (1991, 331).

References

Arnold, R. D. 1991. *The Logic of Congressional Action*. New Haven: Yale University Press.

Bennett, W. L. 1991. "Toward a Theory of Press-State Relations in the U.S." *Journal of Communication* 40: 103–25.

Brace, P., and B. Hinckley. 1992. *Follow the Leader*. New York: Basic Books.

Brody, R. A. 1991. *Assessing the President: The Media, Elite Opinion, and Public Support*. Stanford: Stanford University Press.

Cohen, B. C. 1973. *The Public's Impact on Foreign Policy*. Boston: Little, Brown.

Congressional Quarterly 1990 Almanac. Washington, D.C.

Cox, G., and M. McCubbins. 1992. *Legislative Leviathan*. Berkeley: University of California Press.

Drew, E. 1991. "Letter from Washington." *New Yorker*, February 4, pp. 82–90.

Fenno, R. 1978. *Homestyle*. Boston: Little, Brown.

Gamson, W., and A. Modigliani. 1966. "Knowledge and Foreign Policy Opinions: Some Models for Consideration." *Public Opinion Quarterly* 30:187–99.

Gaubatz, K. T. 1991. "Election Cycles and War." *Journal of Conflict Resolution* 35: 212–44.

Jacobson, G. 1993. "Congress: Unusual year, Unusual Election." In *The Elections of 1992*, ed. Michael Nelson, Washington, D.C.: CQ Press.

James, P., and J. Oneal 1991. "Influences on the President's Use of Force." *Journal of Conflict Resolution* 35:307–32.

Key, V. O., Jr. 1961. *Public Opinion and American Democracy*, New York: Knopf.

Kingdon, J. 1989. *Congressmen's Voting Decisions*. Ann Arbor: University of Michigan Press.

Mueller, J. 1973. *War, Presidents, and Public Opinion*. New York: Wiley.

Mueller, J. 1994. *Policy and Opinion in the Gulf War*. Chicago: University of Chicago Press.

Ostrom, C., and B. Job. 1991. "The President and the Political Use of Force." *American Political Science Review* 79:541–66.

Sigal, L. 1973. *Reporters and Officials*. Lexington: D. C. Heath.

Sinclair, B. 1981. *Majority Leadership in the U.S. House*. Baltimore: Johns Hopkins University Press.

Smith, J. E. 1992. *George Bush's War*. New York: Henry Holt.

U.S. News and World Report, 1992. *Triumph without Victory*. New York: Norton.

Woodward, B. 1992. *The Commanders*. New York: Pocket Books.

Zaller, J. R. 1992. *The Nature and Origins of Mass Opinion*. New York: Cambridge University Press.

Conclusion

thirteen

David L. Paletz

Just Deserts?

Perhaps apocryphally, it is said that the writers of Laurel and Hardy movies always included one wild man. Usually silent at script conferences, he would suddenly burst out into initially bewildering words and phrases that often, but not always, turned out to be creative contributions. For one film, the writers had placed Laurel and Hardy in the Alps where they are trying to move a piano across a narrow suspension bridge that is precariously strung over a sickening chasm. Inspiration failed the writers. What next? They all looked at the wild man. He sat there silent and morose. Then he spoke: "gorilla." A gorilla in the Alps? (Un)Naturally. Meet him Laurel and Hardy do, right in the middle of the bridge. In the film the scene ends with the piano and gorilla crashing down into the gorge. The gorilla survives and later reappears, on crutches, to chase Stan and Ollie away.

In the wild man tradition (would that I were wilder) this essay is an idiosyncratic, usefully provocative (I hope), and inevitably ruminative and speculative response to some of the ideas and arguments contained in this book, and their contributions to an understanding of the relationships between the media, public opinion, policy-makers, and foreign policy. It also attempts to fill in some of the inevitable gaps among the chapters. I am particularly indebted to David Swanson for contributing some of the ideas herein and articulating others from my initial formulations.

My approach is possible because all of our authors root their chapters in the larger literature of the areas studied: for example, Brody (Chapter 10) on public rallies, Hallin and Gitlin (Chapter 7) on popular culture, Manheim (Chapter 6) on public diplomacy, and Iyengar and Simon (Chapter 8) on priming and framing. Moreover, in Chapter 1 Lance Bennett admirably integrates the book's chapters into an approach to understanding the relationships of elites, the media, public opinion, foreign policy, and the war. He effectively outlines many of the myriad elements involved and the connections between the factors shaping the production of news, the ways in which news content can affect public opinion and political participation, and how news and public opinion constrain (and, I would add, offer opportunities for) policy officials.

Among the reactions provoked by my *Just Deserts?* chapter title have been incomprehensibility, outrage at the pun, incredulity, dismay, questions about spelling, doubts, sympathy, curiosity, confidence, pleasure, enthusiasm, and delight. Appropriate, therefore, for me to indicate its meaning, at least in part. The title accords with and sustains my purposes, which are to provoke and challenge, reveal complexity and relationships, and to raise questions. Thus most obviously the phrase has a complex of meanings. For some people Kuwait and the surrounding lands were indeed just deserts, unworthy of one drop of American blood; for others, they were the repository of the oil that they believe motivated President Bush's actions; for yet others, aggression must be challenged even in deserts.

In its second meaning, the title questions whether the acts of the protagonists (George Bush, Saddam Hussein, King Hussein of Jordan, the U.S. military, the press—to mention just a few) deserved *and* received their appropriate rewards or punishments. There is an underlying ambiguity or as least irony here. For the *deserts* do not all seem quite right: Saddam Hussein survives, President Bush suffered reelection defeat. And the many thousands of dead and wounded in the war surely deserved a better fate.

Just Deserts also applies to each of the elements covered by the book: the news media, U.S. foreign policy, public opinion, and the Gulf War itself. For their sins of relying excessively on governmental sources, their having been softened by the application of pools and procedures in Grenada and Panama, and their "patriotic" (or bellicose) boosterism, the reporters, editors, and executives of the American press found their coverage deemed one-sided before the war, censored, and often controlled by the government during the war, and variously criticized by all sides throughout. These were their *deserts*, but were they just?

With respect to foreign policy, there were several alternatives to the Bush administration's "crisis" reaction to the invasion and subsequent deployment of troops. But the policy-making process and media content virtually precluded these alternatives, with variously applauded or denounced *just deserts*. Would this policy process have been subject to greater political opposition or media scrutiny had public opinion not been so easily swayed by the Bush administration or, more charitably, had the complexities of opinion been revealed by conventional polling? Throughout the crisis, the *just deserts* of the public were to be manipulated then relegated during the war to a supporting chorus. And of course the war itself was the culminating *just deserts* of the interplay of politics and communication documented in this book.

Public Relations

I start with Saddam Hussein. For while this book analyzes the public information, management, manipulation, or relations efforts (the word chosen indicates the writer's attitude towards the action) of President Bush, the Pentagon, and to some degree the Kuwait government in exile, Saddam Hussein remains essentially in the background.

Consider what might have transpired had Saddam Hussein hired Hill and Knowlton or its equivalent (assuming such a firm would have been willing to accept his business). His public-relations hirelings could have portrayed him as America's staunch ally against Iran, chronicled his intimate relationship with the Reagan and Bush administrations, detailed his country's grievances against Kuwait, portrayed Kuwait as an autocratically ruled medieval society in comparison to the more modern and secular Iraq, and shown how his control of Kuwait's (and Saudi Arabia's) oil reserves would benefit the U.S. by assuring this country of an abundant and cheap supply. Such a campaign (more plausible and possible than it may seem now) could have filled in the Saddam Hussein image gap identified by Gladys Engel Lang and Kurt Lang in Chapter 2 and made it harder for President George Bush to pin the Hitler label on him (see Dorman and Livingston, Chapter 3).

Instead, the Iraqi president contributed mightily to George Bush's public-relations success. He publicly displayed hardly any diplomatic flexibility (soothing words, a persuasive willingness to negotiate), or strategic adroitness (a partial withdrawal from Kuwait). He seems not to have undertaken a considered public-relations campaign aimed at the United States and its allies. As demonstrated by his treatment and release of the Western hostages-guests, he and his representatives used the American media ineptly, when they tried to use them at all. True, it would have been awkward for Saddam Hussein to expose his autocratically ruled country to the scrutiny of the Western media. However, numerous televised scenes of the widespread death and destruction being wrought by the allied air attack could have told powerfully on worldwide television.

Saddam Hussein seems never to have realized that public relations is an indispensable ally, especially for an inflexible leader with insufficient power contending against an inflexible leader such as George Bush with more than sufficient might at his disposal.

Instead, with the conspicuous and oft-criticized exception of CNN's Peter Arnett, who remained in and sporadically but vividly reported from Baghdad, the war itself was overwhelmingly depicted by the U.S. media from the perspective of U.S. decision-makers, the U.S. military base at Dahran, and the Israelis under Scud attacks in Jerusalem and Tel Aviv.

Indeed, the U.S. military leaders stand in direct contrast to Saddam Hussein in their skill in media management or manipulation (see also Paletz and Ayanian, 1986). The technology, instantaneousness, and ubiquity of reporting seem to have been more than matched by the growing sophistication of the leaders of the U.S. military whose actions were being reported. Whether this skill would have survived a protracted conflict involving numerous American casualties was, fortunately, not put to the test.

Media Processes and Content

PREWAR

Prewar coverage obscured the historical background of the Bush and Reagan administrations' support for Saddam Hussein. Properly reported, this story might well have emboldened some congressional Democrats to oppose the war more forcefully. Coverage also failed to raise alternatives outside the sanctions or war frame, virtually ignored the ways the U.S. corralled U.N. Security Council members, and dismissed the possibility of any justification for the Iraqi action or negotiating position. Iraqi spokesmen did occasionally appear on U.S. television "Nightline" in particular, but their arguments were almost always contested by the interviewer and other guests. Their language and that of Saddam Hussein, flowery and metaphorical, was taken literally, their case essentially discredited.

Criticism of the news media for failing to generate a national "debate" on the wisdom of President Bush's policy, and to provide a panoply of alternative policies, slights the fact that the news media are organized to report the news and see that as their fundamental purpose. Provoking debate is at best an incidental artifact of this activity. That is why disagreement and conflict among policy-makers are so important: when reported, they spur policy discussion (see Chapter 4 by Entman and Page). But elite disagreement by U.S. policy-makers is often relatively quite narrow, in contrast, for example, to the ideological range found in France (see Timothy Cook's introduction, Chapter 5). And reporters are often uncomfortable covering uncommon policy positions. For the Gulf, these ranged from approval of the conquest of Kuwait (and of the possible invasion of Saudi Arabia) to dropping nuclear bombs on Baghdad; or from refusing to participate in the war to volunteering for it. Even had these extreme policy possibilities been reported as part of the range of opinions, they would have been submerged under the chorus of official voices. Giving them prominent and sustained attention was to exaggerate their representativeness.

The debate function, then, is usually the province of editorialists, op-eds, newspaper columnists, television and radio commentators, and politically oriented magazines. But their views are more often asserted and announced than joined or judged. Moreover, despite the abundance of opinion-mongering, the range of perspectives in the mass media is quite limited; few reactionaries and even fewer radicals have prominent platforms.

The media's difficulty in promoting debate was exemplified in their coverage of the antiwar movement. Depending upon one's perspective, the mass media minimized, dismissed, or denigrated the antiwar movement in the U.S., or bestowed upon it too much favorable and legitimizing attention. For the media the issue (not necessarily expressed consciously) was whether the movement should be covered according to its size and prevalence or for its significance as a dissent from the relatively narrow range of policy options under consideration by policymakers. If the former, coverage would be relatively limited and in turn would likely discourage the movement's growth. If the latter, the movement's numbers would be exaggerated, its impact on policy increased. When the war began, the issue became moot; the media essentially dismissed the antiwar movement.

I would speculate, however, that in the future the television and radio talk and interview call-in shows, even MTV, so prominent in the 1992 presidential election, could be involved in the policy debate, inspiring an outpouring of public sentiment. Given the public's occasional vulnerability to demagogy, the opinions expressed and options preferred might not necessarily please either the policy-makers or the proponents or opponents of particular policies.

DURING THE WAR

Criticisms of the media's coverage of the war abound. Journalists themselves provided a prevalent source of discourse consisting of various combinations of personal accounts, self-scrutiny, and indictments of governmentally imposed restraints. Books by John J. Fialka (1991) and

John R. MacArthur (1992) show sometimes compellingly, sometimes tendentiously, how during the war the U.S. media were a too-often willing subject of censorship and propaganda by the U.S. government and military and by some of their allies.

The military gave uninformative or at best guarded briefings, denied unfettered access to the battlefield, deployed an access-limiting system of reporter pools, used public affairs officers to supervise interviews, engaged in story-delaying reviews of copy, rendering stories obsolescent, and imposed outright censorship. These tactics could be attacked for providing political protection for policy-makers and depriving the American public of detailed knowledge about and understanding of the war. And defended on the grounds of reasonableness and necessity, given the size of the press corps.

The Gulf War revealed technology's potential for inaccuracy and exploitation, inherent in instantaneous transmission of events without editing, contextualizing, or framing by reporters. Televised briefings were a particular concern. The military briefers were able to bypass reporters and communicate their points of view directly to the public. In contrast, reporters at these briefings came across as distinctly unappealing: their customarily excitable demeanor (with which most people had been unfamiliar) was exacerbated by the process of demanding information from those reluctant to provide it. Reporters' visibility to the public may have contributed to their appearance of being inadequately prepared to cover the war, lacking knowledge of military matters, and sometimes displaying downright incompetence.

Given the difficult circumstances and onerous restrictions under which reporters labored, their coverage of the war was inevitably vulnerable to criticism. Television was the primary culprit. Its coverage was nationalistic (if not jingoistic), overwhelmingly relayed the Bush administration and Pentagon perspectives, relied on U.S. sources, adopted the military's sanitized lexicon of war, and transmitted U.S. military disinformation.

Coverage of the air war in particular so depended on the Pentagon and U.S. military that it overemphasized the bombing's precision and brutally underemphasized the suffering and punishment inflicted on Iraq's innocent civilians and the destruction of nonmilitary targets and the infrastructure of their country.

Secretary of State James Baker may have been joking but his comment has more than a grain of truth: "The Gulf War was quite a victory. But who could not be moved by the sight of that poor demoralized rabble—outwitted, outflanked, outmaneuvered by the U.S. military. But I think, given time, the press will bounce back" (quoted in the Raleigh *News and Observer,* March 27, 1991, p. 2D).

NEGLECT

Several significant subjects were neither adequately reported by the mass-media nor raised by columnists and commentators. Only after the war was over would the Reagan and Bush administrations' prewar policy of building up Iraq be documented. Background to the Iraq-Kuwait conflict was similarly neglected, as were the internal politics and external ambitions of such states as Saudi Arabia and Syria.

Also neglected, no doubt because they were not willingly revealed to reporters, were the Bush administration's internal debate over strategy and tactics towards Iraq after the invasion; the behind-the-scenes maneuvering of the U.S. in the UN; and the Kuwait government in exile's public-relations activities in the U.S. (see Manheim, Chapter 6). Unreported, no doubt because they were unavailable and inaccessible, were the calculations of the rulers of Iran and Saudi Arabia. Little attention was paid to reactions to the Iraqi invasion and to the conflict by the governments and in the media of non-English-speaking Western states and of third-world countries, especially those not sharing or opposed to the U.S. perspective. Barely covered by the U.S. media was the mass migration of hundreds of thousands of Yemenis from Saudi Arabia when that country's government suspended their residence privileges.

There was a related failure to use stories from foreign media, for example, from the Swedish reporters who, barred from the pools, produced stories about the weak and poorly armed Iraqi cannon-fodder front-line defenders, and about how the involvement of Kuwaiti troops in the liberation of Kuwait City was staged.

EXPLANATIONS

Explanations for the media's behavior are hard to disentangle and document with certainty (see Paletz and Entman, 1981). Journalists' deference to presidential primacy in foreign affairs was important. Certainly, the foreign policy beat reporters in Washington, D.C., rely on their sources and place stock in their statements; otherwise they are likely to be marginalized. These reporters were the main providers of most of the news. Stories by investigative reporters, who are outside the process, or have an outsider's perspective, were uncommon until after the war.

The war began with a news blackout because, as Lieutenant General

Thomas Kelly told our research group: "war is messy at first." During the war, confinement by Pentagon rules, dependence on military sources, reliance on technology, and the restraints inherent in objectivity—these and many other factors could all be invoked more or less to explain the limitations of coverage. Insufficient dedication to the freedom of the press, fear of provoking governmental outrage, shared frames of reference with governing elites, and the pursuit of sales and ratings (read profits) are among the factors that can help explain the acquiescence to government curbs, no matter how reluctant, of media executives. As Timothy Cook's discussion of institutional routines in Chapter 5 shows, these explanations all transcend the specific context of the war and apply generally to the media–foreign policy relationship.

POSTWAR

The combination of time-consuming research, dilatory writing, and reluctance to rush to judgment endows fortunate scholars with the opportunity for hindsight and for contextualizing events. Because mine is the last essay written for this book, I enjoy the additional benefit of including postwar activity.

If President Bush had a postwar media-management strategy, it does not appear to have been conspicuously successful. Television coverage of the flight of the Iraqi Kurds compelled the administration and its allies to intervene with humanitarian aid. Saddam Hussein's intransigence forced a continuing series of well-publicized confrontations with Iraq. Reporters for the prestige press, notably the *Los Angeles Times,* kept digging and turned up more and more evidence of prewar support by the Bush and Reagan administrations for Saddam Hussein. Representative Henry B. Gonzalez (D.—Texas), chairman of the House Banking Committee, began to extract documents about that aid from executive branch agencies and read them into the *Congressional Record,* thus enabling the press to report their contents. Hearings on the war by the Democratically controlled Congress were also reported. The negative aspects of the Pentagon's final report to Congress on the *Conduct of the Persian Gulf War,* released in April 1992, were widely publicized in the press. These included the deaths and injuries caused by friendly fire and the inadequacies of some the weapons deployed. Most of this information had been suppressed or only revealed in part during the war.

The prestige press has also continued occasionally to scrutinize the crawl towards democracy in Kuwait and the persistence of autocratic rule in Saudi Arabia (e.g., Chris Hedges in the *New York Times,* February 14, 1993, pp. 4E and 3).

Books have been published, most of them critical, documenting and attacking the government's attempts to control the press (Fialka 1991; and MacArthur 1992). In another of his "instant histories" Bob Woodward (1991) has traced (apparently mainly from the point of view of chairman of the joint chiefs of staff General Colin Powell) how the Bush administration took the United States to war. And Michael Kelly (1993) has written a devastating account of the horrors of postwar Iraq.

In other words, the war directed journalistic attention to the Gulf. Despite their propensity to move on from one topic to another, the news media have not entirely lost interest in that area of the world and in the intended and inadvertent repercussions wrought by American foreign policy there. This stream of reports and revelations has contributed to reasserting the independence and resilience, if not redeeming the reputation, of the American press.

Normative

Social science researchers tend to eschew explicit expressions of their policy preferences in scholarly tomes. Thus, while discerning readers might find considerable skepticism about, if not outright hostility to, the war in some of this book's chapters, these sentiments are relatively restrained (compared, for example, to Mowlana et al. 1992). One reason is that the application of normative perspectives is not always easy. One might deplore the success of the Bush administration and the Pentagon in managing the media and public opinion for the war in the Gulf, while approving President Franklin D. Roosevelt's "achievement" in moving U.S. public opinion from isolationism to intervention in the years leading up to the Second World War.

The normative views of most of the book's authors do shine through in their assumption that a public debate about President Bush's responses to the invasion of Kuwait was both necessary and desirable; that the decision to go to war requires an extensive, open, public discussion of the range of possible alternatives. In my view, a modicum of skepticism or at least caution is required about the benefits of public debate. Such debate may be laudable, but its effects are not necessarily desirable; the public could well espouse a range of problematic actions, from nuclear bellicosity to isolationism.

I also wonder whether ascribing the purpose of reporting as enabling and supporting informed public debate about policy questions through representing (and evaluating) the range of policy alternatives worth considering in such a debate places an untoward, even unachievable ex-

pectation on the news media. Surely our Gulf War case makes it clear
that the conventions and practices of reporting stem from the institutional, economic, cultural, historical, and social contexts of American
journalism. It is hard to think of a time when the American press has
achieved the debate norm, although it probably comes closer than the
media of most countries.

Technology, however, might change this situation in the future. With
five hundred channels available on cable, one at least could be devoted
to foreign policy, with enough time to offer the widest diversity of views
and proposals. One effect might be that Zaller's media-oriented public
(Chap. 9) would no longer follow the elite's lead.

Public Opinion

Public opinion is customarily portrayed as responding to, dependent on,
even subservient to elite cues and media content. This is not entirely fair
to the American public. For as John Zaller argues in Chapter 9, the Bush
administration engaged in a major effort to mobilize public opinion
through the media; and yet, opinion was divided right up to the war.
Indeed, in early December 1990, some 37 percent of those polled favored war, while 30 percent supported sanctions over force. The other
third shifted between the categories or expressed no opinion (Kagay
1992, 108). Only with the start of hostilities did the overwhelming majority of the U.S. public rally round the president. The point is that public
opinion is just that, opinion. No matter how intense (how intense was it
on the Gulf War?), it may oppose, even resist, but when policy-makers
are determined, as George Bush was in this case, it is unlikely to prevail.
Usually, the boundaries public opinion sets for foreign policy actions are
spacious. It countenances invasions of Grenada and Panama, the sending of troops to the Gulf, and war against Iraq. Thus while public opinion
can sometimes limit or broaden policy-makers' options, or serve as a resource for them, the public's predominant attitude on issues of foreign
policy can be characterized as government knows best.

As a result, public opinion would appear to be primarily retrospective. Policy-makers have wide leeway to act but are then judged by the
perceived results of their actions. And the judgment is rendered in the
relatively short term—meaning, for presidents, the next election. The
makers of foreign policy know this (especially if they read Dick Brody,
Chapter 10) and it influences their behavior in several ways. They usually (but not always) calculate the anticipated reactions of public opinion to their proposed actions and adapt their justifying rhetoric, and

sometimes adjust the policies themselves accordingly (see John Zaller, Chapter 12). They are cautious about embarking on open-ended military action abroad. Grenada, Panama, and the Gulf War were all relatively limited actions with specific, reasonably clear objectives. Quagmires are to be avoided.

This analysis overlooks the fact that, as Zaller points out, and as the Hallin-Gitlin chapter assumes, surveys cannot always adequately convey the public's primordial feelings and instincts, moods and sentiments. The end of the Gulf War may have moved Americans from Hallin and Gitlin's "ritual metaphor" to what I would call a "hangover metaphor." This would help explain why the pundits and pollsters were so wrong in predicting George Bush's reelection from the height of his warending public opinion "popularity." For the public saw (through the media) the president galvanized by foreign affairs in general and his antipathy to Saddam Hussein in particular, and compared this behavior invidiously to his apparent indifference to domestic problems. As Iyengar and Simon in Chapter 8 essentially predict, President Bush suffered from the reemergence of the apparently dismal condition of the U.S. economy to a prominent position in the news. The contrast between the apparent efficiency of the allies' military machine and the U.S. government's inability to solve problems at home was striking. The war ended with the Iraqi president still firmly ensconced in power, the U.S. economy seemingly in further decline, and, as conveyed by the media, President Bush unable to do much about either situation. As a Democratic campaign slogan put it: "Saddam Hussein still has his job. Do you?" So the president won the battles, won the war, and lost the election; with the concomitant uncertain effects of a new administration on the content and conduct of U.S. foreign policy.

Foreign Policy

We are faced with an apparent paradox. Most of the chapters in this book confirm the continuity between the Gulf War case and previous foreign policy episodes. This may not seem at first to be a startling revelation. But it becomes one if we reflect on how news processes and coverage of this case contrast so strikingly with the coverage of foreign conflicts in the past. The Gulf War featured live, daily television coverage from the war zone punctuated by periods of saturation reporting; the transmission of on-the-spot, more or less accurate information instantaneously worldwide, often requiring instant reactions from leaders and officials; opportunities for foreign representatives including "enemy"

spokespersons to voice their viewpoint in the U.S. news media; and the
daily reporting of polls showing levels of support for the war, thus putting upon public opinion a greater and more omnipresent significance
than ever before. In this context of innovation and change, the finding
that the process of policy formulation and implementation proceeded in
ways that resembled more than departed from established models seems
both newsworthy and noteworthy.

It therefore becomes essential to consider the variables involved in
any foreign policy decision. The situations may range from routine to
crisis, from issue areas to events: summit diplomacy and long-term
arms-control negotiations are not synonymous. Policy-makers can have
clear objectives with carefully developed tactics to achieve them, or they
may just try to muddle through, reacting to events over which they have
little control. Elite consensus or dissensus may exist over means or ends
or both. Coverage in the mass media can range from prominent and
continuous (Americans held hostage in Iran) to sporadic (the civil war in
El Salvador) to virtually nonexistent (repression in Myanmar).

Thus David Gergen, who worked in the Reagan White House (and
returned to that abode under President Clinton), has observed "that
television had an enormous impact on our policy in Lebanon. We with-
drew those marines from Lebanon in part because of television. We
asked the Israelis to stop bombing in part because of the television pictures that were coming back from Beirut." In contrast, according to Gergen, "television has had precious little impact" on America's Gulf War
against Iraq (Smith 1992, 237). The policy was decided on by the executive branch without much regard to television. At the same time,
though, he concedes to television the role of "international party line"
over which many of the parties involved in the crisis communicated
publicly. To what extent, one wonders, did this influence the policy of
any of the governments, not just that of the Bush administration?

Given that it was a situation in which President Bush sought to convince the media and public opinion of the rightness of his cause and thus
ensure that Congress would not obstruct him, what are some of the gen-
eralizable conclusions about the conduct of foreign policy and media-
manipulation efforts by elites, about the relations between government,
media, and public opinion, derivable from our Gulf case study?

We can conclude that when an event is defined by the president or by
the news media as a crisis, it automatically requires a response and narrows policy flexibility. That given past experiences (the Vietnam War
still looms large), the relative impatience of public opinion, and the

likely shift of the media from gung ho to negativity over the course of a prolonged conflict, presidents will seek to avoid open-ended military entanglements abroad. Rhetoric, pronouncements, symbolic behavior, proposals without implementation, are all possible alternatives.

Certainly, the Gulf War disproves the post-Vietnam conventional wisdom that, because of television, the U.S. might never again be able to fight a war. It appears, instead, that the Vietnam experience determined the kind of war the U.S. can fight. Knowing that had the Gulf War lasted longer or, worse, gone poorly, the media, especially television, would likely have had greater impact on President Bush's foreign policy objectives and conduct, future presidents will be far more likely to set specific, manageable objectives and to try to accomplish them with overwhelming power. And they will seek to justify decisions and actions with specific, persuasive arguments. Although in future they may not want to demonize opponents unless their destruction is an actual and achievable policy goal.

Even when their policies are set, policy-makers are usually smart to undertake a public information policy, to be concerned about how the media will report and comment on their proposals and actions and how this coverage influences elite and public perceptions at home and abroad (on a related subject, see Paletz and Schmid 1992). For negative perceptions can easily turn into serious problems. One could argue, for example, that Iraq's invasion of Kuwait revealed the failure of U.S. diplomacy, intelligence gathering, and policy. President Bush's accomplishment was to obscure, if not transform this failure, by refashioning the issue into Saddam Hussein's Hitlerite aggression and threat to the "free world."

Bernard Cohen is concerned in his "provocation" that television will impose humanitarian over political decisions in foreign policy. And we now know, if we did not before, that television pictures can alter the content (in at least some details) and the conduct of foreign policy. In the face of television coverage, the Bush administration had to condemn the brutality in Tiananmen Square.

In certain circumstances, policies themselves are modified, even changed. For example, cameras in Manila showing crowds stopping tanks, revealed the failing repression of the Marcos regime, thereby causing the Reagan administration to withdraw its support and contributing to the overthrow of the Philippine president. Similarly, when the Israeli government expelled some four hundred people from Gaza, it erroneously assumed Lebanon would accept them. The vivid television pictures of the expellees' plight in the no-man's-land between the two states contributed to Israel's announced decision to take some of them back immediately and the rest later.

Media characterizations of policies (e.g. as "Star Wars") can make them vulnerable to attack and difficult to accomplish. And in rare circumstances (one thinks of Irangate), media exposure can ensure the termination of a policy entirely and discourage its pursuit by policy-makers in the future.

Such occurrences are striking but uncommon. Especially in autocratic states, governments control access and visibility. The making, conduct, and even the implementation of much foreign policy is kept from the television cameras—creating crises without images. Even in democratic societies, much foreign policy coverage on television consists of the coming and going of dignitaries, but not their deliberations or decisions.

And even when television does capture horrendous crimes and atrocities and their effects, as in what used to be Yugoslavia, and shows them to the world, the perpetrators may be impervious to world opinion, outrage, and threats of military intervention.

I am not convinced, finally, that untrammeled news coverage necessarily precludes effectiveness in foreign policy decision-making and diplomacy. It is probably true that publicity reduces diplomatic flexibility. But this can be a negotiating tactic, with public opinion invoked to preclude particular concessions. Nor is visibility invariably constraining on policy-makers. Depending on the direction and intensity of public opinion, news coverage of policy positions and negotiations could encourage support or opposition, obduracy or flexibility on the part of policy-makers.

Conclusions

As Patrick O'Heffernan points out in Chapter 11, policy-makers and journalists are locked in an approach-avoidance relationship of interdependence. But as the "provocations" in this book by Marvin Kalb and Lieutenant General Thomas Kelly demonstrate, it is a relationship that neither side relishes acknowledging. When questioned by an interviewer of John Zaller's calibre, politicians can be brought to be relatively candid about the situation, but both sides have normative conceptions of their roles, embedded in professional canons for the journalists, that discourage public admission of interdependence. These normative conceptions seem to function as ideals guiding journalists' and politicians' public representations of their actions, although not necessarily their actual practices. Thus both during and after the war, journalists vented their righteous wrath about having been manipulated and censored by the military. For their part, military officials justified their handling of the press by pointing to journalists' irresponsible actions, almost complete inability to agree on any procedures, and downright silliness as complicating their military objectives. Neither side eagerly acknowledged its indebtedness to the other, as the press proved (to reporter's frustration) to be an enormously effective public-relations voice for the military and the military's actions turned out to be a circulation and viewership bonanza (although at considerable expense) for the news media.

The Gulf War case also reveals the clash between the mythologies of journalists and politicians in American culture, mythologies that establish norms and roles that are more or less carried out in practice. For journalists, the myth is that of the skeptical adversary of the government and official power. Accordingly, during the war, at least in the national media, they made the attempt (often unsuccessful) to maintain the same nonpartisan, distanced perspective that they claim (hope) characterizes peacetime reporting (a notable example was Dan Rather repeatedly correcting himself for using phrases like "our tanks" as though these phrases were a role violation). The government's mythic conception of itself during the war was of being involved in a great enterprise in which secrecy, limiting access to information, and engaging in disinformation (this last rarely admitted) were justified by the objectives sought and the costs of failure. According to poll data, and to the distress of many journalists and the proponents of a free, untrammeled press, the public overwhelmingly espoused the wartime government mythology over the mythology of peacetime journalism. Perhaps we need a mythology of wartime journalism—whatever that may be.

In sum, the contributors to this book encourage us to put the Gulf case in historical and comparative perspective with other foreign policy issues. They alert us to the differences between routine and crisis foreign policy decision-making, the stages of the foreign policy process, and variations in the attempts by and successes of elites to influence the media and public opinion at each stage. They identify the connections, interactions, and reciprocal relations between elites, media, media content, and public opinion. And they show some of the effects on the formulation, promotion, timing, and content of policy. In the process, they raise a host of philosophical issues: the relationships between the media and government, press responsibility (if any), limits on the public's right to know, censorship, and what is entailed by freedom of the press. This is no mean feat.

References

Department of Defense. April 1992. *Conduct of the Persian Gulf War: Final Report to Congress.* Washington, D.C.: U.S. Government Printing Office.

Fialka, J. J. 1991. *Hotel Warriors.* Washington, D.C.: The Woodrow Wilson Center Press.

Hedges, C. 1993. "Kuwaiti Parliament Is Acting Like One"; and "Saudi Rulers Resisting Pressure from Two Sides." *New York Times,* February 14, pp. 4E and 3.

Kagay, M. R. 1992. "Variability without Fault: Why Even Well-Designed Polls Can Disagree." In Thomas E. Mann and Gary R. Orren, eds., *Media Polls in American Politics.* Washington, D.C.: The Brookings Institution, pp. 95–124.

Kelly, M. 1993. *Martyrs' Day: Chronicle of a Small War.* New York: Random House.

MacArthur, J. R. 1992. *The Second Front: Censorship and Propaganda in the Gulf War.* New York: Hill and Wang.

Mowlana, H.; G. Gerbner; and H. I. Schiller. 1992. *Triumph of the Image.* Boulder: Westview Press.

Paletz, D. L., and J. Z. Ayanian. 1986. "Armageddon, the Pentagon and the Press." In Peter Golding, Graham Murdock, and Philip Schlesinger, eds., *Communicating Politics.* New York: Holmes and Meier, pp. 197–208.

Paletz, D. L., and R. M. Entman. 1981. *Media Power Politics.* New York: The Free Press.

Paletz, D. L., and A. Schmid, eds. 1992. *Terrorism and the Media.* Newbury Park, Calif.: Sage Publications.

Smith, H., ed. 1992. *The Media and the Gulf War.* Washington, D.C.: Seven Locks Press.

Woodward, B. 1991. *The Commanders.* New York: Simon and Schuster.

appendix

Gulf Conflict
Event Guide

1990

July   18   Saddam Hussein openly threatens to use force against Arab oil-exporting nations if they do not curb their excess production.

          25   Bush administration says U.S. has dispatched two aerial refueling planes to United Arab Emirates and sent combat ships to sea in rare exercise with Persian Gulf nations after Iraq threatens military force.

August   2   Iraqi troops cross Kuwaiti border.

          3   UN votes to condemn Iraq's invasion of Kuwait.

          5   European Community embargo on oil imports from Iraq and Kuwait.

          6   Bush demands total Iraqi withdrawal.

          7   UN orders trade and financial boycott of Iraq and occupied Kuwait.

          8   Bush sends thousands of paratroopers, an armored brigade, and jet fighters to Saudi Arabia.

          9   Saddam Hussein declares annexation of Kuwait.

          10   U.S. and allies announce naval blockade of Iraq.

          13   Bush orders U.S. military to block exports of Iraqi oil and of all imports to Iraq except some food shipments.

          17   Tens of thousands of American troops land in Saudi Arabia in largest American troop deployment since Vietnam.

          22   U.S. calls up 40,000 reservists.

          23   Bush signs order putting 40,000 military reservists on active duty by end of month.

          26   UN adopts resolution giving U.S. and others right to enforce economic embargo.

September 2   Iraq releases 700 foreign women and children it had been preventing from leaving the country.

          4   U.S. secretly deploys combat aircraft in several Persian Gulf nations to help defend Saudi Arabia.

	9	Bush and Gorbachev arrive in Helsinki for summit on crisis.
	26	UN votes to extend economic blockade to include air traffic.
October	3	Senate approves resolution that supports Bush's actions so far in Gulf.
	9	Bush administration shuts down government for a day due to budget impasse.
	13	UN approves compromise resolution condemning Israel for violence in Jerusalem that resulted in Palestinian deaths and injuries.
	18	Senate Foreign Relations Committee members demand that Bush get congressional approval before any military attack on Iraq.
	24	Bush is politically weakened by budget crisis, which becomes an issue in midterm election campaign.
	25	Congressional leaders reserve right to reconvene Congress in case Bush administration decides to go to war against Iraq.
	28	Republican candidates damaged by Bush concessions in budget talks.
	30	UN approves resolution warning of further, unspecified measures unless Iraq withdraws from Kuwait.
November	5	Defense Department decides to call up major combat units from reserves, totalling thousands of troops, to join force in Persian Gulf in next few months.
	6	Election day: Democrats gain in Congress.
	8	Pentagon announces that Bush administration will send at least 100,000 additional troops to Gulf by late December, bringing total to approximately 350,000.
	9	Bush orders more than 150,000 additional American ground, sea, and air forces to Gulf area to provide "adequate offensive military option."
	14	Bush urged by both parties to convene special session of Congress on Gulf Crisis.
	15	Bush assures Congress he would consult with it before using force in Gulf.
December	1	Bush invites Foreign Minister Tariq Aziz of Iraq to Washington.
	5	House Democrats adopt nonbinding policy statement that Bush should not initiate any offensive military

action in Gulf without formal approval of
Congress.

7   Saddam Hussein says he will free all foreigners held
hostage in Iraq and Kuwait.

10   More than 1,000 foreigners leave Iraq.

15   George Mitchell (Senate majority leader) and other
Democratic senators visit Saudi Arabia. Although U.S. is
closer to war, Congress won't automatically support it.
Gephardt and other House Democrats complain about
financial contribution lag from coalition partners.

1991

January 3   NATO to send three squadrons of jet fighters to Turkey to
strengthen its border with Iraq.

4   The 102d Congress convenes.

5   Iraq accepts U.S. offer for meeting in Geneva between
Secretary Baker and foreign Minister Tariq Aziz.

5   Senate sets debate on Gulf War resolution.

7   Saddam Hussein tells his armed forces to prepare for war.

9   Bush calls on Congress to adopt resolution supporting
use of force against Iraq if it does not withdraw from
Kuwait by January 15.

11   Congress begins debating resolution supporting force in
Gulf.

12   Congress, by slim majority in Senate and solid majority
in House appears ready to authorize Bush to attack Iraq.

13   Congress approves military action in Gulf by votes in
Senate (52–47), and House (250–183).

14   UN secretary meets with Saddam Hussein.

15   Iraqi Parliament votes unanimously to follow Saddam
Hussein into combat with U.S.

17   U.S. and allies open drive to oust Iraq from Kuwait with
night air strikes.

18   Saddam Hussein launches missile attacks on Israel.

26   Iraq releases millions of gallons of Kuwaiti crude oil into
Persian Gulf.

29   More than 80 Iraqi planes fly to Iran.

31   More than 20,000 reservists are called up as part of
deployment of Individual Ready Reserves.

February 19   House rushes to pass bill to help troops deal with
economic hardships at home.

21 Ground war begins; more than 450 Iraqi prisoners of war are taken.

27 Iraqi troops retreat across Kuwait; allied forces enter Kuwait City.

28 Bush says he has ordered halt to offensive combat in Gulf War; says "Kuwait is liberated" and Iraq's army defeated.

March 3 UN approves resolution effectively endorsing Bush's call for allied troops to remain in Gulf until Iraq complies with his peace terms.

6 Baghdad radio reports that Saddam Hussein has voided annexation of Kuwait.

8 House votes 380–19 to appropriate $15 billion to pay for Gulf War. Democrats join Bush in celebrating victory.

11 U.S. troops return from Gulf.

14 House of Representatives approves benefits package for veterans.

15 Senate approves package of benefits for veterans of Gulf that is less generous than the one voted by House.

20 Senate approves $15 billion appropriation for Gulf War.

21 April Glaspie appears before Senate committee.

22 Kurdish rebels claim military victory in Kirkuk, Iran, in campaign to topple Saddam Hussein.

23 UN Security Council lifts embargo on food supplies to Iraq.

27 Bush decides to let Saddam Hussein put down rebellions in his country without American intervention.

April 1 U.S. Army will begin withdrawing about 20,000 troops from southern Iraq within two weeks.

4 UN approves resolution that offers to end Gulf War and progressively lift most sanctions against Iraq if Saddam Hussein accepts series of tough military and financial conditions.

7 Iraq accepts without condition UN terms for formal cease-fire in Gulf War.

22 General Schwartzkopf returns home.

May 7 General Schwartzkopf addresses joint session of Congress.

10 U.S. reaches agreement with Saudi Arabia and other Persian Gulf governments about storing of American military equipment and other steps to maintain long-term military presence in region.

contributors

W. LANCE BENNETT is professor of political science and chair of the department at the University of Washington. He has authored numerous books and articles on political communication, public opinion, and the role of symbolism in political processes. Recent works include *News: The Politics of Illusion* and *The Governing Crisis: Media, Money, and Marketing in American Elections*. He is a member of the Foreign Policy Studies Committee of the Social Science Research Council and chaired the Media and Foreign Policy workshop series upon which this book is based.

RICHARD A. BRODY is professor of political science at Stanford University and a fellow of the American Academy of Arts and Sciences. He is a student of political behavior with an emphasis on public opinion, voting, and media and politics. His most recent books are *Reasoning and Choice: Explorations in Political Psychology*, co-authored with Paul Sniderman and Philip Tetlock, and *Assessing the President*.

BERNARD C. COHEN is professor emeritus of political science at the University of Wisconsin-Madison. He is the author of *The Political Process and Foreign Policy, The Press and Foreign Policy, The Public's Impact on Foreign Policy*, and has a work in progress on "Public Participation in Foreign Affairs in the United States and the Netherlands."

TIMOTHY E. COOK is professor and chair of the Department of Political Science at Williams College. An American Political Science Association Congressional Fellow and a guest scholar at the Brookings Institution in 1984–85, he is the author of *Making Laws and Making News: Media Strategies in the U.S. House of Representatives* and many articles on political communication in the United States, political socialization, and representation in Congress.

WILLIAM A. DORMAN is professor of journalism at California State University, Sacramento, where he also teaches in the Peace and Conflict Studies Program. He is an associate of the Center for War, Peace, and the News Media at New York University. Dorman has written extensively on the press and foreign affairs for journals and periodicals ranging from the *Columbia Journalism Review* and *The Bulletin of the Atomic Scientists* to *World Policy Journal* and *The Nation*. He is co-author of *The U.S. Press and Iran*.

ROBERT M. ENTMAN is associate professor of communication studies, journalism, and political science, and faculty fellow of the Center for Urban Affairs and Policy Research at Northwestern University. He also directs Northwestern's Program in Political Communication. He is the author of *Democracy without Citizens: Media and the Decay of American Politics* and co-author of *Media Power Politics*.

TODD GITLIN is professor of sociology and director of the Mass Communications Program at the University of California, Berkeley. Among his books are *The Sixties: Years of Hope, Days of Rage; Inside Prime Time; The Whole World is Watching;* and, as editor, *Watching Television*. He also is a published poet.

DANIEL C. HALLIN is author of *The "Uncensored War": The Media and Vietnam*, and numerous articles on media and foreign policy, media and elections, and comparative analysis of the news media. His writings have appeared both in academic journals, including the *Journal of Communication*, the *Journal of Politics*, and *Theory and Society*, and in such popular publications as *The Quill*, *The Bulletin of the Atomic Scientists*, and the *Columbia Journalism Review*. He is associate professor of communication at the University of California, San Diego.

SHANTO IYENGAR is chairman of the Communication Studies Program and professor of political science at the University of California, Los Angeles. He is the author of *Is Anyone Responsible? How Television Frames Political Issues*, co-author of *News That Matters: Television and American Opinion* and *The Media Game*, and co-editor of *Explorations in Political Psychology* (forthcoming).

MARVIN KALB is Murrow Professor of Press and Public Policy at Harvard University and director of the Shorenstein Barone Center on Press, Politics, and Public Policy at the Kennedy School of Government. For thirty years he was diplomatic correspondent, first for CBS then for NBC, moderator of "Meet the Press," and anchor for NBC's White Paper documentaries. He is the author of eight books, including two best-selling novels.

THOMAS W. KELLY, Lieutenant General, U.S. Army (Retired), was the director for operations for the Joint Chiefs of Staff. He served as the chief operations officer for the U.S. effort in the Gulf and as the Pentagon's top briefer during the Gulf War. Previously, General Kelly had been assigned as commanding general, United States Army Security Affairs Command. Currently he is a consultant to NBC News.

GLADYS ENGEL LANG is professor of communication, political science, and sociology and **KURT LANG** is professor of sociology and communication, both at the University of Washington. They are joint recipients of the Edward L. Bernays Award of the American Sociological Association and of the Annual Award of the American Association of Public Opinion Research for exceptionally distinguished achievement. Their co-authored books include *Politics and Television-Reviewed,* and *The Battle for Public Opinion: The President, the Press, and the Polls During Watergate.* Kurt Lang is also author of *Military Institutions and the Sociology of War.*

STEVEN LIVINGSTON is assistant professor of political communication at the National Center for Communication Studies, The George Washington University, Washington, D.C. He is currently researching post-cold-war news coverage of foreign affairs with the assistance of an award from the Social Science Research Council's Advance Fellowship in Foreign Policy Studies, supported by a grant from the Ford Foundation. He is the author of *The Terrorism Spectacle.*

JAROL B. MANHEIM is professor of political communication and political science, and director of the National Center for Communication Studies and of the Political Communication Program, at The George Washington University. He is the author or co-author of eight books on U.S. politics, political behavior, and research methods. These include *Empirical Political Analysis* and *All of the People, All the Time: Strategic Communication in American Politics.*

PATRICK O'HEFFERNAN is director of foundation relations and adjunct professor in international affairs at the Georgia Institute of Technology. He is the author of numerous articles and books, including *Mass Media and American Foreign Policy: Insider Perspectives on Global Journalism and the Foreign Policy Process.* He is a member of the Academy of Television Arts and Sciences and a regular contributor to its journal, *Television Weekly.*

BENJAMIN I. PAGE, the Gordon Scott Fulcher Professor of Decision Making at Northwestern University, has written extensively on various aspects of American politics including public opinion and elections, the mass media, the presidency, effects of government programs, and U.S. foreign policy. He is co-author (with Robert Shapiro and Glenn Dempsey) of "What Moves Public Opinion," and (with Shapiro) of *The Rational Public.*

DAVID L. PALETZ is professor of political science at Duke University. He is the co-author of *Media Power Politics, Politics in Public Service Advertising on Television,* editor of *Political Communication Research,* co-editor and contributor to *Glasnost and After: Media and Change in Central/Eastern Europe, Terrorism and the Media,* and author of some sixty other publications. He is the chairperson of the Political Communication Research Section of the International Association for Mass Communication Research.

ADAM SIMON has an A.B. in communication studies from the University of California, Los Angeles, where he is currently a graduate student in political science. He was formerly employed by the Financial News Network. His work on this project was supported by a graduate fellowship from the National Science Foundation.

JOHN ZALLER is associate professor of political science at the University of California, Los Angeles. His principal research interests are political culture, the mass media, elections, and the role of elites in shaping public opinion. He has written *The Nature and Origins of Mass Opinion* and, with Herbert McClosky, *The American Ethos: Public Attitudes toward Capitalism and Democracy.*

index

ABC: content analysis of news broadcasts, 172, 173, 179–83; coverage of gassing of Kurds, 55; coverage of opposition to Gulf War, 123–24; coverage of prewar debate, 84–90, 93, 96; newsbeats of, 105–6; "video postcards" broadcast by, 5. See also *Nightline* (ABC)
Accountability, 22, 23, 37
Acheson, Dean, 214
Adams, Brock, 216
Agenda-setting, 167, 168–70, 175, 176–78
Agon, war as, 152–56
Albritton, R. B., 135
Allison, G., 244
Allsop, Dee, 70, 141, 143
Almond, G. A., 190
Alter, Jonathan, 6
Amaize, O., 135
American Jewish Congress, 44
Amnesty International, 55, 140
Anderson, R., 135
Appeasement, 44
Apple, R. W., Jr., 216
Arab-Americans, discrimination against, 123
Arafat, Yasir, 225
Arens, Moshe, 70, 71
Arnett, Peter, 5, 30, 234, 242, 280
Audience: condemnation of journalists by, 30; and definition of news, 94; as factor in news management, 30–31; feedback from, 21–22; skepticism of, 14–15; for television, 14–15, 16
Aziz, Tariq, 92, 105

Baker, James, 92–94, 105, 119, 216, 282
Bakir, Ahmed al-, 48
Bateson, G., 170
Bay of Pigs (1961), 212
Bazoft (British journalist), 46, 56–57

Begin, Menachem, 51
Behr, R. L., 169
Bennett, W. Lance, 65, 73, 82
Bernays, Edward L., 16, 134
Bernays Foundation, 134
Bipartisanship, 97, 216, 263
Bosnia-Herzegovina, television coverage of, 10, 28
Boucher, Richard, 119
Bowen, Jerry, 123
Brady, Matthew, 10
Briggs, Fred, 123
Broadcast networks. *See* ABC; CBS; NBC; Television
Broder, David, 253
Brody, Richard A., 33, 211, 212
Brokaw, Tom, 153, 154
Budget deficit, 173, 176, 178, 216
Bush, George: congressional support for, 255–57, 260–70; interviewed by David Frost, 140; media independence from, 82–101; popularity ratings of, 5, 178–79, 183, 269; populist press under, 4; postwar media-management strategy of, 284; press coverage of, 26; public support for, 65, 168, 213, 217, 219–25, 258–59; reaction to Iraqi invasion of Kuwait, 17, 26, 32, 35–36, 64–69, 106–7, 251, 252–55; reelection defeat of, 278, 287; relations with Saddam, 57, 59, 66–71, 73–75, 287; relations with Saudi Arabia, 70

Cantril, Hadley, 190
Capitol Hill newsbeat, 110–11, 112–19, 126. *See also* Congress
Carter, Hodding, 3
Carter, Jimmy, 13, 35, 37, 48
Casualties, estimates of, 198–99, 284
CBS: coverage of gassing of Kurds, 55; coverage of Gulf War by, 153; coverage

301